THE POWERBROKER

THE
POWERBROKER

MARK LEIBLER

AN AUSTRALIAN JEWISH LIFE

MICHAEL GAWENDA

MONASH
UNIVERSITY
PUBLISHING

The Powerbroker: Mark Leibler, An Australian Jewish Life

Monash University Publishing
Matheson Library Annexe
40 Exhibition Walk
Monash University
Clayton, Victoria 3800, Australia
www.publishing.monash.edu

Monash University Publishing brings to the world publications which advance the best traditions of humane and enlightened thought.

Monash University Publishing titles pass through a rigorous process of independent peer review.

ISBN: 9781925835809 (hardback)
ISBN: 9781925835823 (pdf)
ISBN: 9781925835816 (epub)

www.publishing.monash.edu/books/powerbroker-9781925835809.html

Series: Biography

Design: Les Thomas

Cover photograph of Michael Gawenda © Husky Gawenda
Cover photograph of Mark Leibler © Earl Carter

A catalogue record for this book is available from the National Library of Australia.

CONTENTS

ACKNOWLEDGEMENTS

I want to thank Sue Hampel who helped sort and research the very large archive of documents, notes Leibler wrote about meetings he had with a whole range of politicians, taxation officials and Jewish leaders, private and official letters, newspaper articles and the hundreds of pages of minutes of meetings of all the organisations that Mark Leibler has been involved with over almost half a century. Her work was invaluable.

Mark Leibler made all of the material in his archive available to me and I thank him for that. He understood that this was to be an unauthorised biography and that there were bound to be judgments by me and by others that he would not necessarily like, but he was always generous with his time, always available for yet another interview.

My friend and colleague James Button edited the manuscript. There is no doubt that James, who is an outstanding editor and writer, made it a much better book.

I want to thank Louise Adler who always believed in this book. It was Louise who brought the manuscript to Monash University Publishing. I am glad she did because the Monash team has been terrific, easy to work with, encouraging and always professional.

Finally, I want to thank my wife Anne who read every draft of the manuscript and offered invaluable advice, most of which, even when it made me grumpy, I accepted. Books are a sort of marathon and she ran the distance with me.

CHAPTER 1

In the morning of a late summer's day in 2019, Mark Leibler is getting ready to travel to Israel. The 75-year-old has a sense of purpose and controlled urgency about him—he has no time to waste, certainly not on small talk. Several times he calls out for his long-time assistant to get him something or call someone, quickly, immediately, for time is marching on. We are sitting at a small table in his office, but he is oblivious to the sweeping views of the city that shimmers in the sunlight on this warm summer's morning.

Dressed in a white shirt and red silk tie, with his thinning sandy hair neatly combed and his pencil-thin moustache carefully trimmed, Leibler does not look or sound like an elderly man. He is someone who believes he still has much to do, in his professional life, in the law—one of his great passions for more than half a century—and as a leader of the Jews in Australia and around the world. Asked to look back and describe what he has achieved and what his failures might be, he becomes impatient, as if the questions imply that his life is almost over.

This trip is the first of three visits to Israel Leibler will make this year—this first one in summer, another in mid-winter and the last one in spring. He has made these visits for 25 years, ever since he was elected to the two major international Jewish organisations that help determine how the substantial sums of money raised in diaspora communities will be spent on projects in Israel and, increasingly, in diaspora Jewish communities, especially the six-million-strong community in the United States.

Even when he is in Israel, when his days are packed with meetings, he will be in constant touch with his office at Arnold Bloch Leibler (ABL), where he has been a partner for almost 50 years. He is always available to clients and to lawyers at ABL who might want to discuss with him some aspect of a case they are handling. He will take and make calls at any time of the day and night, talking to Jewish community leaders, Indigenous leaders who regularly seek him out for advice, powerful people in all walks of life. Mark Leibler is a man of many parts and he has learnt to move across these parts—from lawyer to Jewish leader to activist on behalf of Indigenous causes—so that each part enriches the others.

He is not well known to most Australians. His name does not appear in the newspapers often, though he has become, over the years, the go-to tax lawyer for financial journalists. For journalists covering the Middle East, Leibler is frequently the first person they turn to for comment, but amongst the general population his is hardly a household name. Yet his influence far exceeds his public profile. Of the 200 people and families on the *Australian Financial Review*'s 2019 Rich List, nearly one in five are clients of Arnold Bloch Leibler. Partly as a result of this client base, Leibler is widely recognised as one of Australia's most influential tax lawyers. He has given advice and put the case for changes to tax laws to every Australian Treasurer since John Howard had the job in the 1970s.

Over 40 or more years of public life, Leibler has developed and sustained close relationships—he calls them friendships—with senior Australian politicians, from Bill Hayden when he was Foreign Minister in the Hawke government to Prime Ministers John Howard, Paul Keating and Julia Gillard. Keating calls Leibler a friend. Gillard says that, in her most difficult days as Prime Minister, she felt from him

"a care and concern about me as a human being." Indigenous leader
Noel Pearson considers Leibler to be not just a mentor who taught
him about the workings of power, but a father figure.

Others, such as Kevin Rudd when he was Prime Minister and
Foreign Minister and Bob Carr when he replaced Rudd as Foreign
Minister, do not share such warm assessments of Leibler. Both Rudd
and Carr came to believe that Leibler and the "Israel Lobby", as they
called it and which Leibler led, was a malign force in Australian politics,
one that distorted Australia's policies on the conflict between Israel
and the Palestinians, and turned many politicians and journalists into
the Lobby's puppets, or, to use Carr's word, "poodles".

Leibler is a man of contradictions. He is considered to be a political
conservative, yet most of his closest relationships with politicians
have been with Labor prime ministers. He is an Orthodox Jew who,
nevertheless, publicly supported the yes case in Australia's 2017 same-
sex marriage postal survey. He is a lifelong Zionist who, as a Zionist
leader, urged and encouraged Australian Jews to go and settle in Israel
as the ultimate fulfilment of a Jewish life, yet he never did so himself.

This is perhaps the greatest contradiction in the life Leibler has led.
The idea of the ingathering of all Jews into a Jewish state was central to
the establishment of Israel, and, in theory at least, it remains central to
Zionism today. The Hebrew word Aliyah ("going up") has been used
since the Jews were dispersed by the ancient Greeks and then by the
Romans to describe any Jew who returns to the Holy Land. Zionism's
leaders and philosophers adopted the term to describe any Jew who
makes the move to what was once Palestine and is now Israel, in order
to create a national home for the Jews. The Israeli Law of Return grants
virtually automatic and immediate citizenship to any Jew—defined as
anyone who has at least one Jewish grandparent—who makes Aliyah.

Since the late 1990s, when his older brother, Isi, pre-eminent leader of Jews in Australia and a major figure in world Jewry, settled in Israel, Mark Leibler has been recognised as Australia's most influential and powerful Jewish leader, and has become increasingly influential in international Jewry. The *Jerusalem Post* has described him as one of the world's 50 most influential Jews. He has had, and still has, relationships with Israeli politicians, including prime ministers, and with senior Israeli public servants, among them Yuval Rotem, head of the Israeli Foreign Ministry and close adviser to Prime Minister Benjamin Netanyahu. It was Rotem who convinced Netanyahu to visit Australia in 2017, the first Israeli prime minister to do so. Prime Minister Malcolm Turnbull chose Leibler to chair the official lunch for Netanyahu he hosted at Sydney's Convention Centre on 22 February 2017, an event Leibler described as one of the greatest of his life.

Anyone who has lived such a public life and has been involved in so many different and seemingly unconnected areas is bound to have critics and even enemies. Leibler has both. Former senior Australian Taxation Office officials who have had dealings with Leibler have said that he has a reputation as a bully who intimidates junior staffers conducting audits of his clients. Within the Jewish community, he has a reputation for being arrogant and a formidable and difficult opponent. Academic and writer Mark Baker, a lifelong Zionist, believes that Leibler has tried and has largely succeeded in shutting down any criticism of Israel in the Jewish community. Only a minority of Australian Jews share Baker's view of Leibler. But, in the age of social media, the voice of the minority is loud and often personal in its criticism of Leibler.

None of Leibler's critics, however, deny that Leibler has influence and power and knows how to use them. Leibler's power is unquestionably built on the strength of the 120,000 in Australia's Jewish community.

CHAPTER 1

Over three generations, the Leibler family has shaped and been shaped by that community, contributed significantly to its vitality, its cultural and political richness, its success across business, the law, medicine, the arts, and philanthropy. In many ways, the Australian Jewish community is a multicultural success story.

Leibler's law firm, Arnold Bloch Leibler, was built on the remarkable successes of Jewish refugees, many of whom had lost their families in the Holocaust. They became clients of the firm as they ran their milk bars and tailoring shops in the rundown minor streets of Melbourne's central business district and inner suburbs, where they lived after arriving from the displaced persons camps or the ruined cities of Eastern Europe. Within a couple of decades of their coming to Australia, many had become wealthy, perhaps beyond their wildest imaginings. Their history is also Leibler's history—his Australian Jewish story.

In his office on the 21st floor of a central Melbourne office tower, he answers questions with some impatience on this summer morning, as he has things to do before he flies to Israel. But we are comfortable with each other, as comfortable as a writer and his subject can be. We have spent a lot of time together and we have come to know each other, not as friends, but with a knowing that comes from talking for a long time about our lives—about his, of course, more than mine.

It has been more than a year since I decided to write Leibler's biography. It had not been an easy decision. I was getting old. I had spent more than four decades of my life in journalism, and I wanted to spend the years left to me writing whatever took my fancy. I had written a memoir based on memories that came to me when I walked along the beach with my dog each morning. I had published a small book of poems I had written every fortnight during my grandson's first year of life. There had been some journalism—mainly columns during federal election campaigns—but I wanted to write more poetry, including some in Yiddish after I had studied Victorian Certificate of Education (VCE) Yiddish, the language of my childhood.

I had never written a biography. When the possibility first arose of writing Mark Leibler's biography I was not inclined to give up whatever time it would take and delay my dreams of writing poetry. But the more I thought about it, the more intriguing the idea became. It would be, I came to realise, not just a biography of Leibler, but my story as well to a certain extent, and the story of the Australian Jewish community in which I had grown up but had rarely written about as a working journalist.

The time was right. Anti-Semitism of the right and the left was on the rise. Among non-Jews, and among a significant number of Jews, Israel had long ceased to represent the miracle of Jewish resurrection that it had been after the virtual destruction of European Jewry by the Nazis and their helpers. For the first time, I had a growing sense of foreboding about the future of the Jews. I wondered whether that time after the Holocaust—the time in which Leibler and I grew up and lived most our lives, when anti-Semitism was totally unacceptable and anti-Semites were given no oxygen, no legitimacy—was over.

There had now been more than a year of talking and questioning and reliving episodes of his life and, as it turned out, of my life as well. We talked not only in his office but in the study of his home in suburban Caulfield, which many Jews in Melbourne call the *shtetl*—the Yiddish word for the Jewish villages of pre-war Eastern Europe. The walls of his office and his study are adorned with photographs of Leibler with Australian and Israeli prime ministers and foreign ministers and senior cabinet ministers: John Howard, Paul Keating and Malcolm Turnbull, and Israeli Prime Ministers Itzak Shamir, Shimon Peres and

Benjamin Netanyahu. It would be unfair not to mention that there are also photographs of Leibler with his wife, Rosanna, and of their four children and 14 grandchildren. On a shelf behind his desk stood a framed photograph of his parents in their mid-20s, two well-dressed young middle-class members of the Antwerp Jewish community, taken several years before they escaped to Australia and just months before the start of the war in September 1939. It had become clear over time that Leibler had few close friends and had never had many. He had his family, he would often say, and that was enough.

Leibler and I are around the same age. We were both children of parents who, despite the best efforts of the Nazis, had managed to remain alive and escape to Australia—his before the war and mine afterwards. My parents had escaped to the Soviet Union with their two young daughters just as the German army invaded Poland in September 1939 and had spent the war in Siberia. I was born in a displaced persons camp in Austria in 1947. We are both the children of "reffos", of Holocaust survivors. We both grew up in a Jewish community that had been reborn with the influx of more than 20,000 Holocaust survivors after the war, more of whom settled in Australia proportionately than in any other country other than Israel.

In 1948, just three years after the darkness they had lived through, when so many of their family and friends and so many Jews had been murdered, and when many of them were still in the displaced persons' camps of a ruined Europe, these survivors witnessed the establishment of the State of Israel. Many of them felt that this miracle changed and saved their lives, and redefined their Jewishness. Jews were no longer powerless victims; they were, for the first time since the destruction of the second temple, actors in their own destiny. Israel brought light and hope into lives that had been consumed by darkness. These survivors were Zionists of the most visceral kind. It was not so much about ideology but about feeling again that there was a future for them and for the Jews.

For these Jewish refugees and migrants, Australia became a *goldene medine* (golden land) in the post-war years. This was not just about how wealthy the Jewish community was to become, but the way it was able to foster Jewish life and Jewish institutions while at the same time contributing mightily to every facet of Australian life, from business to the professions to politics and culture.

Apart from these connections, however, Leibler and I lived in different Jewish Australian worlds. He had grown up in the religious and fiercely Zionist Mizrachi community. I grew up in that small part of the Australian Jewish community that was militantly secular and either anti-Zionist or, after the establishment of Israel, non-Zionist. Our community was of the left, anti-Communist but socialist and universalist in its outlook. Nevertheless, it was committed to Jewish peoplehood through an attachment to Jewish history and culture, specifically Yiddish culture.

My Jewish home was in the Bund, the democratic socialist party of Eastern Europe that from its founding at the end of the 19th century until World War 2 was the party of the Jewish working class. Hundreds of thousands of its members, perhaps millions if you included its supporters, were murdered by the Nazis. Of those who survived, several thousand managed to come to Australia, my parents among them. The Bund was reborn in Melbourne. These people set up a youth group, organised summer camps for the children, and became actively involved in the Australian Labor Party (ALP). Like the Zionists, they were determined not to be defined as victims. My father and mother worked in the textile industry after their arrival in Australia—my mother in a sock manufacturing factory, my father weaving carpets. They were life-long supporters of the Bund and the ALP. This was not Mark Leibler's story. Had we met as young people, there would have been very little on which we would have agreed.

Over the years we had hardly spoken to each other, even when I was editor of *The Age* and representatives of the Australia/Israel & Jewish Affairs Council (AIJAC), the highly influential lobbying outfit that Leibler chairs, contacted me regularly to complain rather robustly about the newspaper's coverage of the Middle East. Later, when I was a foreign correspondent in Washington, Leibler and Rosanna, and retail magnate Solomon Lew and his then wife, Rosie, came to Washington to meet officials of the administration of George Bush Junior, including the then Secretary of State Condoleezza Rice, whom I had been trying unsuccessfully to interview for two years. Lew, a major funder of AIJAC, invited me to have lunch with them and their wives. My memory of the lunch is that the wives were engaging and Leibler interesting on American politics, but Lew spent the whole lunch with a phone piece in his ear, making and receiving calls.

In the mid-1990s, before I became Editor of *The Age*, I had written a long feature article about Lew when he was the embattled Chairman of Coles Myer. The journalist and shareholder activist, Stephen Mayne, then owner of *Crikey*, at the time a rather cheeky, gossipy news website, wrote that I should have declared that I was Jewish in the article. Mayne's view was that this would have explained why I had been soft on Lew. This was the first time that the fact that I was Jewish was raised in reference to my journalism; it was not the last. When I was Editor of *The Age*, it seemed to be an issue for activists on both sides of the Middle East conflict; for example, when I refused to publish a cartoon by the beloved Michael Leunig that, in my view, equated the

Israeli armed forces with the Nazis, my decision was fiercely debated in the media.

I often wondered why some people thought it important that I declare the fact that I was a Jew in my journalism and when I was an editor, even when—as in the profile of Lew—there was no apparent reason for me to do so, unless you thought that a Jew writing about another Jew was somehow problematic. And it could only be considered problematic if you thought that Jews stuck together, that their first loyalty was always to each other, that Jews, in other words, had dual and even conflicting loyalties. For Jews, this is an accusation with a long and bloody history, and it has, no doubt, been leveled at Mark Leibler.

As Leibler prepared to fly to Israel on this summer's day, it had been 25 years since hope of peace between Israel and the Palestinians had flowered. There had been the optimism of the early 1990s—the Oslo years—which had culminated with the handshake on the lawns of the White House between Yasser Arafat, leader of the Palestine Liberation Organisation, and Israeli Prime Minister Yitzhak Rabin, with a beaming President Bill Clinton looking on. The assassination of Rabin by a right-wing Jewish terrorist in November 1995 was the beginning of the end of the Oslo dream. In 2000, the second Intifada ushered in the time of no hope and no way forward, the years of the rise of Hamas with its anti-Semitism and terrorism and its commitment to Israel's destruction. It ushered in the rise of Benjamin Netanyahu and his right-wing coalition partners, some of whom remained committed to a greater Israel, which would mean the annexation of the West Bank and permanent rule over millions of stateless Palestinians.

During those 25 years of hope, and then dashed hope, Leibler's commitment to Israel never wavered, either publicly or privately. His Zionism, indeed the Zionist dream of a Jewish state which would foster the ingathering of the Jews scattered in diaspora communities around the world, remained as strong as ever, even as increasing sections of the left, in the United States and Europe and Australia, came to use the words Zionism and Zionist as terms of abuse. Leibler's conviction that without Israel the Jews of the world would be lost, reduced again to powerlessness and despair, remains unshakeable.

Whatever issues he might have with the government of Benjamin Netanyahu—and there is some evidence that he is not necessarily a great supporter—Leibler would never publicly criticise either the Israeli government's handling of security issues or its handling of the conflict with the Palestinians. For him, it is all a matter of principle; Israel is constantly under threat and it is not for Jews who have chosen not to live in Israel to tell the democratically elected Israeli government what to do when it comes to the country's security. Leibler's steadfast position has often made him seem like a policeman of the boundaries of what his fellow Jews could legitimately say about Israel. Often, in the past, Leibler has been scathing in his criticism of these Jews whom he felt had crossed those boundaries. In recent years, while he may still feel that these Jews are betrayers of the Jewish people, he does not say so publicly. To do so, he says, would be to "make these people more important than they actually are."

Leibler's life is a story about Jews and power. Making that connect-ion is fraught with risks, for it is one that has been made throughout history by anti-Semites and by those who think the Jews somehow have an almost magical ability to influence and change—always for self-interest and for the worse—the course of history. Questions about Jewish power have consumed Jew-haters, and their answers have led to discrimination and hatred and, sometimes, to unspeakable, historically unprecedented, violence.

But just because anti-Semites believe the Jews have power does not mean it is untrue. Leibler's story cannot be told without an examination of the way he has developed and used power and influence. Mark Leibler's life is located in the story of how Jews became a force in Australian life, of how this community became influential way beyond its numbers in business and the arts, in the law, the media and medicine, of how this community was able to maintain its identity and culture while it maintained deep involvement in Australian life. This is a biography of one man. It is also the story of one community in a multicultural nation. It is a story about Australia.

CHAPTER 2

The journeys of the refugees and migrants who came to Australia in the 20th century, the trajectory of their lives, the lives they built anew, the astounding velocity of change down the roads their lives travelled, the suffering of many in the Great Depression and in two World Wars, are truly among the greatest stories ever told, and sometimes untold. Not just in Australia of course, but in Australia as much as anywhere, the stories of the refugees and migrants and their children changed the country's story. It changed, in the most fundamental ways, how Australians saw themselves and their country.

Abraham Leibler, his wife Rachel and their four-year-old son, Isi, were among the "39rs"—the 5000 or so mainly German and Austrian Jews who, in 1939, had managed to raise the £200 they needed to qualify under the Australian government's mandated quota of 7000 Jewish German and Austrian refugees and be given the chance to escape Nazi persecution. The Leiblers were not strictly speaking eligible for the scheme. They were not German or Austrian Jews whose lives had been destroyed, economically and politically, in the years after Hitler became German Chancellor in 1933.

Abraham Leibler had established himself in his family's diamond enterprise in the Belgian city of Antwerp, which by the mid-1930s was the centre of the diamond business in Europe. In Antwerp and in Brussels there were growing communities of Jews, most of them migrants from Eastern Europe, especially from Poland, where Abraham Leibler's parents had been born. It was a middle-class community of diamond dealers and clothing manufacturers.

Abraham was 29 years old when sometime in late 1938—there are no records of his departure from Antwerp—he set off by boat on a business trip to Singapore and Australia to sell diamonds. Rachel Leibler also came from a family of diamond dealers. Photographs of her at 27 with Abraham and their young boy, Isi, show a dark-haired, attractive young woman, dressed in the nicely tailored clothes that were the fashion among the middle-class young women of Antwerp. Her family, like Abraham's, was Orthodox; they were religious Zionists. They led an upper middle-class life that probably had all the trappings of such a life in pre-war Belgium—a nice apartment, a couple of housekeepers, a nanny and the financial means to take part in the cultural life, both Jewish and non-Jewish, of the city.

While there were ominous signs at the beginning of 1939 that Europe was heading towards another conflict, and that the Nazis represented a particular threat to Europe's Jews, what eventually happened to the Jews of Europe was unimaginable to Abraham and Rachel. Abraham set off for Singapore and then Melbourne and Sydney, with no thought of the dangers that his wife and son and their extended families might face back home. He was in Melbourne, having arrived aboard the passenger ship *Nieuw Holland* in February 1939, when he read the letter from Rachel telling him not to come back to Antwerp and that she was making arrangements to come to Australia with Isi.

Rachel Leibler was already a presence in the Antwerp Jewish community, active in the synagogue that the family attended and involved in the nascent Zionist movement that would be one of her great passions during a life that spanned 103 years. She was a formidable person in the Leibler family and would grow ever more formidable in the years after Abraham died in 1957.

One time, when talking about his mother, Mark Leibler speculated about what might have happened to his parents and his brother, had it not been for her foresight, her sense that Europe was about to be consumed by war and that the Jews faced the most implacable enemy in their history. It was not as if the Jews of Belgium faced any imminent danger. They were not in the same precarious position as the Jews of Germany and Austria, or of Eastern Europe for that matter.

Rachel Leibler's parents, like many of the Jews in Belgium, did not flee the country. They stayed in the place where they had built their lives. In 1943, both of them were transported to Auschwitz, along with thousands of the country's Jews. Rachel's parents died in Auschwitz; no-one knows whether they were murdered shortly after their arrival or whether they were gassed later, when they could no longer work.

According to records kept at Melbourne's Immigration Museum, Rachel Leibler (nee Akermann) and her four-year-old son, Uziel Joseph, arrived in Melbourne on 13 June 1939 aboard the passenger liner, *Strathaird*. Abraham Leibler was at the dock in Port Melbourne to meet them. He had not seen Rachel and Isi for more than nine months. He had been sharing a small flat in the bayside suburb of Elwood, but had rented a bigger flat for his family in a nearby street, not far from the house (*shtibl*) where the Jews of the area went for the Sabbath service and Jewish festivals. It would later become the Elwood Synagogue, where Arnold Bloch, the founder of the legal firm in which Mark Leibler was to spend his professional life, was an imposing presence after his arrival in Australia from England in 1948.

Did the Leiblers come with money? Abraham must have had diamonds with him when he left Antwerp for Singapore and Australia in late 1939. And when his mother and Isi left for Australia, there were no obstacles for Jews leaving Belgium to sell their property and take their wealth with them. Leibler did not know what his parents had brought with them to Australia, but, from the time of their arrival in Melbourne, the family lived a comfortable, middle-class life. They had a car (a Holden), and never needed help from the Jewish welfare agencies that were overwhelmed with the needs of the pre-war refugees and, later, the mostly destitute Holocaust survivors.

The war in Europe was just three months away when, in June 1939, the Leiblers settled into their flat in Elwood and Abraham set up his diamond business in Little Collins Street in the Melbourne central business district. Australia was an outpost of the British Empire. While it was independent to a certain extent and about as far away from Britain as was geographically possible, its population of seven million was mostly Anglo-Saxon and loyal to what they saw as their motherland, though a significant population of Irish Catholic background most certainly felt no great allegiance to the Empire or the British Crown. In those days the word "diversity" pertained only to plant and animal species, not to human beings, and the word "multicultural" was still many decades away from becoming a description of Australian society.

As for the Jewish community that the Leibler family was to help reshape and revitalise, it mirrored the general Australian community in many ways. A majority were largely assimilated Anglo Jews, dedicated supporters of King and Empire. But even in 1939, years before the arrival of tens of thousands of Holocaust survivors, the transformation of the Jewish community in Australia was underway, with the influx of some 7000 Jewish migrants and refugees, including the 39rs. These refugees and migrants, small in number, began the revolutionary changes that would accelerate in the post-war decades and would transform the Australian Jewish community.

When the Leiblers settled in Melbourne in 1939, there were close to 29,000 Jews in Australia, 6000 more than in 1933, when the Jewish population had been declining for some years because of inter-marriage and assimilation. There had been a Jewish presence in Australia since the landing of the First Fleet in 1788, with seven or eight alleged Jewish thieves among the convicts transported to the penal colony. Small but significant numbers of Jews arrived in Australia during the gold rushes of the 1850s and 1860s, most from Britain and some from Germany. In the early 20th century, most Jews who migrated to Australia were British, mostly English, Jews and, as a consequence, the Jewish community up to the early 1930s was a sort of microcosm of Australia. In every synagogue hung a portrait of the British king or queen, and one of the prayers of the Sabbath service on Saturday mornings was that God protect and look after their beloved monarch.

The Jews considered themselves Anglo-Australians of the Hebrew, or Mosaic, persuasion. John Monash, the great Australian World War 1 general, and Isaac Isaacs, the nation's first Australian-born Governor-General, were part of that Anglo-Australian culture, although their ancestors had come to Australia from Germany and Poland respectively. They were assimilated Jews, with a deep understanding and knowledge of British history, British institutions and the classics of English literature. For a while Monash was honorary President of the newly established Zionist Federation of Australia, but he was the exception rather than the rule. Men like Isaacs, while they were not ashamed of being Jews, did not consider being Jewish particularly significant. They were not Zionists. They would have found the concept of Jewish peoplehood or of a Jewish nation entirely alien.

In their 2018 book, *A Second Chance: The Making of Yiddish Melbourne*, Margaret Taft and Andrew Markus write that around

2000 Jews managed to escape the pogroms and persecutions in Eastern Europe during the 1920s and make their way to Australia. These Jews were radically different to the Anglo Jews. They spoke mainly Yiddish and were steeped in Yiddish culture and traditions, and, critically, they did not define their Jewishness narrowly, as a matter of religious adherence. Many were Zionists who believed in Jewish nationhood. Even the several hundred anti-Zionist Bundists who came to Australia just before World War 2, and as Holocaust survivors after it, had a concept of Jewish peoplehood that involved a connection with Jewish history and a deep involvement with Yiddish culture.

Unsurprisingly, the established Jewish community and its leadership in Melbourne and Sydney were hostile to these strange Jews, with whom they had little in common. They worried that the strangeness —the way they dressed and spoke—would provoke an increase in anti-Semitism. As Taft and Markus write:

> The established community gained acceptance through deliberate adoption of British customs and protocols, through their promotion to positions of public office and their loyalty and patriotism to the British Empire in times of crisis.

> For example, a large proportion of young Jewish men answered the call to arms with the outbreak of the Great War in 1914. Thirteen per cent of the eligible male Jewish population voluntarily enlisted compared to nine per cent of the total population.

By the time Abraham and Rachel Leibler and their son, Isi, embarked on their new life in Elwood, the Anglo establishment that ran the Jewish communities in Melbourne and Sydney was starting to feel challenged, both by the "reffos", mostly from Eastern Europe, who had come to Australia in the 1920s, and by the 7000 or so Jews accepted as refugees under the Australian government's quota for Jews fleeing Nazi persecution. From the time they arrived, Abraham Leibler identified with the reffos rather than with the Anglos. While they did not live in the inner city suburb of Carlton, north of the Yarra River, where the Eastern European refugees had established themselves and had set up their cultural institutions, which were to become some of the great examples of what multiculturalism could achieve, the Leibler family had no great affinity with the establishment leadership of the Jewish community. They may have lived in the heartland suburbs of Anglo Jewry—St Kilda and Elwood—but their hearts were elsewhere.

In essence, the conflict between the Anglo-Jewish establishment and the reffos was about Jewish identity. Were Jews essentially Australians of the Hebraic faith—"Hebrews" as they were referred to in some Anglo circles—or were they more than a faith community? Were they a people, even a nation, as the Zionists believed? When the Leiblers arrived in Australia, the Jewish community in Melbourne and Sydney had advisory boards that consisted of representatives of the Orthodox congregations—there were no Reform congregations on these boards—and only "established" congregations were represented. The reffo synagogues in Melbourne and Sydney were not.

It was inevitable that the refugee Jews would challenge this narrow concept of Jewish identity and the community organisations that embodied it; it was inevitable, too, that the battles between the Anglos and the refugees and migrants would be hard-fought and bitter. The politics of Jewish community life in 1939, through the war years and the post-war period into which Abraham Leibler immersed himself, were not for the faint-hearted. There was much at stake. Abraham Leibler was a religious Zionist whose conception of Jewishness involved, at its heart, the dream of a Jewish state for the Jewish nation. This idea was anathema for much of the Anglo-Jewish establishment before the establishment of Israel in 1948 and, for some, even after its establishment.

Abraham Leibler believed that things had to change in Australia. It was a disgrace that the fledgling Zionist organisations were not represented on the Jewish advisory boards in Sydney and Melbourne. Nor were the Bundists represented, for that matter. Leibler believed that broad-based community organisations were needed, with delegates representing every facet of Jewish life—Zionists, non-Zionists, religious congregations of every kind, secularist Yiddish cultural activists. It was not just the Zionists like Leibler who believed that the community organisations had an outdated and inadequate concept of Jewishness. The secular Yiddishists and even the anti-Zionist and militantly anti-religious and socialist Bund banded together to agitate for reform of the community leadership held tightly by the Anglo establishment.

The idea that the established congregations should form only part of the leadership of the Jewish community was revolutionary. In a sense, it was the first battle in Australia between proponents of assimilation and the proponents of cultural and even national expressions of identity, who argued that such expressions of identity did not contradict total loyalty to Australia.

From the time the Leiblers arrived in Australia, they advocated for this ideology—that Jews were not just a faith community but a people, and that one day, once Israel became a reality, they would be a nation. In the Australia of the 1940s and 1950s, this was not an easy position to hold publicly. The almost familial ties with Britain were all-encompassing. Australia was monocultural and before the arrival of hundreds of thousands of migrants from Europe in the 1950s, ethnically homogeneous. Even in the 1950s, more migrants arriving in Australia were from Britain than from any other place. The immigrants from

Europe were expected to assimilate into the general community as quickly as possible. No alternatives were offered.

In this context, the idea that the Jews were somehow part of a nation or a people and not just Australian was puzzling at best and threatening at worst. The Anglo Jews understood this. It is why, during World War 2, when it became clear that the Nazis were perpetrating a genocide of Europe's Jews, their leaders were loath to protest too vociferously, to demand too stridently that the Allies, Australia included, do more to rescue the Jews who had not yet been murdered. The charge of dual loyalties haunted them.

It was a charge made regularly against the Jews in Europe. The Jews were loyal to each other and not to the countries where they lived. This accusation dogged the Jews for centuries; it dogged them across different Jewish communities—both those, like the German Jewish community, that were assimilated and whose members saw themselves as patriots of the nations they lived in, and the Eastern European communities, where the Jews lived in ghettoes separated from the rest of the population by government edict and by the rituals and its dietary laws of their Judaism. Sometimes the dual loyalties' charge was expressed as an accusation that Jews were a fifth column of traitors hidden in the general population. Hitler famously ranted about the Jewish stab-in-the-back of the German people during World War 1.

It was, however, a relatively new concept in Australia, where, until the arrival of the refugee Jews in the 1930s, Australia's Anglo Jews had, in the main, done everything they could to avoid being accused of such a terrible thing. After the establishment of Israel, the dual loyalties' charge morphed into a charge that Jews were more loyal to Israel than to the countries where they lived and had often lived for generations.

Abraham Leibler and Rachel were religious Zionists. From the time they came to Australia, Abraham immersed himself in the Jewish community, which was going through a time of profound change. Inevitably, they would have had to deal with the charge of dual loyalties, but Mark Leibler could not recall his father or mother ever talking about it. Looking back, he could not remember ever being subjected to any sort of anti-Semitism, even though he was a lifelong Zionist and a veteran Jewish leader. Could this be true? He insisted to me that it was. In part this was because he had lived his childhood wholly within the Jewish community. In part it was because Australia had no history of the sort of vicious and often murderous anti-Semitism of Europe, but it was also about the way that Leibler lived his life from when he was young.

Born in 1943, at the height of the genocide of the Jews in Europe, when most of the six million or so Jews who were to be murdered during World War 2 had already been killed, Leibler's memories of his childhood in Melbourne are sketchy. He does not remember any prolonged family discussions about what was happening in Europe, which is hardly surprising given that he was only two years old when the war ended, but nor could he recall his parents ever talking to him later about what had happened to the Jews during the war.

Isi Leibler remembers that time rather differently. He was nine years older than his brother. As is often the case with siblings born many years apart, they had the same parents but different childhoods. Isi said that his father influenced him profoundly in two ways. First, Abraham was an outspoken promoter of moderation within Orthodox Judaism through his involvement with Mizrachi, a religious Zionist organisation that in Australia is like a self-contained community, with its own synagogues, day schools and youth movement, Bnei Akiva.

Founded at an international conference in Lithuania in 1902, Mizrachi would become part of Israel's first official religious Zionist party, contesting seats in the Knesset for the first time in 1951. Bnei Akiva (Hebrew for the children of Akiva) was established in Palestine 1929 as the youth organisation of the religious Zionists. It is named after Rabbi Akiva, a rabbinical authority on Judaism's major texts, who was executed by the Romans in the aftermath of the failed Jewish revolt against Roman rule in 66CE.

In Australia, Mizrachi and Bnei Akiva have had an impact on Jewish life far beyond the size of their membership. From the start, the international Zionist movement was overwhelmingly a secular nationalist movement that included left and right groups and parties. The religious Zionists were always in the minority, internationally, in Israel, and in Australia as well. But Mizrachi has produced some of the Australian Jewish community's most influential leaders; the Leibler family is just one of the country's prominent Mizrachi families.

The second major way that Abraham Leibler influenced Isi's life was in moulding his eldest son's political outlook. From early in his life, Isi knew that his mother's parents had been gassed at Auschwitz. The Shoah (Hebrew term for the Holocaust) was uppermost in Isi Leibler's mind.

Abraham, according to Isi, was a born leader. Until he became president of the Victorian Jewish Board of Deputies, it had always been controlled by the Anglo Jews, whom Isi described as "more respectable, more conservative—and absolute arseholes to the Holocaust survivors and the East European Jews." These survivors and refugees were his father's constituency. Later, they became Isi's constituency and remained so ever after. Isi has often told veteran journalist Sam Lipski, who had known Isi since they were boys at

Bnei Akiva, that Abraham was a huge influence on the sort of Jewish leader he, Isi became.

When Isi Leibler spoke to me of that time, he remembered that his father had been a leader of a Jewish faction of Zionists and anti-communist socialists who were opposed to the Jewish Council to Combat Fascism and Anti-Semitism, a left-wing Jewish organisation formed during the war which by the 1950s and 1960s had become a major force in Australian Jewish community politics. According to Isi Leibler, the Jewish Council in the 1950s was virtually running the Jewish community. This is undoubtedly an exaggeration, but there is no doubt that the Jewish Council was a major force in the community. Many of its members and leaders were either communists or fellow travellers. Abraham Leibler taught his sons that, now that fascism had been defeated, communists were the enemy. He led the battle to expel the Council from the Board of Deputies in Victoria.

It was during this time, when he was still a teenager, that Isi got involved in Jewish politics, which led to his involvement and eventual leadership of the global movement to free the Soviet Jews. As a result of this movement more than a million Jews were allowed to leave the Soviet Union. The largest number went to Israel and transformed the country. The vast majority of them were enemies of the left, having grown up and lived in what was supposed to have been socialist paradise. These immigrants, who had seen socialism up close, entrenched the rule of right-wing Israeli governments. About 10,000 Soviet Jews settled in Australia.

In 1990, on the 33rd anniversary of Abraham Leibler's death, Yiddish journalist Shmuel Bennet wrote a tribute to him entitled "Historical Sketches of Jewish Australia". The article was published in "Yiddishe Nayes", the Yiddish section of the *Australian Jewish News*. When Mark

Leibler found it among his papers some years ago, he could not read it. Not only can he not read or write Yiddish, but he speaks hardly a word of the language his father seems to have loved. In a sense, this merely reflects the way Zionist movements became determined over the years to establish Hebrew as the language of the "new" Jews and to consign to history Yiddish, a language of the powerless Jews of Eastern Europe who were annihilated by the Nazis.

In the article, Bennet described Abraham as a gentle, tolerant and much-loved leader of the Melbourne Jewish community. He was a founder, Bennet wrote, of the Elwood Synagogue, a long-time president of Mizrachi, and president of the Jewish Board of Deputies. "His attitude to Yiddish, which he often used at Board meetings, made him popular with the Jewish masses, particularly the refugees. He was a warm man and a tolerant man, tolerant of all Jewish political parties and groups." This description of Abraham does not sound much like his two sons, Isi and Mark. Even their most loyal supporters would agree that the Leibler brothers played their politics hard, that they were always up for a fight, and that they could be vicious about and towards their opponents. They made enemies. They regularly fell out with people; indeed, in the early 1990s, they fell out with each other.

While influence is never easy to pinpoint, it is hard to see how they modeled themselves on their father. Perhaps a stronger influence was their mother, who lived a long life and was for many years a leader of the Mizrachi women's organisation, both in Australia and around the world. Rachel Leibler, by all accounts, was a woman to be reckoned with.

When I asked Mark about his father, and what the family talked about at those Friday night Sabbath meals, he said that he was still very young when his father died and could not remember the specifics of those meals. He could remember that his father talked about leadership issues and about the Jewish community. Sometimes, he said, they had important visitors from Israel, politicians, and the Israeli ambassador to dinner. Mark got to meet various Israeli politicians and community leaders when he was still a small child.

What he remembered most vividly, he said, was being taken to a Yom Ha'atzmaut, the Israel Independence day celebration. Thousands of people were at Festival Hall in West Melbourne and his father was up on the stage, sitting at a long table with other community leaders. This must have been before 1957, Mark said, the year his father died. He had always known that his father was a leader of the Australian Jews.

Was he also—at a tender age—witness to the often bitter inter-community leadership disputes in which his father must have participated? More than once Mark said that his father had been a major influence on his early ambitions to become a leader of the Jews, but that his mother, Rachel, had been far more influential than his father, who died when Mark was 14. When he spoke about his father, he tended to speak in platitudes.

He seems to have had a rather idyllic, materially comfortable childhood. Although he was born at the height of the Holocaust, it did not play a significant part in his early years, before his father died. It did not, as far as he could tell, hang like a dark memory over his family, as it did over many of the families of the Jewish children he went to school with at Mount Scopus College. It seems that Abraham and Rachel Leibler had decided early on that they would not burden their children with talk of the Holocaust, how it had consumed the lives of Rachel's parents and destroyed the comfortable middle-class life they had lived in Jewish Antwerp.

CHAPTER 2

One thing Mark Leibler did remember was coming home from school one day and seeing a beautiful Jaguar parked in the driveway of their house in Caulfield. It was about 1954, after his father and mother had been back to their house in Antwerp to retrieve from its brickwork a bundle of diamonds that his mother's parents had hidden before they were sent to Auschwitz. Now his parents could afford to splurge a little. A Jaguar would have been his father's idea. His father, he said, had always liked nice things.

CHAPTER 3

Sam Lipski vividly remembers what the American writer, Herman Wouk, said about his experience of the Australian Jewish community when he visited Australia nearly 30 years ago. Wouk, who died in 2019, aged 104, would have been in his late 70s when he came to Australia in the early 1990s. His books include the Pulitzer Prize-winning novel, *The Caine Mutiny*, and *Marjorie Morningstar*, which was made into a Hollywood movie starring Natalie Wood and Gene Kelly. Perhaps his best-known books are the historical novels about World War 2, *The Winds of War* and *War and Remembrance*, both of which were made into successful miniseries in the 1990s. At a Library of Congress function to mark his 80th birthday, Wouk was described by a number of literary critics as America's Tolstoy. Wouk also wrote a sort of primer about Judaism, and Orthodox Judaism in particular, entitled *This is my God*. Hundreds of thousands of copies have been sold. It has never been out of print and it remains the biggest selling book by far about the Jewish religion, its history and its major teachings.

Wouk came to Australia at the invitation of his friend, legal academic and former Governor-General, Zelman Cowen. He visited Jewish schools and Jewish cultural institutions in Melbourne and Sydney. He was apparently surprised not just by the number of Jewish schools and the plethora of Jewish cultural and political bodies, but by the vitality of Jewish communal life, given the relatively small size of the Jewish community in Australia.

When he was in Melbourne and was taken to the Kadimah, the Jewish Cultural Centre, which had been Australia's major Yiddish cultural organisation for almost a century, he was reduced to tears. On the stage, in his honour, a choir of primary-school children from Sholem Aleichem College, named after Yiddish writer Sholem Aleichem and the only secular Jewish day school in the world that teaches Yiddish and Yiddish culture, sang for him. The children sang the Yiddish folk songs of his long-ago childhood. These children reminded him of what had vanished from American Jewish life.

Asked to explain why he was so moved, Wouk said something that Sam Lipski has never forgotten. He said that he was not an expert on Australian Jewry, but he had come to believe that there was a confluence of things that made this community unique. It was a post-Holocaust community, meaning that by the late 1940s its population was mostly made up of Holocaust survivors. At that very time the miracle of Israel's birth took place. For these people, the two events created a path from darkness and hopelessness to light and hope. After their unspeakable suffering, Australia offered recovery, and the establishment of Israel offered them redemption. These two things happening simultaneously was the key, Wouk said, to understanding the Jewish community in Australia.

The irony in all this was that these children who had reduced Wouk to tears went to a school that was established by the leaders of the Bund. Although Sholem Aleichem College was never a Bundist school—it could never have attracted enough students if it had been—it was not a Zionist school either. The Bundists, while a minority in the Jewish community, had had their own form of resurrection after the Holocaust. In Australia, these refugees and survivors somehow retained their commitment to building a better world, their belief in the international brotherhood of man and, critically, in Jewish continuity and survival. Part of their commitment involved keeping alive the Yiddish culture of old Europe, from which Jews had almost entirely vanished, by teaching its music, stories and language to their children.

It was in this larger Australian Jewish community that Wouk so admired, in which recovery and redemption were fused, that Mark Leibler and his older brother, Isi, would become leaders. Sam Lipski was also raised in this community and was to become the best-known Jewish journalist of his generation, a public intellectual who moved effortlessly between the world of Jewish journalism and journalism in the general community. He was a columnist for *The Bulletin* magazine, a Washington correspondent for *The Australian* newspaper, and executive producer of the Australian Broadcasting Commission (ABC)'s nightly current affairs program, *This Day Tonight*.

Like all migrant and refugee families—but especially so for the Jewish refugees of the 1930s and the Holocaust survivors of the late 1940s and 1950s—Abraham and Rachel Leibler were committed to the continuity and strength of their own community before they developed an attachment to Australia and came to consider themselves Australian. This was also true of Isi Leibler, who was born in pre-war Antwerp, and it was true for Mark, even though he was born in Australia. But Isi Leibler's experience of being a Jew was different in some fundamental way to his younger brother's.

In a long feature article on the Leibler brothers in the *Australian Financial Review* in 1987, Isi Leibler described his childhood encounters at Melbourne High School in the late 1940s and early 1950s, when non-Jewish boys formed gangs that taunted and beat up migrant and Jewish boys. The experience, he told journalist Ruth Ostrow,

> transformed me into the person I am. That brought out my aggressive responses. They have stayed with me. I was one of six Jewish kids collected by the older boys and beaten up. I was

so outraged that, for the next year, I organised teams of kids to systematically beat up the people who had humiliated me.

He remembered the hostile world his parents escaped in 1939, when he was four years old. According to Ostrow, he "remembered hearing, as a small boy in Australia, of his grandparents' extermination at the hands of the Nazis."

In the article, Mark Leibler also talked about his school years, but he had gone to a different school where he had suffered none of his brother's childhood traumas, no taunts about being Jewish and no beatings. There was no evidence that he was ever aware of what his brother had experienced. Ostrow describes him as a "tough and stubborn character," a terror who could not be controlled by his teachers. "I was impossible at school, obnoxious," he is quoted as saying. "I opposed anyone who tried to impose discipline. The headmaster wanted to know how a boy from an intelligent, fine family could behave like that. I hated having to conform." Nevertheless, by the last two years of his schooling, Mark Leibler knew that he wanted to be a lawyer. He studied hard, even though he often skipped classes, and had lost none of his dislike of authority. He was looking forward to going to university.

It is as if the brothers grew up in different epochs and came from different families. Their different childhoods reflected the way the Jewish community had changed in just a few years, from the time Isi went to school in the 1940s to the mid- to late-1950s of Mark's school days.

In 1948, after a period of intense community debate, in which many argued against any move to set up a Jewish day school because they feared that it would promote insularity and separation from the general community, a group of business people and education activists, having raised enough money to get started, established Mount Scopus College, Australia's first Jewish day school. This was a brave move for a small community. There were no government grants for private schools, which had to be funded entirely from donations and fees.

Mount Scopus College opened its doors in St Kilda Road, Melbourne, in February 1949 with 123 students. Among them was five-year-old Mark Leibler. Now based in outer suburban Burwood, to which its students are bussed from faraway Caulfield, St Kilda and Elsternwick, Mount Scopus College was to grow into the largest Jewish day school in Australia and one of the largest in the world, with more than 1500 students. (Sydney's Moriah College enrolments have now overtaken those of Mount Scopus.) It was to become part of a network of Jewish day schools in Melbourne and Sydney that by the 1980s and 1990s surpassed, in its reach and its impact on Jewish life, any Jewish day school system in the world.

The establishment of Mount Scopus College and Moriah College in the 1940s and early 1950s was a sign of the Australian Jewish community's transformation in the immediate post-war years. The schools were a consequence of the community's rapid growth and increasing wealth and of the determination of the pre-war Jewish refugees and post-war Holocaust survivors to rebuild a rich Jewish life in Australia—the sort of life that had been destroyed in Europe.

Asked about his memories of Mount Scopus College, where he spent 12 years of his childhood, Mark Leibler remembered most vividly that he was a rebellious boy who did not like being told what to do. In Form Four (Year 10), when only prefects were allowed to go up the middle stairs of the school building, he would always go up the middle stairs, and he was regularly suspended as a result. That did not worry him. He said that it helped to explain why, apart from a couple of years when he started as a lawyer, Leibler had never worked as an employee for anyone or any organisation.

How important was it that he had gone to a Jewish school, unlike his older brother, who had gone to state schools for the whole of his education? How different, as a result, were their experiences?

As Mark talked about his early life, something emerged that perhaps he had not realised before; unlike his brother, he had led a wholly Jewish life until he was 18 and started university. He was raised in an Orthodox Jewish home, which meant that he went to synagogue on Saturday morning and sometimes for the Friday night services. With the rest of the family, he observed the Sabbath. He never went to the pictures or to a game of football on Saturday. He went to a Jewish school and, three days a week after school, he went for extra religious instruction. Every Saturday afternoon, from the age of eight, he went to Bnei Akiva, and for 10 days every summer he went to a Bnei Akiva camp. In the summer holidays, he sometimes went with his mother and father and Isi to St Kilda Beach, which was a meeting place for Jewish families.

Did he have any non-Jewish friends? Did he, like Isi, experience anti-Semitism when he was growing up? He replied,

No, I don't think I did have any non-Jewish friends. I was basically mixing with Jews all the time. It was one of the downsides of a Jewish day school education, but I think that the upsides, in terms of one's Jewish character, clearly outweigh the downsides. But it is a disadvantage in the sense that you know only Jews. Of course later on, when I went to university, I came into contact with non-Jewish people and even later, at ABL, we had non-Jewish clients and non- Jewish lawyers, so all that changed. But I had very few close friends, Jewish or non-Jewish.

When asked about Isi's experience of anti-Semitism when he was young and about how this experience had been fundamental to making him the sort of leader and person that his brother became, Mark Leibler said that he was not really able to answer the question.

Did Isi ever talk to him about his experiences? He didn't think so. They were, he said, different people. He had never felt threatened as a Jew in Australia. He had never experienced anti-Semitism—not when he was a child and not at university, nor when he started in the law, even when he knew that the establishment law firms had a sort of unofficial ban on hiring Jewish lawyers, no matter how outstanding their results in law school.

Life in the Leibler family was marked by the rituals of Jewish family life: synagogue; family meals on Friday night and Saturday afternoon; Abraham more and more involved in his community work, out at meetings a couple of nights a week; Rachel at home looking after her husband and three sons. Allan, who was two years younger than Mark, was eventually to go into the family diamond business, but he never followed in the footsteps of his father and brothers in terms of leadership position in the Jewish community.

Mark Leibler's memories of his life before his father died are vague and hazy. Much of his childhood seems to be submerged deep inside him. At times, when asked for details, he is embarrassed that his memories are so meagre and lacking in detail.

Did the family eat together other than on the Sabbath? What did he remember about his mother and father and their relationship? Was he close to them? To Isi? He had said that he always had very few friends—was he a lonely boy?

He thought that his family probably did not eat their evening meal together. He would come home from school on the school bus and sometimes his mother was not home, so the housekeeper would prepare a snack for him and for Allan. He could not remember whether Isi was there; he was older and didn't go to school with them. His parents, as far as he could remember, never fought. They had an old-school way of bringing up their children. His mother was most concerned that her children got a good Jewish education and general education. "I don't know because I was so young, but I think my parents were close. There were never any fights." But his mother was never particularly demonstrative. He could not remember ever going into his parents' bedroom and hopping into bed with them for a cuddle.

His parents travelled a lot, but never with their children. They visited Israel regularly—unusual for Australian Jews in the 1950s—and America, where his father had close family. Both parents were busy with their community work, and his father worked hard to build up his diamond business. Leibler says he never felt neglected or unloved. It was just a form of parenting common in the 1950s.

In the decade to 1957, the Australian Jewish community had almost doubled in size, from about 32,000 to more than 55,000. The vast majority of Jews lived in Sydney and Melbourne, with around 25,000 in Sydney and 29,000 in Melbourne. The post-war mass migration program that saw hundreds of thousands of migrants from Italy, Greece, central and Eastern Europe and Scandinavia settle in Australia peaked in the 1950s. The nation was being transformed, although British culture remained dominant for at least another decade and the consensus across the political parties was for assimilation, for the absorption of these multitudes of migrants from non-English-speaking backgrounds into the general population as quickly as possible. Wherever you had come from, leave that baggage behind! Whatever you had suffered, leave that behind as well! Become Australian, like the rest of us!

For the vast majority of the nearly 30,000 Jews who came to Australia in the 1940s and 1950s, the notion that they could shed their individual and collective past the moment the ships bringing them to Australia docked was unimaginable. Having lived through the near genocide of European Jewry, they were not about to "complete Hitler's work", as many of them put it, by assimilating, by becoming Australians of the Hebrew persuasion like the Anglo-Australian Jews.

As historian Suzanne Rutland observed in *The Jews in Australia* in 2005, being Jewish for these survivors of the Holocaust meant much more than being adherents of Judaism. In their pre-war Eastern European communities they had considered themselves Jews first and foremost, rather than Poles, or Hungarians or Russians. "They were well-versed in Jewish scholarship, often deeply religious and in many cases, passionately Zionist," she wrote. "They were generally imbued with European culture and were experienced in organisational politics."

By 1957, these Jews not only outnumbered the Anglo Jews but had taken over the leadership of all Jewish community organisations. The unique nature of the Australian Jewish community, its rich cultural institutions and reinvigorated religious life, the exponential growth of Zionist organisations and their flourishing youth movements, all came from this fusion, as Herman Wouk so vividly put it, of survival in Australia after the Holocaust and the redemptive power of the establishment of the state of Israel. Even the Bund and its youth movement, the SKIF, in which I grew up and which profoundly influenced my understanding of the world, grew out of the Wouk fusion. After the establishment of Israel, the Bund's anti-Zionism was replaced with a sort of non-Zionism that nevertheless recognised the importance of Israel for Jews everywhere.

It was wholly within this community, which his father had helped shape, that Mark Leibler lived. Then, on 18 June 1957, when he was 14, Leibler was told that he and his brother Allan had to go straight home on the school bus. Abraham Leibler had spent three weeks in bed after suffering a heart attack. His son recalled that his father had recovered a bit and was planning to go back to his diamond business:

> I remember that day very clearly. We had an appointment to go to the dentist and I can remember being told that the appointment had been cancelled. We had to go straight home. I was quite apprehensive because my father had become sick three weeks earlier.
>
> I remember being dropped off at the corner with Allan and the two of us rushing home and my mother telling us that our father was gone. He had died at home. I was quite shocked and distressed. We had a sort of shed in the back yard and I think I must have locked myself in there for an hour... maybe an hour and a half.
>
> I remember the funeral the next day at Fawkner Cemetery. It was pouring and there were a lot of people at the cemetery. Isi was not there. He was living in Israel, studying political science. He had planned to become an Israeli diplomat. But he had to come home eventually to run the family business.

Did Mark talk to his mother about his father's death? Or to Isi, when his older brother came back to Australia a year afterwards? What he remembered was that the day his father died, his mother did not cry, and never cried from that day on. Neither she nor Isi ever talked to him about his father's death. His mother never married again, and they never talked about that either.

After his father died, a family friend called Joe Feiglin, whose family were major fruit growers near Shepparton in regional Victoria and were active in the Melbourne Jewish community, took Mark to synagogue and after-school religious instruction lessons. Feiglin, although Leibler liked him, didn't talk to him about his father's death either. Instead, he says, he spent his time thinking. He thought about mortality all the time, and, if he talked to anyone, he talked to himself.

Isi Leibler remembered how he had tried, after his father's death, to be a surrogate father to Mark. But his brother had always resented his older brother telling him what to do. This resistance had often been the cause of conflict between them. Isi said that the impact of their father's death on Mark was different from how it affected him. Isi was in Israel planning to become an Israeli diplomat. He wanted to come home for his father's funeral but his mother said he had to stay in Israel and learn about the diamond trade before he took over the family business. He spent three months in Israel before going to Antwerp for three of the most miserable months of his life. But these months changed the direction of his life, as until then he hadn't known the difference between a diamond and a piece of glass.

Even though the impact on Isi's life was ostensibly greater, from the time his father died, Mark said, he knew that he wanted to be a leader and that he had the qualities a leader needed. Even as a teenager, he believed that the strength and vitality of any organisation was determined by the strength and vitality of its leader and that virtually nothing else mattered.

Despite his rebelliousness, he was an ambitious boy in his final years of school. He was announced dux of Mount Scopus College at the end of his matriculation year in 1961. In the following January his mother wrote to him at the Bnei Akiva summer camp. He was unwell and she urged him to postpone a planned trip to Sydney:

My dear Mark

First let me congratulate you on your brilliant results so far…I am terribly proud and excited. Last night I went out for tea and a show with Mrs. Bloch and on my return, I was pleasantly surprised to find your letters and hope you have got rid of your cough.

For once, you should take my advice and postpone your trip.

I hope to see some more good results from you…

All is well here…

My fondest love

Mother

At the bottom of the aerogram is a note from Isi: "Well it looks as though I'm soon going to be dwarfed academically by a brother who, if he can keep going, will certainly have a brilliant academic career ahead of him. Congratulations. I am really delighted and proud of you."

There is no evidence that Mark Leibler delayed his trip, as his mother had urged him to do. He was 18 years old, and for the first time was about to enter, at least in part, the non-Jewish world.

CHAPTER 4

In the lounge area of her husband's study, Rosanna Leibler sits forward on the edge of the couch, holding a cup of instant coffee. She looks younger than 72, with no grey in her dark hair, and she is nervous because she has never before talked about her life this way, not even with her close friends. She tells the story of the day Rachel Leibler summoned her to the Leibler home.

Rosanna had met Mark six years earlier at Bnei Akiva, where they had gone every Saturday afternoon since they were children. Although they were together for five years before they married, Mark and Rosanna knew early on that they would be a couple, and she knew that, when he asked her to marry him, she would not have to think for more than a second or two before she gave her answer. One day, Rosanna says, Rachel Leibler

> called me up and asked to see me. Mark had proposed by then I think, but anyway, the families had been close for a long time, since we were children, so she didn't call me to check me out, no. We had all lived pretty close to each other, the two families. My father had great respect for Abraham Leibler. Everyone did. I loved him even though I was just a small girl. I can remember how his death was such a shock to everyone, to the whole community. Isi was in Israel when Mr. Leibler died. He didn't come back for his father's funeral. That must have been terribly hard.

When Rachel Leibler sat down with her future daughter-in-law,

> she said to me, "Now listen, you have to be an obedient wife, you have to do whatever he wants because he's going to be the breadwinner and he's got a career and he's going to be a leader, and it means you won't have a career and you have to do everything

and be supportive so that he can reach his potential." That's how she spoke to me.

Mark Leibler and Rosanna Weiss were married at the Mizrachi Synagogue in Caulfield on 6 June 1966. He was 22 and she was 21. By then, Rachel Leibler, widowed at the age of 42, had taken on the task that her husband would have seen as his responsibility had he lived long enough. She had quickly become the head of the family, the guide and planner of the future she wanted for her sons, the future she felt was their destiny.

Rosanna Weiss was a vivacious and outgoing young woman. She was in the final year of an Arts Degree at Melbourne University when Rachel Leibler set out her future so bluntly. Rosanna was not surprised by what she said. Her mother-in-law was the strongest person Rosanna had ever met. Rachel Leibler never talked about the trauma of losing her husband when she was young, and never talked about why she had never remarried even though, Rosanna said, she must have had suitors. She was an attractive and smart woman and the family was not poor. The only sign Rosanna saw that Rachel had been through hard times was that she could never cry. Rosanna had majored in psychology and understood this as a sign of the post-traumatic stress that Rachel had suffered after the death of her husband.

Did Rosanna heed her mother-in-law's command and become the sort of wife that Rachel felt Mark would need in order to fulfil his potential? She did. She might have resented her mother-in-law's intervention, but she never really thought that she would do anything other than live the sort of life that Rachel had mapped out for her.

Rosanna Leibler has an openness, with none of the lawyerly calcul-ation that her husband has developed and refined over the years. She says that Mark has always been rather awkward socially, not much good at small talk. When she first met him at Bnei Akiva, when they were teenagers, he was known as a dag. He never wore jeans to the meetings on Saturday afternoon, nor did he wear jeans at summer camp. Mostly he wore his Shabbat pants with three pleats. What attracted her to him?

> He was so smart. Intellectual. I loved the lectures he gave at camp, and he was so shy. Hadn't gone out with a girl before. I was not so shy. I think he liked that about me. I came from a very religious home, but I went to state schools. We girls were not allowed to wear pants but I would go out in a skirt with my pants on underneath, rolled up, and then take off the skirt and go meet the other girls and go to some party somewhere. I was cheeky. I loved life. I think Mark loved that about me.

Rosanna was unusual in another way, too. "She was very sort of demonstrative," says Mark Leibler. "She taught me to be demonstrative with our children. I don't know where she got it from because she came from a very strictly Orthodox family and you know cuddling children in bed or anywhere would have been unthinkable."

Rosanna was three years old when Eugene and Margaret Weiss arrived in Australia in 1948 with their seven daughters. Before the war the family had been prosperous and well known in the Jewish community of Bratislava, Czechoslovakia. Eugene, the father of nine children, had been a textile magnate.

Asked about her family's struggles during the war, Rosanna Leibler said that her parents never talked about it, and never answered any question that she or her sisters asked them about that time. It was not until 2014, when her eldest sister, Eva Slonim, published a memoir, *Gazing at the Stars*, that Rosanna learnt in detail what her parents and sisters had been through. The family's story has also been recorded in interviews with family members and is part of the testimony of Holocaust survivors stored at Yad Vashem, the Holocaust memorial in Jerusalem. It is a tragic story, and also one of almost miraculous survival.

After the Germans invaded Czechoslovakia, Eva, Marta and Judith Weiss were transported to Auschwitz. They were barely teenagers. Judith died there, but Eva and Marta survived and were liberated by Soviet soldiers. The rest of the family had been hidden with non-Jews in Czechoslovakia and Poland. This was possible, Rosanna said, because they had been a wealthy family, who could afford to pay people to save them. Later, when they wanted to come to Australia, the Weiss family was able to get a sponsor because Eugene had hidden money and diamonds in Bratislava. Just before they came, the family's one son, Kurti, drowned in an accident.

After arriving in Melbourne, the family quickly became part of the nascent Mizrachi community. The girls went to Bnei Akiva and, according to Sam Lipski, were all considered to be very intelligent and good-looking. The family went to synagogue every Saturday morning. Asked whether she still went to synagogue every Saturday, Rosanna said that she did not. Even when she was young, when her father forced her to go to synagogue, she had wondered how her parents could remain believers after what had happened to the Jews and to their family in particular. When she summoned up the courage to ask her father how God had allowed it all to happen, he said that God had his reasons.

As far as Rosanna could remember, her family's story and her views about God had not come up when she was Mark's young girlfriend. Nor had these things been talked about in the first years of their married life, when they were living in a small apartment in Caulfield and Mark was doing his articles at Arnold Bloch and Associates. By then she was pregnant. It was only later that she and Mark talked in depth about what had happened to her family.

One day early in their marriage, Mark came home from work and told her that he had been accepted into the Masters program in law at Yale. Taking a degree at one of the world's most prestigious universities was always a likely path for Mark Leibler. From the moment in 1962 when he walked as an undergraduate into the 19th century law building at Melbourne University, Leibler felt liberated. Hardly anyone ever told him what to do. There were no school rules. He studied hard, was focused, and felt at home in a way he never had at Mount Scopus College.

At university, for the first time in his life, Leibler had contact with non-Jews, though he cannot recall making any close friends at university. Nor did he have more than a few friends at school or at Bnei Akiva. Among the non-Jews he met at Melbourne University were lecturers, including Lloyd Churchwood, a communist. Listening to Churchwood's lectures, Leibler said, was an unusual experience because he disagreed with Churchwood about everything. When he started studying law, the baby boomers were still a few years away from the mass invasion of Australia's universities that was to transform the universities from a cosseted place for the wealthy and privileged to a place of student revolt by the mid-1960s.

Louis Waller, legal academic and Dean of Law at Monash University in the late 1960s, had Mark Leibler among his students when he was lecturer in criminal law at Melbourne University. In an interview before his death in 2019, Waller said that he knew the Leibler family through Isi and remembered Mark and Rosanna's wedding reception, which was quite an event in the Jewish community, with all its leaders present. By then, Isi Leibler, still in his twenties, was on the executive of the Victorian Jewish Board of Deputies and was considered destined for great things. The Leibler and Weiss families were widely known in the Jewish community, and Rachel Leibler had emerged as a community leader in her own right, at Mizrachi and in other Zionist women's organisations.

Waller sat at a table with other academics; a number of Mark Leibler's law lecturers were in the big crowd. Waller remembered that Arnold Bloch and his wife Elaine were there. He was close to the Blochs, especially Arnold, whom he considered to be a great lawyer. Isi was in great form that day, Waller said. He and Isi had been good friends since their Bnei Akiva days. Waller said that Isi was brilliant academically. He had graduated in political science with first class honours and could have done anything, but he had always wanted to study in Israel and join its diplomatic service.

After two years of teaching at the University of Pennsylvania, Waller returned to Australia in 1965 to take up a chair in law at Monash University. By this time, Leibler was in his final year at Melbourne University and contacted Waller to ask him to give a talk to the Melbourne University Jewish Students' Society, of which he was president. "He was on his way to becoming a leader in Jewish politics," Waller said. "He had blossomed. He ended up with a very good degree. Outstanding." In his final year, Leibler won the Supreme Court Prize for the university's top law student in 1965. Despite this achievement, he did not receive a single job offer from any of the established law firms. At the time these firms were known not to hire many Jews, as indeed established business did not accept Jewish businessmen. Hardly any, if any at all, sat on the boards of big public companies or owned shares in these companies. When I asked whether his failure to receive such an offer upset him, Leibler said that it hadn't; in fact, he did not think about it much at all. Perhaps he always knew that he would end up being hired by a Jewish firm.

By the time Leibler graduated, at 22, he also knew that the law and his ambition to be a Jewish leader, specifically a Zionist leader, would be the two great passions of his life. And he knew that the law and his community work would overlap—that what he had learnt studying law would be central to the sort of leader he would become. Law had taught him to think rationally about the way the world worked.

Did it inform the sort of leader he hoped to become, and especially his decision to focus on Zionism to the virtual exclusion of any other Jewish issue? His brother Isi, by contrast, saw himself as a community leader involved in and leading every aspect of Jewish life in Australia and internationally. I asked him whether he chose the narrow path because he did not want to compete with his older brother. In his view, I asked this question too many times. Surely, he said, there were more important things to discuss. Anyway, he had never thought about it. He had never in his life avoided anything in order not to step on someone's toes or invade their political territory, and that included his older brother.

Nevertheless, the differences between the brothers, both in terms of their childhood and school experiences and of the sort of Jewish leaders they were to become, were profound. From the start, Isi Leibler saw himself as a Jewish leader who, like his father, understood and formed relationships with every Jewish group: the religious Zionists, the secular Zionists, the Yiddishists, even the Bundists, whom he still saw as committed to Jewish peoplehood and continuity, even as he fiercely rejected their non-Zionism.

In the late 1960s, Isi Leibler developed a friendship with Bono Weiner, one of the Bund's leaders in Australia. Weiner was a Holocaust survivor whose formidable leadership skills had been honed in the pre-war Bund organisation in Poland and, later, in the Lodz Ghetto, from which he was transported to Auschwitz in 1944. In Australia, Bono Weiner quickly became active in the Australian Labor Party and helped shape Arthur Calwell's policy for the post-war migration program that was to transform the country. Weiner was also active on the Victorian Jewish Board of Deputies, on which he was the secular Jewish left's main spokesman. There he met and became friends with Isi Leibler. In the 1970s, Isi Leibler bought into a small but growing travel business that Weiner had established in the early 1960s. The business flourished. After Leibler bought out Weiner, who wanted to retire and travel the world, Jetset grew quickly to be one of Australia's biggest travel agencies. The friendship between the two men remained strong until Weiner's death in 1996.

It was through Weiner that I met Isi Leibler in the late 1970s. We did not see each other often, but when we did, Isi Leibler would invariably ask whether I was still a Bundist and would promise not to tell Weiner if I admitted that I was no longer a card-carrying member of the Bund. Weiner had been my mentor from my teenage days in SKIF. He had helped shape my political views and my sense of what it meant to be a secular, non-Zionist Jew. Later, when I was a journalist writing about politics, I would invariably receive a note or a phone call from Weiner that was almost always critical of what I had written—too soft, too mealy-mouthed, not left-wing enough.

Mark Leibler, by contrast, told me that he had never had a mentor. From the time his father died, he had never turned to anyone for advice. And no, Isi had never taken on the role of father figure after their father's death. A day later, however, he said that he had perhaps made a mistake. Zelman Cowen was Dean of Law at Melbourne University and had taught Leibler constitutional law. Cowen was known for mentoring the brightest students, offering them career advice, supporting their applications for further study at the most prestigious universities in England and America. Cowen helped Leibler get into the Masters program at Yale, so maybe he was a mentor. And yes, Cowen had come to Mark and Rosanna's wedding.

At 22, Leibler was pretty clear about where he wanted to take his life at the end of his law degree. Having won the Supreme Court Prize, he felt as if all the paths he might travel were open to him. He was not sure whether he wanted to become a legal academic like Waller and Cowen, or whether he would become a barrister like some of his Jewish contemporaries. While he found academic study intellectually rewarding, when it came to the law he saw himself as a man of action and committed to measurable outcomes, so he was unlikely to have ever really contemplated a university career. And a career at the bar would not have provided him with the administrative support for his Jewish leadership ambitions that he would have as a partner in a law firm.

To become a solicitor, he first had to do his articles. It had never crossed his mind to go anywhere but to Arnold Bloch, a family friend and Jewish community leader who had known Mark since he was a boy. In 1966, Arnold Bloch and Associates was a single-practitioner firm based in unfashionable Lonsdale Street. It had one associate, a handful of experienced conveyancing clerks, and a list of mostly Jewish clients. Within a decade and a half, many of these clients would be among Australia's richest people.

Leibler did not like the work. As the junior in the firm, he was handed briefs that were unchallenging and boring. Although he had great respect for Bloch, he didn't enjoy being a junior, told what to do by the more senior lawyers. By then, he had decided that when he completed his articles, he would do a Masters in Law at one of the Ivy League universities in the United States. Given that he had won the Supreme Court Prize, he was pretty sure that his application for a place and a scholarship at any of these universities—Yale, Harvard or Columbia—would be successful. Zelman Cowen was his adviser, helping him to settle on Yale, and his main referee for a Fulbright travel grant and a scholarship that covered his tuition and some living expenses.

On 5 June 1967, two months before Leibler left for Yale and two months before his son Anthony was born, war broke out between Israel and its Arab neighbours, following weeks of tension and threats leading up to the hostilities. Every few days, thousands of Jews in Melbourne and Sydney attended meetings to get updates about what was happening. Jews everywhere had a pervasive sense that Israel faced an existential threat, that little more than 20 years after more than a third of the world's Jewish population had been annihilated the Jews of Israel were facing another Holocaust. In a community dominated by Holocaust survivors and their children, there was an almost hysterical sense of foreboding of terrible things to come. Hundreds of young men and women in Melbourne and Sydney queued outside the Zionist headquarters to offer themselves as volunteers to fight for what they thought was Jewish survival. It was a fanciful idea; these young men and women had no military training. I was one of those who lined up; I think I was the only graduate of SKIF to do so, but I believed that Israel was facing extinction. It was only a little over two decades since the Nazis had attempted the genocide of European Jewry. From the time we were eight years old, the words, "never again" had been drummed into us by our elders at SKIF.

Hundreds did manage to get to Israel, but not before the war ended in six days, with Israel the comprehensive victor, occupying the whole of Jerusalem, the West Bank, Gaza, the Golan Heights and the Sinai Peninsula. For many Jews, it felt like a miracle. Few imagined that the Six-Day War would transform Israel into an occupying power with all the moral and political and military consequences that flow from ruling over an occupied people.

For Mark Leibler, the Six-Day War and its aftermath reinforced his commitment to Zionism. From childhood, he had always believed that Israel was central to the Jewish people, but he said that the 1967 war made it clear to him that Israel was central to their survival. Without Israel, they were doomed. From that time on, that idea was central to his Zionism and to his leadership of Zionist organisations. I asked whether he volunteered before or during the war to go to Israel? "No, I didn't. Yes, there were people who volunteered and some went, but I didn't think my presence would make any difference."

Instead, three days after his son Anthony was born, Leibler boarded a plane for the United States. He was so excited on the flight that he could not sleep. He had never been overseas and had only been out of Victoria a couple of times, for family holidays in Surfers Paradise. He had arrived at Yale when Anthony's *bris* (circumcision ceremony) was taking place at Anthony's grandmother's house.

To this day it still upsets Rosanna that Mark missed his son's *bris*, this most profound of ceremonies for a Jewish boy, because he had a deadline to enrol at Yale. When asked about it, Rosanna remembers:

> I organised the *bris*. I lived with my mother-in-law, shared a bedroom with her for God's sake, with this newborn baby and Anthony was premature, quite sick in the prem ward at the hospital. He was allowed to fly finally when he was six or seven

weeks old and she [Rachel] came with me and I had never been overseas, never ever. It was unbelievable, holding this tiny baby on that long flight to New Haven.

Rachel Leibler stayed with Mark, Rosanna and Anthony for two weeks before flying back to Australia. She left them in a small flat in New Haven, up a set of stairs in an old building that was stiflingly hot in summer and very cold when winter came. Mark and Rosanna were to have different experiences of that year. She was lonely and isolated from the start. They had no money. Mark, who loved whisky, could afford to buy only one bottle, which had to last him for the year. Rosanna was stuck with the baby, with no friends or family. She said that she did not really experience America. The only thing she could remember was that, on the day Martin Luther King was assassinated, she had splurged and hired a mothercraft nurse to look after Anthony and had gone out to a department store. After the assassination she was locked in there for hours with everyone else.

When asked, Mark said that, of course it was hard for Rosanna in New Haven, but Yale was magnificent. Leibler was intoxicated by the atmosphere, by the brilliant lecturers and the dazzling brightness of most students. Boris Bittker, his lecturer in tax law, had written the classic textbook on tax. Guido Calabrese, later Dean of Law at Yale and a senior Federal Court judge, taught estate planning. Leibler worked hard and got outstanding results. He focused on tax law, estate planning and trusts, because of his experience at Arnold Bloch and Associates. Bloch had already built a reputation as an outstanding lawyer in these areas.

A few months before he finished his Masters, Bloch wrote to Leibler and offered him a job. Leibler said that, although it took him a while to make a decision, it seems unlikely that he ever considered declining

Bloch's offer and becoming an academic instead. Bloch wrote that there was a future for Leibler in his firm and, while he never spelt it out, it was pretty clear that if Leibler took up his offer, a partnership would be in the offing before long. Leibler had known Bloch, 15 years his senior, since childhood. After talking to Rosanna, Leibler took up the offer. He had huge respect for Bloch and, although he had enjoyed Yale so much and been invigorated by it, he was determined to make a difference in the real world. He wanted to do things that would change things in both the law and the Jewish community.

As he graduated with honours from Yale, his mother returned to New Haven and took Anthony, less than a year old, back to Australia. Rosanna and Mark went to Europe, to Spain and Italy, and then to Israel. It was the summer of 1968, of student and worker uprisings in Paris, so they avoided France. Across Europe and in the United States, it was a time of student revolution. In Australia, the anti-Vietnam war movement was gathering strength and at Monash University student radical leader Albert Langer was leading a revolt against the university administration. All this had almost no impact on Mark and Rosanna Leibler.

Mark remembered best their two weeks in Israel, the only time that he and his wife went to Israel alone just to explore the country:

> Many people kissed the tarmac back then when they got off the plane in Jerusalem. I didn't do that but I was very moved. Israel was very different than I had imagined it. The people, many of them did not look European. Of course they were Jews from the Arab countries, refugees. They had been driven out after the establishment of Israel. It was not the mythical place of my Zionist childhood—full of pioneers living together and working the fields and singing songs. Of course it wasn't. Like any place,

CHAPTER 4

it had its crooks and thieves and even murderers. It's not that I
felt at home there but I felt connected.

That sense of connection was to grow stronger and deeper over the
years. The trip to Israel had opened his eyes to the fact that the image
he had had of the country was mythical, but this did not shake his
commitment to what he has often called the nation state of the Jews.

Seven years after they returned from the United States, Mark and
Rosanna built a house in Caulfield. Their second child, Simone, had
been born in 1972. They were settling into the roles that would remain
unchanged and unchallenged for decades to come. As her mother-
in-law had demanded, Rosanna stayed home, raised the children
and supported her husband. In time, with the grace and ease that her
husband lacked, she would play hostess to Jewish leaders and Israeli
and Australian politicians—the growing numbers of important people,
as she describes them with just a hint of irony—whom Mark invited
to dinner at their home.

From the late 1940s, Caulfield had become home to many of the
Jews who had arrived in Australia from the displaced persons camps
in Europe and had started to do well financially—mostly in milk bars
and stalls selling cheap clothes and cloth at the Victoria Market. They
moved from the inner-city working-class suburb of Carlton to the
more salubrious suburb south of the Yarra River, with its Californian
bungalows set on largish blocks of land. Jews often describe Caulfield
as Melbourne's *shtetl*, the Yiddish word for the Jewish villages of
pre-war Eastern Europe. Caulfield was where the extended Leibler
family lived, within easy walking distance of each other, from the
1950s. Mark and Rosanna had grown up there, a few streets apart.
They still live there today.

CHAPTER 5

Not long after he came to Australia, Arnold Bloch taught himself Yiddish. He did so because he wanted to attract to his law practice the Eastern European Holocaust survivors who came to Australia as refugees in the late 1940s and 1950s. Bloch was 21 when he came to Australia from England. Four years later, he set up his own law firm in inner Melbourne. He came from a distinguished English Jewish family. According to those who knew him, he had been a lonely child because his parents had divorced, which was most unusual among Orthodox English Jews. Like many thousands of English boys and girls, Bloch was evacuated to the English countryside during the Blitz of 1940 and 1941. He lived with an Orthodox rabbi, who insisted that the boy study some of Judaism's major texts in the morning before he went to school and at night when he came home. Bloch developed a deep knowledge and lifelong love for the texts of Judaism. He lived with the rabbi for a couple of years before he won a scholarship to Cambridge at the age of 18. After studying oriental languages, he went on to complete a law degree.

In June 1949, Bloch emigrated to Australia. It was a big decision for a 21-year-old single man, but Bloch had his reasons. He wanted to get away from England and his wartime experience. The Australian government was encouraging, even paying for, English migration to Australia, which meant that his mother and sister could follow him once he had established himself.

Given the "Englishness" of his background, Bloch should have become one of the Anglo Jews who were still leading the Australian Jewish community in the late 1940s. But Bloch was a passionate

Zionist, a religious Zionist at that, and the Anglo Jews, in the main, were at best lukewarm about Zionism. Soon after his arrival, Bloch joined a small synagogue in inner-suburban Elwood, close to the flat he shared with a couple of young refugees and, therefore, within easy walking distance of home. On Saturday mornings in this small synagogue in Elwood, a bayside suburb of rather shabby Edwardian houses and mansions that had seen better days, he first met some of the Jewish men, refugees from Eastern Europe, who would become his first clients.

When he was studying for the exam that would allow him to practise law in Australia, Bloch became one of the founders of Bnei Akiva in Australia, and it was there that he first met and began to mentor Isi Leibler. Although just 15 or 16, and six years younger than Bloch, Leibler was already seen by many as a future leader of Bnei Akiva and of the wider Jewish community.

Every Zionist faction, from the religious Zionists to the right-wing secular Zionists who today support Israeli Prime Minister Benjamin Netanyahu, to even left-wing secular Zionists, some of whom were communist fellow travellers, had a youth movement. Each youth movement ran a program of Zionist education at their meetings on Saturday or Sunday afternoons; each ran summer camps where hundreds of young Jews lived and played, studied Jewish history and the history of Zionism and debated the challenges facing Israel. The need to form a deep attachment to the Jewish state was instilled in all these young Jews.

Bloch set up his practice in Ripponlea, a suburb next to Caulfield. Ripponlea was becoming home to Melbourne's ultra-Orthodox Jews, its streets increasingly populated by women in wigs pushing prams and trailing lots of children, and men in fur hats and white stockings and black coats. The young lawyer never did attract Anglo-Jewish clients, not even when he moved from Ripponlea to Lonsdale Street in central Melbourne in the late 1950s, the move undertaken because Bloch was determined, according to those who knew him, never to be a suburban solicitor. Instead, through his Mizrachi contacts and other involvements in the Jewish community, and through his growing reputation as a lawyer, Bloch attracted those Jewish immigrants and refugees who were starting out in business—in milk bars, clothing workshops and small-time buying and selling of property. Many were Holocaust survivors who, like most Australian Jews, came to regard Australia as a *goldene medine*. In time, these businessmen would form the base for the growth of Arnold Bloch Leibler into a firm known for its wealthy Jewish clientele.

This Cambridge-educated Englishman, a lover of art and opera and theatre, widely read in English literature but also steeped in Jewish learning and culture, had, according to many who knew him and became his clients, a visceral affinity with the Eastern European Holocaust survivors, most of whom had not even finished high school, who spoke little English, and felt shunned and rejected by Australia's Anglo Jews. He instinctively understood them and saw them as a remarkable group of people. To get closer to them, he taught himself Yiddish and within a year spoke it fluently.

This anecdote may be apocryphal but, then again, it could be true. One of the Eastern European refugees came to check out Bloch as a potential lawyer to look after his small but growing business interests. They spoke in Yiddish to start with and, when the man switched to English for some reason, his English not exactly fluent, Bloch switched to English as well. The man was astounded: "How did you get to speak English so good?" he cried.

John Gandel, the billionaire property developer, was running the two Sussan stores that constituted the family business when he became one of Bloch's first clients in the 1950s. At the time, the Jewish community was a lot more intertwined, Gandel told me. Most Jews married Jews, lived in Jewish streets, and socialised almost exclusively with each other, which meant that business people like him were much more likely to go to a Jewish firm than they are today. According to Gandel,

> Arnold was a fantastic personality and was very well loved by everybody. He had a wonderful personal touch with clients, never sent them off to juniors, was always there for us. I think he was a great lawyer, yes, but it was his ability to make clients feel special, that is what I remember most about him.

Louis Waller also had a great affection and respect for Bloch as a lawyer and a Jewish leader. Waller, who was to become a world authority on the legal aspects of IVF and other forms of fertility treatments, met Bloch in February 1950, while a 15-year-old student at University High School. Bloch was Waller's group leader at Bnei Akiva and a very powerful influence on Waller, both as a Jew and as a legal scholar. When we spoke almost a year before his death in October 2019, Waller described Bloch as one of the best lawyers he ever knew, adding that the former High Court Judge and Governor-General, the late Sir Ninian Stephen, whom Bloch briefed in leading cases, regarded Bloch as the best solicitor he had ever known.

Bloch was also a first-class Jewish scholar. While still at Cambridge he worked with a professor of mathematics to translate and annotate a chapter of one of Judaism's most renowned works, the Mishnah Torah, written by the 12th-century Jewish scholar and philosopher, Moses Maimonides.

Waller said that in the 1950s, 1960s and even the 1970s, Bnei Akiva was a left-of-centre organisation, with many of its members calling themselves socialists. They were Orthodox left-wingers, religious Zionists of the left, which today might sound like a contradiction in terms. Waller remained a religious Zionist, but he did not share the politics of the religious Zionist parties in Israel or the politics of their followers in Australia. He remained true to the sort of religious Zionist he was when Bloch was his leader at Bnei Akiva—Modern Orthodox in his Judaism, socially liberal and a firm supporter of a two-state solution to the Israel–Palestine conflict.

Sam Lipski was also a member of Bnei Akiva in the 1950s, but, by the time he joined, Bloch was in his mid-20s and had moved on to the young adult Bnei Akiva group. For the past 20 years Lipski has been CEO of the Pratt Foundation, the Pratt family's philanthropic body, but he remains the most respected journalist and commentator on Jewish issues in Australia. He has observed and, in some cases, worked with every major Jewish leader over the past half century, and was particularly close to Isi Leibler in the 1970s and 1980s. His relationship with Bloch spanned several decades.

Lipski said that Bloch was very intelligent, far more intelligent than many of the Jewish leaders:

> He was a big man, rotund, looked like a *gevir* [flamboyantly rich man]. He was impatient with people. It was his great flaw as a leader. He did not suffer fools lightly. I found him stimulating to be with. He had a great mind. Perhaps it was inevitable that he would fall out with the Leibler brothers—over different issues in each case. Politically, he was left of centre, a small-l liberal. I remember he had a front row seat at the Mizrachi synagogue. Back then, many religious Zionists were left of centre. They ran a number of *kibbutzim* in Israel. Some considered themselves to be socialists.

It was inevitable that Bloch would become close friends with Isi's parents, Rachel and Abraham Leibler. They shared the same commitment to Modern Orthodoxy and to Zionism. Before the establishment of Israel, and for some decades afterwards, not all Orthodox Jews, especially adherents of the various Chassidic groups and some of the fundamentalist sects that set up in Melbourne and Sydney in the early 1950s, shared that commitment. These Jews believed that the ingathering of the Jews to the Holy Land could only happen with the coming of the Messiah. Zionism was a secular nationalist movement that the fundamentalists believed had no connection with Judaism.

The Leiblers and the Blochs—in 1952 Arnold married Elaine Friedman, daughter of a prominent Orthodox Melbourne rabbi—were leaders of that small, close-knit community of religious Zionists, with its daily and weekly rituals of Jewish observance, its often intense internal politics, its passion for Jewish and secular education, its commitment to Jewish continuity after the Holocaust, its determination to succeed in business and the professions in Australia, and its overarching dedication to Israel, which represented for them the miracle of rebirth after 2000 years of exile and persecution. Without Israel, these religious Zionists believed, the Jewish people would be powerless, eternal victims in a mostly hostile world.

Mark Leibler remembers that his parents would often have Arnold and Elaine Bloch around for *shabbes* (Yiddish for the Sabbath) lunch on Saturday afternoons at their home. These lunches were long and leisurely and unhurried. Everything was up for discussion, from conflicts in their Mizrachi congregation to Jewish community politics to the politics of Israel. The Blochs and the Leiblers had been to the morning Sabbath services and strolled together with their children back to the Leiblers' home just a few minutes' walk away, the women dressed in their *shabbes* long dresses and black or brown fur coats with scarves around their hair, the men in their *shabbes* dark suits and hats.

Leibler also remembers that his parents often went with the Blochs to the cinema, or to a classical music performance. The two couples took holidays together. His father, who became president of the Jewish Board of Deputies in 1955, and Bloch, who was elected the Board's president 20 years later, would have intense, though never loud or impolite, discussions about the Jewish community and its leadership.

By 1968, when Leibler, fresh from Yale, took up Bloch's offer, Arnold Bloch and Associates had an established clientele of mostly Jewish businessmen who were starting to build their businesses from small to medium size. It was a successful small firm, its reputation due in the main to Bloch's reputation and approach to his clients. From the start, he dealt personally with every client who had come to him from the early days, when they were struggling to get started in Australia. Long-time clients all said that Bloch never delegated their work to other lawyers, not even when their legal issues became ever more complex and they grew ever wealthier. They were his people.

Leibler also speaks of Bloch in glowing terms. While he says he had never had a mentor, it is clear that Bloch was his professional mentor, especially in those areas in which Leibler was to build his reputation—trusts, estate planning and particularly tax. Leibler said that what he learnt from Bloch informed the lawyer he became. Beyond the law, Bloch also taught him how to deal with clients, especially with Jewish clients, who were the basis of the firm's success.

In part what he learnt from Bloch was that involvement and leadership in the Jewish community was not just a good thing in itself—something Leibler had always believed—but that being a Jewish leader would have a profoundly positive impact on the firm, and on its eventual pre-eminence as the law firm for the Jews.

Bloch understood the needs of his clients better than anyone Leibler had ever met. He had a fantastic reputation in the Jewish community as one of its best and brightest lawyers. He never offered his clients just legal advice. Often, they wanted to be told what they should do to minimise risk and grow their businesses at the same time. They wanted an adviser, a relationship.

Bloch taught Leibler about the principle of service. The one lesson that Leibler still teaches his partners and all ABL lawyers, from the most senior to the most junior, is the lesson Bloch taught him: when a client calls you, you return the call the same day. Personally. If for some reason you can't, if you're in court for instance, get your secretary to call and explain that you will call the next day.

When Bloch offered him the position, the senior lawyer had signalled that it would not be long before Leibler, then 25 and ambitious to make a name for himself in the law and in the Jewish community, would be rewarded. Bloch had probably decided that, if things worked out, he would quickly make Leibler a partner. Bloch was a hard-working lawyer but he liked to take trips overseas, often for eight weeks at a time, travelling in the Melbourne winter with his wife to Europe, Asia and the United States. He needed someone to run the firm while he was away and, even back then, Leibler was an obsessive organiser who drew up daily lists of what he had to do each day.

Despite the family friendship, Leibler did not know Bloch very well. They were 15 years apart in age. Arnold Bloch and Associates was still very small, with a junior lawyer and a number of conveyancing clerks who were responsible for the firm's substantial focus on small-time property transactions. But from the day he rejoined the firm after his time at Yale, Leibler loved the work. Bloch threw him off the deep end, handed him cases that were far from straightforward. In 1969 he made Leibler his partner, with a 25 per cent stake in the business, and added Leibler's name to that of the firm. Of Bloch, Leibler said:

> Arnold was a very strict teacher. A lot of the drafts of stuff I did, even when I was a partner, came back from him with big scribbly red lines. He was known for his use of language, for the quality of his briefs. He was an extraordinary lawyer with a brilliant mind.

At every possible moment, when he is talking about the values and ethical rules that govern ABL, Leibler emphasises that it was Bloch who set those standards, and that even today Bloch remains a big presence in the firm's work.

Daphne Stamkos agrees that Bloch had a profound influence on the firm and the people in it. She has worked as a receptionist for ABL for more than 40 years, since she was a teenager not long out of school. Before coming to the firm in 1976, she had worked part-time for an accounting firm that had two Jewish partners. Some of its clients were post-Holocaust refugees who were also clients of ABL. These men— they were exclusively men—were also Bloch's clients and had been since he had set up his firm in the early 1950s. It was one of these men who suggested to Stamkos that she should apply for a job with ABL.

Stamkos had seen the way ABL had changed over the years. When she remembered Arnold Bloch's death in 1985 from cancer—a young man of 56, she said—there were tears in her eyes. She loved him, she said. And she loved the Eastern European Jews who were the clients, whom she described as

> salt of the earth, those people, when I first met them. They were very interesting. They were determined to make sure their children were safe and looked after. Educated. Had what they

needed. I loved their sense of doing business, their way of doing things. I had no idea about the Jewish community. It's a very close community. I think Jewish people are very committed to their community, to their businesses. They look after each other and use each other as a resource. They have been challenged. I think that's made them stronger, a bit more creative in their thinking. I think it's a little bit of a survival thing as well.

Over the centuries, Jews have often been accused of clannishness, of separating themselves from the general community, of forming closed communities in which they practise their Judaism and business affairs, and conduct their disputes, their political rivalries and their family lives. In many ways the Australian Jewish community was such a community, but this was not just a matter of choice. In Jewish history, it was never just a matter of choice, a decision the Jews made to wall themselves off in physical and metaphorical ghettoes. In the 1950s and 1960s, and even into the 1970s, in Australia, which has no history of vicious anti-Semitism, Jews were unofficially shut out of the business community and of large law firms and out of some of the clubs and associations where the political and business elites gathered.

Since Jews were forced to live within this space that in some ways was like a ghetto, a space where everyone knew everyone else and where, in business, people both cooperated and fiercely competed with each other, it was little wonder that the politics inside their community bubble was not for the faint-hearted. Bloch and Leibler were both involved in Jewish politics, Bloch as a senior leader, and Leibler beginning to make his way. The younger man was prepared to spend three or even four nights a week at long and often tedious meetings of various Jewish organisations in order to make the contacts that would eventually see him elected to leadership positions.

It was a different time. Now it is a struggle to get young people to take on leadership roles in the community. Many have no desire to sit in meetings. Wives and partners are not prepared to make the sacrifices that Rosanna Leibler made so that her husband could pursue his leadership ambitions. In the past, people wanted to make sacrifices. They wanted to lead. They thought that working for the community was important. That was true for most of Leibler's generation, including his brother Isi. It was also true for Arnold Bloch.

Although Bloch and Leibler were both Modern Orthodox, members of Mizrachi, and religious Zionists, Leibler says they hardly ever talked about community politics in those years. Their relationship was all about the law. Bloch loved art and the theatre and opera; Leibler did not. It was the law that bound them together, but it would be community politics that eventually caused considerable conflict between the two men.

It is hard to exaggerate just how intense and how contested Jewish politics in Australia was in the first few decades after the war, and even into the 1980s and 1990s. The speed with which the community worked to recreate as far as possible the rich life of European Jewry before the catastrophe of Nazism was unmatched anywhere else in the world. Religious and cultural organisations, libraries, theatre groups, Jewish schools, Zionist and non-Zionist organisations were established at an extraordinary pace. Thousands of Jews, many of them Holocaust survivors, gave up every spare minute of their time to work as volunteers for these new institutions, and scores of Jews jockeyed and plotted to lead these institutions and the community.

It is remarkable how these post-war Jewish Australians, many of whom had lost everything, including most of their families, rebuilt their individual lives—quickly married, or remarried, if they had lost their wives or husbands, had children, began building businesses, and became passionately involved in community work and the chase for community leadership roles. The intensity—some would say viciousness—of Jewish community politics can in part be explained by the determination of the post-war refugees to live again, as intensely as possible. They were determined to rebuild everything that had been lost.

Out of this community, Isi and Mark Leibler—and to a certain extent Arnold Bloch, though he was an English Jew—emerged as leaders in the 1960s and 1970s. The community shaped the sort of law firm that ABL was to become. And the sort of firm it was partly explains how professional differences and competition in Jewish politics played such significant roles in two of the major crises of Mark Leibler's life: the end of the partnership with Bloch in 1981 and his feud and falling out with Isi 10 years later.

By 1973, Mark had made it clear within the community that he would concentrate his leadership ambitions on the Australian Zionist organisations—the State Zionist Council of Victoria and the national Zionist Federation of Australia, which was affiliated to the World Zionist Organisation. By then, Isi Leibler was president of the Victorian Jewish Board of Deputies and an internationally recognised leader of the campaign to persuade the Soviet Union to allow Jews to emigrate to Israel. Scores of Soviet Jews, the so-called refuseniks or Prisoners of Zion, had been sentenced to jail or work camps in Siberia for applying for exit visas to Israel. From the time he was a student, Isi Leibler had campaigned for Soviet Jewry. His story was told by Sam Lipski and Suzanne Rutland in their 2015 book, *Let My People Go: The Untold Story of Australia and the Soviet Jews 1959–89*. Eventually, by the early 1990s, over two million Jews from a population of about three million were granted permission to leave the Soviet Union. More than half went to Israel, with about 700,000 going to the United States and between 10,000 and 20,000 coming to Australia.

Mark Leibler was concerned, as far as possible, not to enter into any leadership competition with his older brother. He played no role in the Soviet Jewry movement. Unlike his brother, who saw himself as a community leader across every issue, from anti-Semitism to the school network to support for Israel by Australian governments, Mark narrowed his focus to Zionism: to the Jewish community's connections with Israel, to the promotion of Aliyah, and to lobbying Australian governments for support of Israel at the United Nations and in other international bodies.

In 1973, when Mark was still very much a junior Jewish leader and no threat to Isi, this demarcation of leadership areas was possible, but it was always tenuous and, in hindsight, was never going to hold. Once Mark became recognised as a senior Zionist leader, it was inevitable that the two brothers would fight a leadership turf war that would be intense, public, personal, long-lasting and very bitter.

In 1980, Mark was elected president of the State Zionist Council of Victoria. By then, it was clear to most of the Jewish community that he was on the road to becoming a significant player in Jewish Australian life. At ABL he had started to establish himself as an up-and-coming tax lawyer. He was 36 years old, growing in stature as both a lawyer and Jewish community leader. He and Rosanna had two boys and two girls; his youngest child, Jeremy, was a few months old. Life was good; his path ahead was clear.

Then, on 3 April 1981, Leibler found a memorandum on his desk. It was from his senior partner. Arnold Bloch wrote that he was going to go into business with Abe Goldberg and Marc Besen, both clients of ABL. At the same time, the memorandum made it plain that Bloch intended to continue to play a professional role at the firm he had established and made so successful—the firm that carried his name. That was never going to be acceptable to Mark Leibler.

CHAPTER 6

He has a lawyer's demeanour and a mask of calm when answering questions. He considers every question part of a cross-examination and, like every good lawyer, he is determined to answer every question as briefly as he can, giving away as little as possible. He anticipates where questions are going and, when they don't go in that direction, he can be annoyed, the mask slipping for a moment. Anger can flare, a sort of impatient anger, as if the questions he had not anticipated are just stupid, irrelevant, out of order.

Sitting at the table in his office, he sometimes fiddles with a pile of papers that he thinks he might need to consult in order to ensure that some issues are properly understood. What he seems least able to anticipate are questions about those times in his life that were difficult—the crisis times, when he couldn't just be the lawyer or the community leader, when the public face was threatened by things he could not control. Falling out with Arnold Bloch was one of those times.

On 3 April 1981, Bloch sent a memorandum to Leibler and the other two partners at ABL, stating that he had decided to resign as ABL's senior partner. The memorandum set out his terms for staying with the firm. Among other things, he wanted to stay on as a consultant two days a week. For that, he expected to be paid at a certain rate—more or less the hourly rate for senior lawyers at ABL—and he would, at the same time, be free to do consultancy work, but not legal work, including for clients of ABL.

The memorandum shocked Leibler. He had had no inkling that Bloch was planning to leave and to go into business in a company jointly owned by Marc Besen, the retail magnate and owner of the Sussan chain, and the textile manufacturer and property developer, Abe Goldberg. Both were clients of ABL. While Leibler had been in the dark about Bloch's plans, a number of people were not. Apart from Besen and Goldberg, Bloch had told John Gandel, a long-time ABL client, that he had decided to leave the law and go into business some months before sending the memorandum to Leibler and his other ABL partners.

Sam Lipski had also known for some time that Bloch had decided to leave ABL. In February or March of 1981, Bloch told Lipski that, amongst other things, he wanted to buy the Melbourne-based *Australian Jewish News* and install Lipski as publisher and editor, to which Lipski had agreed. He admired and respected Bloch and thought that, with Bloch as owner, they could transform the *Jewish News* into a great Jewish newspaper. But on the day the sale was to be finalised, Bloch called Lipski to say he had decided not to buy the paper. He had had another look at the numbers and had realised that it was going to make a loss. Lipski was surprised and disappointed, and still has no idea why Bloch pulled out of the purchase. Lipski was not angry, but they had less to do with each other after that.

Besen had formed a partnership with Goldberg to buy a controlling interest in the public company, Entrad. He offered Arnold Bloch chairmanship of the company, along with a 10 per cent holding. Bloch accepted the offer before he informed the ABL partners of his decision to resign as ABL's senior partner. Goldberg was one of the business high-flyers of the 1980s. He owned the Linter group of textile companies that included such iconic brands as King Gee, Speedo and Pelaco. At one stage, Goldberg was the fourth richest man in Australia on the *Business Review Weekly* Rich List. He would take Linter public in 1985, but, after the stock market crash in 1987, bought it back as a private company and went massively into debt in order to do so.

In early 1990, Goldberg's bankers appointed KPMG to look over Goldberg's books. The auditor discovered that Goldberg's companies had liabilities of $1.7 billion with assets of about $425 million. In other words, Goldberg had been technically bankrupt since the stock market crash. But, before he could be held accountable for the hundreds of millions of dollars he owed the banks and other creditors, he fled to Poland where he renewed his Polish citizenship. At the time Australia did not have an extradition treaty with Poland. Goldberg went back into business in Poland, amassing a significant fortune as a property tycoon before he died there in July 2016, having not paid back a cent of what he owed his creditors in Australia.

Goldberg was a crook, a 1980s crook, like Christopher Skase and George Herscu and Alan Bond. His wealth was built on a mountain of debt obtained from banks that were, to say the least, not much into due diligence. But, in 1981, he was a high-flying businessman in partnership with respected entrepreneur and businessman Marc Besen. In 1988, Besen would sell his share in Entrad to Goldberg in exchange for Goldberg's stake in the Highpoint Shopping Centre in suburban Melbourne. When asked, Besen agreed that the deal was one of his better business decisions.

Besen had probably been one of Bloch's first clients when Bloch had put out his shingle in Ripponlea. They first met at the Elwood synagogue. Besen considered Bloch to be a brilliant lawyer. When he bought Entrad with Goldberg, he needed someone to join the company as chairman, because he felt he needed someone to keep Goldberg in line. And Bloch was looking for something in business. According to Besen, Bloch and Leibler were clashing because Leibler wanted more recognition. Besen felt that, by making Bloch chairman of Entrad, a public company, it would give him what he wanted, a way out of the law. According to Besen,

> Arnold did very well out of his move to Entrad. He finished up with 10 per cent of the company's shares and after he died, his wife sold those shares for a very good price. He made more money, a lot more money, than he would have made had he stayed at ABL.

Bloch never spoke to Besen, his new business partner, about the conflict with Leibler; nor, apparently, did he speak to John Gandel, with whom he had been close for many years. Bloch's family had also never talked about it over the decades. When I approached Bloch's son, Geoffrey, a barrister at the Victorian bar, to talk about his father as a lawyer and a Jewish leader, his reply to my email was: "While assisting in Mark Leibler's biography is hardly a first order priority for me, doing what I can to ensure that there is no historical inaccuracy concerning my late father, or any misappropriation of his achievements, is another thing."

In time, having consulted his mother, Elaine, who remained bitter about the way her husband had left ABL, Geoffrey Bloch agreed to be interviewed. The family had never spoken publicly about these events before. Bloch's sister, Susan, was also present at the interview. She had taken part in a symposium run by the Jewish Museum that honoured her father's life, at which former Federal Court judge, Ron Merkel, spoke, as did Louis Waller. Much of what Geoffrey told me was off the record, but he said enough to illustrate how complex and contested Bloch's departure from ABL had been, and remained more than three decades later. Geoffrey Bloch had done his articles at ABL and had been there for two years when he left soon after his father's falling out with Leibler and the other partners. His two years at ABL are not among his most cherished memories.

He would not talk directly about the issues that were at the heart of the conflict between his father and Leibler. He said he did not want to reopen old wounds, but made it clear that his father had been hurt, angry, distraught, and, in the view of the Bloch family, he never recovered from the trauma of it. Geoffrey Bloch believed that the rupture with ABL had contributed to his father's death from cancer in 1985.

After our conversation, Geoffrey Bloch wrote a letter to Mark Leibler trying to explain why his father had been so upset and why his family had refused any contact with Leibler for so many years. Leibler was shocked by the letter, but he wrote back a short note that he thought had left open the possibility for Geoffrey to respond. He never did.

For Leibler, the accusation that he had helped to cause Bloch's death cut him, angered and distressed him. In our interviews he rejected it absolutely, as he always had. I asked him why the Bloch family was so upset about the falling out between Arnold Bloch and him. He said he didn't know, that I would have to ask them. "I always gave Arnold credit for his leadership, his ability as a lawyer, for everything he taught me. [After the break with Bloch] I never spoke a bad word about him. I just accepted it. Didn't think much about it really."

Was he shocked by what Bloch wrote in the memorandum? "It was a huge shock," he said. But there had been tension between them for some time? To which he replied,

> Yes, there had been tension, but not professional tension, not over ABL issues. Over Jewish communal issues, yes. The reason it came as such a great shock was because I could never imagine

myself doing something like that. I just could not imagine myself in effect going into business. As a lawyer, it frankly amazed me that he did it. I mean with the benefit of hindsight, because he made significant money, it could be considered a good move, but at the time, I considered it a disastrous move for Arnold.

Did he try and talk Bloch out of going into business? "I did not. He had made up his mind."

Abe Goldberg turned out to be a crook? "As it happened," Leibler replied, "Arnold was extracted and bought out from that… shall I say, just in time. I am not suggesting that he knew what would happen with Abe Goldberg. None of us knew."

I asked whether there were any other reasons for the tension that clearly existed between him and Bloch before the professional separation. On Jewish community issues, leadership struggles, that might have caused Bloch to want to leave ABL? "There were clashes," Leibler said, "but these had not affected their professional relationship. Not at all? No, not significantly."

Perhaps it is true that the disputes between Bloch and the Leibler brothers over Jewish community issues did not play a significant part in Bloch's leaving ABL. It is probably true that, as Lipski said and Besen implied, Bloch wanted to make significant money to fund some of his rather grandiose dream projects—the purchase of an old and venerable publisher of Judaica in London, and the funding of an institute in Israel for research into Jewish education and Judaism.

The first time I asked Leibler about severing ties with Bloch, he said that, before reading the memorandum, he had had no inkling that Bloch wanted to leave, and that he, Leibler, was not dissatisfied in any way. No, they had not clashed, nor had Leibler felt that he deserved more recognition than he was getting. After all, he was just 36 years old and Bloch, 15 years his senior, was widely recognised as a great lawyer. He completely accepted Bloch as the senior partner and that most of ABL's clients had come to the firm because of Bloch.

In that first interview about Bloch's leaving, Leibler said he had forgotten many of the details of that difficult time. It was only months later, in response to more questions, that he went to the ABL archives and read the Bloch memorandum again for the first time in more than two decades. Then he remembered the issue that had caused the deepest conflict—the fact that Bloch planned to set up a consultancy that he proposed to call Arnold Bloch Professional Services.

Leibler said that all the partners had considered this to be a totally unacceptable, even outrageous, plan. They thought Bloch's resigning as the firm's senior partner represented an existential threat to ABL. Bloch's reputation as a lawyer far exceeded that of the other partners, Leibler included. His intention to use part of ABL's name for his consultancy would confuse clients, who would already be unsettled by his departure. It is accepted practice that a named partner who leaves a law firm cannot force the firm to change its name and cannot set up a rival firm using his or her name.

Leibler said that memories of the time flooded back as he read the memorandum and the other partners' responses to it. One memory was particularly painful. Sometime before Bloch delivered the memorandum, without informing Leibler or the other partners, he had used one of the shelf companies that ABL held for clients and tried to change the company's name, without informing the nominal directors, to Arnold Bloch Professional Services. In Leibler's view, this was ethically dubious. When we first spoke, Leibler had forgotten about this. It was as if he had not wanted to remember this about the man he had so admired professionally.

The Leibler–Bloch story is about much more than a professional break-up. It is about how the overlapping professional, personal and communal ties of the close-knit Australian Jewish community mean that relationships are often intense and volatile, politics are played hard and often ruthlessly, and fallings out are frequent and often permanent. These conflicts are rarely about ideology, but about what Sigmund Freud described, in a different context, as the "narcissism of the small difference." As Freud put it, "it is precisely the minor differences in people who are otherwise alike that form the basis of hostility between them."

In 1981, the Australian Jewish community of around 80,000 people was small, but its politics were fierce, and its wealth had grown spectacularly since the arrival of more than 20,000 Holocaust survivors in Australia after World War 2. Most survivors were Polish Jews; most of them settled in Melbourne. The next biggest survivor group were the Hungarians, most of whom settled in Sydney. Before the war there had been long-standing cultural and political rivalries between Hungarian and Polish Jews in Eastern Europe. The survivors brought some of these rivalries with them to Australia and translated them into a political struggle between the Jewish leadership in Melbourne and Sydney. It was in part to contain this struggle that the leadership of the Executive Council of Australian Jewry, the federal umbrella body of the Jewish community, alternated between the communities of the big two cities every two years.

In many ways, Isi Leibler has been an outstanding leader not just of Australia's Jews but of world Jewry. Yet his many battles and fallings out with fellow leaders in the community have almost invariably been about the narcissism of small difference. In the main, they have not been about ideology or policy differences, but about tactics and personal status, about who speaks for the community and, above all, about who has access to prime ministers and senior government ministers.

In 1978, Arnold Bloch and Isi Leibler fought over how the Jewish community should react to what most Jews agreed was the virulent anti-Zionism—even anti-Semitism—of some of the programs run on the Melbourne community radio station, 3CR. The dispute vividly illustrates the way power struggles and tactical differences, rather than ideological disagreements, caused the deepest and longest lasting rifts among men—they were all men—who had been close friends, often from childhood. In Jewish politics, as in all politics, there were no friendships, just shifting alliances.

At the time, Bloch was president of the Victorian Jewish Board of Deputies, Isi Leibler was president of the ECAJ. At least when Leibler was president, the ECAJ considered itself to be an elected national body that spoke for Australian Jewry on every issue that affected the Jewish community. In Leibler's view, the Victorian Jewish Board of Deputies, the body that Bloch led, was in every way subservient to the ECAJ. In practice, this meant that Isi Leibler considered his old friend, the man who had once been his *madrich* (leader) at Bnei Akiva, a man steeped in Jewish learning and seen as one of the country's sharpest lawyers, to be a sort of junior Jewish community leader who should do only what he, Leibler, told him to do. It was inevitable that at some point, Bloch, who was not exactly a shrinking violet either, would bridle at Isi Leibler's view of his leadership duties at the Board of Deputies.

For several years, the leadership of the Jewish community had grappled with how to respond to some of the pro-Palestinian programs on 3CR. Even the Australian leaders of the non-Zionist Bund, the Jewish socialist organisation that in Eastern Europe before the war had hundreds of thousands of members, most of them Jewish workers, supported the view that these programs often slipped beyond anti-Zionism into anti-Semitism. When Sam Lipski, then a columnist at *The Bulletin* magazine, wrote a column arguing that several of 3CR's programs broadcast not just extreme anti-Zionism, but anti-Semitism, Bloch decided that the Board of Deputies should take 3CR to the Australian Broadcasting Tribunal. He briefed well-known Jewish lawyer Alan Goldberg (no relation of Abe Goldberg) to run the case before the Tribunal. Isi Leibler was not consulted about this move. Bloch argued that it was a Victorian issue and therefore his to handle.

There was no state racial vilification legislation, so the only course open to Bloch and Goldberg was to argue that 3CR had breached its licence obligations and take the case to the federal Broadcasting Tribunal. The Tribunal held two hearings at which it became clear that the case presented by Goldberg on behalf of the Board of Deputies was unlikely to succeed. The Tribunal ordered 3CR and the Board of Deputies representatives to meet to see whether some agreement could be reached about modifying the broadcasts. An agreement was reached, but, as Lipski said, while he had supported going to the Tribunal, the case was as good as lost.

Isi Leibler was furious. He had warned that taking 3CR to the Broadcasting Tribunal was fraught with danger—the danger of losing the case. He publicly castigated Bloch for wasting money and going ahead with a case that, if it were lost, would give comfort to anti-Zionists and anti-Semites. And Bloch had not consulted him, the leader of the Australian Jewish community, who spoke for the community on every issue. Leibler went after Bloch without mercy, as he was to go after other people he felt challenged his leadership, including, a decade or so after the 3CR controversy, his brother Mark.

Yet while the friendship between Bloch and Isi Leibler was severely strained over the 3CR issue, it did not end until 1980, during the controversy over whether the Australian Olympic team should participate at the Moscow Olympics. In a sense, this was the only conflict between Leibler and Bloch on an issue of substance. Isi Leibler's Jetset Tours was the official travel company for the Australian team and the travel firm for Australian package tours to the Olympics.

At the time Leibler was also heavily engaged in the movement to free Soviet Jewry and had for years used his Jetset connections to travel to the Soviet Union, ostensibly for business, but in fact for meetings with Soviet officials and leaders of the movement, the so-called refuseniks. Leibler publicly urged that there be no boycott of the Moscow Olympics. Some people argued that Leibler was putting his business interests ahead of the principled position of boycotting the Olympics in protest against the Soviet invasion of Afghanistan. Bloch, still president of the Board of Deputies, publicly disagreed with Leibler. He even organised a public meeting in the Jewish community at which he passionately advocated support for a boycott of the Olympics.

Lipski, who was closely involved with Isi Leibler in the Soviet Jewry movement, said he was absolutely certain that Leibler had not opposed the boycott because his Jetset company was the official travel agency for the Australian Olympic team. He said that Leibler was desperate to maintain his contacts with the refuseniks and Soviet officials with whom he had established links. "I think Arnold reflected a majority position in the Jewish community at the time," Lipski said, "but he did not take into account the Soviet Jewry issue. That's what so infuriated Isi Leibler."

As it was, although the Fraser government pushed hard for a boycott, the Australian Olympic Committee decided that Australian athletes would compete in Moscow, but under the Olympic, not the Australian, flag. Jetset remained the official travel agency and Isi Leibler was able to travel to Moscow and further his campaign to free Soviet Jewry. But he never forgave Bloch, and the friendship ended irrevocably.

After decades of friendship, the families ended all contact. Rachel Leibler stopped seeing her close friend, Elaine Bloch, at least for a time. In 1979, Mark Leibler was a few months away from becoming president of the State Zionist Council. He was an emerging Jewish leader, but not yet a senior leader like his brother or Bloch. While he had had no real involvement in the 3CR matter, he publicly sided with his brother. Although he did not know it, at this time Bloch was already thinking of leaving the law. Leibler said that he sided with his brother not because of family loyalty but because he agreed that taking the case to the Broadcasting Tribunal was a bad decision. He reflected, "Did it affect my professional relationship with Arnold? I don't think so. I don't even think it affected our personal relationship. I never have taken these things personally. I don't think you will find a single person who would say otherwise."

Leibler played no role in the Olympics controversy. All things being equal, he would have supported the boycott, but he understood his brother's position. He never discussed the issue with Bloch and said that, again, he did not think it affected their professional relationship. He accepted that Bloch may have seen things differently, given the bitterness of the split with Isi Leibler.

Then, in May 1981, just as Bloch was ending his association with ABL and in dispute with Leibler and the other partners about the way he was leaving the firm, came a major falling out between Bloch and Mark Leibler over a significant Jewish community issue. Their dispute was over the direction of Jewish education and the way it shaped Jewish identity. For Mark Leibler, this was his first involvement in a community controversy outside his proclaimed areas of interest, Zionism and Israel. For Bloch, it was a subject that had inspired him all his adult life. The dispute between them, given their professional falling out, was bound to be scarring and it was.

Bloch had been committed to Mount Scopus College from virtually the moment he arrived in Australia in 1949, the year the school was established. He sent all his children there and served for many years as president of the school's board of governors.

With over 1500 students on two campuses, a primary school in East St Kilda and a secondary school in the outer eastern suburb of Burwood, Mount Scopus College is now one of the largest Jewish day schools in the world. It and Moriah College in Sydney are the standard bearers of a day school network unmatched by any Jewish community in the world, including the United States. More than half of Australia's Jewish children go to a Jewish day school. In Melbourne, these schools range from the ultra-Orthodox schools run by Adass Israel and Chabad, to Yavneh College, the school of the religious Zionists, where all of Mark Leibler's children and grandchildren have been educated, to Bialik College, a secular Zionist school, and King David, a school, run by the Liberal, or Reform, congregations. There is even Sholem Aleichem College, a small secular primary school where Yiddish and Yiddish culture forms the basis of its Jewish studies program. It is the only Yiddish-focused day school in the world.

In 1981, however, few Jewish schools in Melbourne and in Sydney went beyond primary school, apart from Mount Scopus and Moriah College and the relatively small ultra-Orthodox schools. Most children who went on to a secondary Jewish education went to the two big community schools, Mount Scopus and Moriah College.

Although Mark Leibler was in the first intake of students at Mount Scopus, in 1949, the Leibler family was never a major supporter of the college. They had always seen it as a community school, with all the shortcomings of community schools. It had to cater to a wide range of parents, from the Orthodox to those who wanted their children to go to a Jewish school in order to minimise the chances of their "marrying out." These parents had no real interest in their kids learning Hebrew or studying and practising Judaism. What they cared about most was maximising the chances of their children getting good Year 12 exam scores and marrying other Jews.

In Mark Leibler's view Mount Scopus College did not, indeed could not, play the role that supporters of the school, especially Bloch, wanted it to play, which was to ensure that Jewish Australian children had a deep sense of their Jewish identity, a knowledge of and love for Judaism as bulwarks against assimilation and intermarriage. Leibler believed that Mount Scopus played an important role in Jewish life, but he believed that the community needed schools with clear ideologies that fostered their particular kind of Jewish identity.

For two decades, the Leibler family had been committed to supporting a secondary school for Yavneh College, a small primary school run and supported by Mizrachi. Founded in 1962, the school enrolled its first class of Year Seven students in 1979. In Mark Leibler's view, Yavneh College gave its students what a school like Mount Scopus could not—a particular Jewish identity that was Zionist and Modern Orthodox. That identity might be considered narrow in scope, but it was deeply held and it promised to produce Jews secure in their Jewishness, knowledgeable about and able to practise Judaism with an unshakeable commitment to Israel.

Bloch, even though he was a religious Zionist and a leading member of Mizrachi, vehemently opposed any expansion of Yavneh College into a secondary school. Indeed, he had opposed the establishment of Yavneh College in 1962. Bloch was certain that the establishment of a Jewish school like Yavneh College, with its committed parent base and support from the close-knit and influential Mizrachi organisation, would rob his beloved Mount Scopus of the sort of parents and students that it desperately needed, if it was to foster a true and deep Jewish education at what was one of the biggest Jewish schools in the world. Without the Mizrachi community's support, Mount Scopus College would be in danger of becoming what Mark Leibler said it already was—a Jewish school that was unsure of what sort of Jewish identity it was fostering in its students.

In order to refute the arguments of people like Leibler about the weaknesses of Mount Scopus College, Bloch commissioned Dr Barry Chazan of the Hebrew University in Jerusalem, an expert in Jewish education, to conduct a study of the Jewish schools in Melbourne and their role in fostering Jewish identity. No doubt Bloch hoped that Chazan would confirm Bloch's view that Mount Scopus College was not just doing a fine job fostering a strong Jewish identity, but that there was no need for new, ideologically narrower, Jewish secondary schools. The Chazan report did not support Bloch's position, though after Bloch received it and asked Chazan to "clarify certain matters", Chazan obliged with an addendum that was implicitly critical of Mark Leibler, who had argued that the Chazan findings supported his position that there was a need in Australia for schools with a clear Jewish ideology.

Leibler was furious. He accused Bloch of forcing Chazan to water down his findings in the report's addendum. He demanded to see the correspondence between Bloch and Chazan. At a public meeting to discuss the report, Bloch accused Leibler of "improperly utilising Barry Chazan's report for the purpose of flaying Mount Scopus College." This was a serious charge to make against his long-time junior partner at ABL. Neither Leibler nor Bloch held back in their criticism of each other. Leibler said that commissioning the report had been a big mistake. "Bloch," he said, "was very intelligent and a great lawyer, but he was not a very good politician. You didn't commission a report like that when you didn't know its outcome."

Even so, Leibler did not believe this dispute had affected the way the partnership with Arnold Bloch had ended. Leibler said that he could always compartmentalise his Jewish community work from his work as a lawyer and his commitment to ABL. He had thought Bloch could do that, too. Now, well, he was not so sure. Perhaps their disagreement about schooling and public criticism of each other had made their professional divorce harder.

But did he understand why Bloch had wanted to leave ABL? Leibler said that he understood how working with seriously wealthy clients could affect lawyers like Bloch—or like him, for that matter. Bloch had long advised clients who were much wealthier than him. He was intellectually brilliant. Perhaps he had thought that what they had achieved he, too, could achieve.

I asked Leibler whether it affected him, working for such incredibly wealthy people? He replied,

> In a practice like ours, you see clients making heaps of money. And yes, it sometimes crossed my mind that I would be making a lot more if I went into business. I did see people, clients making a lot of money, but so what? I did alright, I was quite comfortable. How much money do you need?

I repeated that question back to him, "Well, you know, that's the question," he said.

Within a matter of weeks the partnership was dissolved on terms suggested by Alan Goldberg, the lawyer who was close to both Leibler and Bloch. Under the agreement, the name of the firm would remain Arnold Bloch Leibler, for which Bloch would be financially compensated. Bloch would continue to use the firm for legal work. The process was smooth and straightforward, Leibler says. He felt no ill will towards his long-time partner and mentor. Bloch had set his mind to go into business—fair enough—but there were consequences, the main one being that Bloch had to leave ABL. Leibler says that Bloch eventually accepted that he had to go.

The disagreement over whether Bloch could stay as a consultant at ABL was only a small part of what made the rupture between Bloch and Leibler so bitter. Bloch not only had to leave, but he had to agree to do nothing that would be seen as putting himself in competition with ABL, which meant he could not use his name for any consultancy that he planned to set up.

What Leibler didn't say when he was first interviewed about Bloch's departure was that he felt as if ABL had been in danger of going under. At the time he was still a young lawyer who was unsure whether ABL's long-time clients, Bloch's clients, would stay with the firm. It was the most stressful and difficult time of his life up to that point. A very close and successful relationship was ending, and he faced the greatest fight of his professional life—keeping ABL afloat.

In that environment, Leibler undoubtedly said things that were wounding and that Bloch felt were designed to destroy his reputation as a lawyer if he did not abandon his plans to use his name for the consultancy he was planning. When asked about these things, Leibler

CHAPTER 6

said that, yes, while he had forgotten the specifics, there had been pretty fierce confrontations with Bloch, especially over the consultancy issue and the way Bloch had gone about establishing the consultancy without telling his partners.

In the end, Bloch set up a consultancy called Arnold Bloch Professional Services, and some of the old ABL clients used his services, about which there is no doubt Leibler would not have been happy. The consultancy operated for a couple of years before it petered out. There was a non-compete clause in the separation agreement that meant the consultancy could not do legal work. Some clients, such as John Gandel, did use Arnold Bloch Professional Services for a while, but never for legal work. That remained with ABL.

Leibler said that creating the consultancy was never the issue. From the start, he had formed the view that, if Bloch wasn't actively practising law, no consultancy could take clients from ABL. For Leibler the problem was use of the name. The firm's practice was built on long-term high-net-wealth individuals. Leibler's job was to hang on to them and build the firm at the same time. For Bloch to use part of ABL's name for his consultancy was a step too far. And registering the name secretly was, in Leibler's view, ethically dubious.

Bloch's desire to use his own name for his consultancy when he had been compensated for the fact that Arnold Bloch Leibler would remain the firm's name, infuriated Leibler. It also troubled Joe Gersh, a young and recently hired lawyer at ABL. Gersh remembers that Bloch's new offices looked just like a legal office, even though Bloch had signed a non-compete agreement that meant he could not practise law. "Arnold made it worse with his consultancy," Gersh said. "He virtually built himself legal chambers somewhere in Collins Street with legal books lining the walls. It was difficult."

85

Bloch's move into business proved successful, at least in terms of his wealth. He was not in the same league as his business partners, Besen and Goldberg, but he was a lot wealthier than he would have been had he stayed at ABL. He didn't get much time to enjoy it. When Bloch died in February 1985, the *Jewish Chronicle* in London published a glowing obituary that began: "The death of Mr. Arnold Bloch at the age of 56 has deprived Australian Jewry of one of its most dedicated and dynamic leaders." Many hundreds of people came to the funeral in the Jewish section of the Springvale cemetery in Melbourne. Among them were many of the clients, now fabulously wealthy, who had first come to Bloch in the 1950s for legal advice as they started their businesses.

Virtually every significant leader of the Jewish community in Australia attended the funeral. Yet two were missing and their absence caused intense speculation and rumour-mongering among the mourners, though it was never reported in the Jewish press. One was Isi Leibler; the other was Mark. The Bloch family had let it be known that Mark Leibler would not be welcome at the funeral.

CHAPTER 7

Joe Gersh remembers that time well, the couple of years after Arnold Bloch left ABL. Gersh is executive chairman of Gersh Investment Partners, an investment banker for private developers and construction companies. He is a director of Gerard Henderson's right-wing think tank, The Sydney Institute, and has strong contacts in the Liberal Party. He has long been friends with the former Treasurer, Peter Costello, and in 2018 was appointed to the board of the Australian Broadcasting Corporation, as a "captain's pick" by then Communications Minister, Mitch Fifield.

His firm's offices feel as if they have been designed by a tech start-up interior decorator. The young men and women who wander around outside Gersh's small, glass-enclosed office affect an air of casualness that seems contrary to the cliché of investment bank high-flyers. Jeans seem *de rigueur*, and Gersh is dressed in jeans and a blue jumper. As we speak, he gives off an air of slight disappointment, as if the memories of his time at ABL are painful, although he emails me later to say how much he enjoyed remembering those years.

When Gersh joined ABL in 1980 as a 24-year-old articled clerk, he had been involved in Jewish politics from his school days at Mount Scopus College, at Melbourne University and, nationally, through the Australian Union of Jewish Students. In the mid-1970s he was a student representative on the Victorian Board of Deputies and on the ECAJ. He was considered a young man with a bright future. He was already close to Bloch, whom Gersh considered a "giant in the Jewish community" and the sort of leader that Gersh aspired to be. He knew many of ABL's clients through his Jewish community work. It was almost inevitable that he would end up at ABL. As he recalled,

> After I prepared .my articles application, I actually gave it to Arnold at a Board of Deputies meeting. He signed it "ok" at the bottom and passed it on to somebody and that was that. When I graduated, I just rocked up for work and they had half an office ready for me.

Gersh did not know Mark Leibler well, but for a time he had worked for Isi Leibler at Jetset, and had been offered a lucrative position in the company. Gersh felt so much a protégé of Isi's that, when Mark called him in towards the end of his articles to say that he wanted him to stay with ABL and that, if he stayed, he would quickly be made a partner, Gersh went to Isi for advice.

At the time, businessman Richard Pratt had offered Gersh a lucrative job at Visy Industries. Pratt had heard that Gersh was a bright Jewish boy and, according to Gersh, Pratt was then trying to hire every bright young Jewish boy in Australia. By then, however, having consulted Isi Leibler, Gersh had decided to stay in the law and at ABL. Leibler had told him that "things were happening at ABL."

Gersh says he did not know that, by the time he was finishing his articles, Bloch had fallen out with both Leibler brothers and had decided to leave the law. The atmosphere at ABL was tense. Gersh thought that the war between Bloch and Mark Leibler was a subset of the ugly community fight between Isi and Arnold for supremacy at the Board of Deputies and that it had somehow spilled over into ABL. It was an extremely difficult time at the firm, Gersh says. "Mark was in his 30s, still a relatively junior lawyer and we kids might have thought he was all powerful, but he was actually a little bit scared. All the major clients, the backbone of the firm, even today, were all Arnold's clients."

Bloch and Leibler were very different in their approach to young lawyers, Gersh says:

> Mark let us young people show what we could do. He never told clients to come see him rather than one of us. Arnold never did that. He'd say, "Look he's a nice kid, but come talk to me." It was never going to be Mark's show until Arnold left, but that leaving was always going to be fraught.

It was fraught, above all, for Gersh himself. He loved Bloch, but he felt professionally loyal to Leibler. His loyalty was handsomely repaid. Bloch's departure left a hole in the firm's leadership that Leibler and the other partners were anxious to fill. In July 1981, Gersh was made a senior associate; at the end of that year, at just 26 years old, he was made a partner.

Over the next decade Gersh brought to ABL a group of young, mainly Jewish lawyers. They included Henry Lanzer, now ABL's managing partner, Steven Skala, who would work at ABL for 20 years, and Leon Zwier, who had a reputation for imagination, legal brilliance and unorthodox thinking. These men were young and sharp, and nearly all were active in the Jewish community. Gersh, Lanzer and Zwier, in particular, were to play a pivotal role in building ABL's reputation as a creative, aggressive firm, modelled on some of the big, mainly Jewish, law firms of New York. They were not just lawyers who gave their clients legal advice based on black letter law. They were advisers who saw their mission as getting to know their clients and giving advice based on this knowledge—for instance, on their knowledge of a particular client's appetite for risk. All three had gone to Mount Scopus College, studied law at Melbourne University and been active in Jewish student politics. They knew each other well, and, as lawyers and as young Jewish community leaders, they knew most of ABL's clients. Gersh and Lanzer persuaded Leibler to take on Zwier. In time, this decision would transform the firm.

Gersh said that the connection and overlap between the Jewish clients and community "was Mark's vision and maybe it had been Arnold's vision, too. Mark wanted ABL to be the pre-eminent law firm in the Jewish community." That aligned with his leadership ambitions. "If you were the pre-eminent law firm, then you had the credibility to be a leader, a respected person in the Jewish community. Back then, that was my ambition, too."

In time, Leibler came to believe that Bloch's departure, while difficult, would be the making of ABL. These outstanding young lawyers, most of them hired on Gersh's recommendation, would form the backbone of the firm and secure its future. They would be Leibler's people. Leibler's fears that Bloch's departure threatened the firm's existence were not borne out. Many of ABL's old Jewish clients remembered Bloch with great affection; some never developed the same affection for Leibler. Nevertheless, nearly all these clients say they never considered taking their legal business elsewhere.

Nechama Werdiger is the widow of property developer Nathan Werdiger, who died in 2015, aged 93. When Bloch left ABL, she and her husband had been friends with Arnold and Elaine Bloch for many years. Nathan Werdiger arrived in Australia in 1949, at the age of 23, having spent four years in a Swiss sanatorium recovering from his experiences in Auschwitz, to which he had been transported with his brother, Nechemia. They were two of six children. At the platform where SS officer and physician Dr Joseph Mengele chose who would live and who would die, four of the six Werdiger siblings were sent to their deaths.

By the late 1960s, Nathan and Nechemia Werdiger had turned a small textile shop into Classweave Industries, one of Australia's largest textile businesses. In the 1970s, when the Whitlam government cut tariffs on textiles, Nathan went into property investment, setting up Juilliard Corporation. It became one of the biggest landlords in Melbourne's central business district. When he died, his son Shlomo took over the business. In the 2018 *Australian Financial Review* Rich List, the Werdiger family fortune was estimated at $859 million.

Nechama Werdiger, a handsome woman in her 80s, speaks carefully and precisely, because she does not want to say anything that might cause controversy or upset her good friend, Rosanna Leibler. The Werdigers were always part of the Chasidic Chabad movement and were major donors to Melbourne's Chabad schools, Beth Rivka College and Yeshiva College. Arising in the 18th century in Eastern Europe, Chasidism was a form of mysticism designed to open up Judaism to poor and uneducated Jewish men who were unable to practise the sort of deep learning demanded by traditional Judaism of the Talmud and other holy books that interpreted the Torah, the first five books of the Hebrew (and Christian) Bible.

From Poland to Hungary a number of Chasidic sects sprung up, each with its own Rebbe (leader). These sects, especially after the Holocaust, set themselves up in America, famously in New York's Williamsburg district where thousands of Chasidim of various sects live. In Australia they established themselves in Sydney and, in greater numbers, in Melbourne, around the Ripponlea streets where Arnold Bloch first set up his legal practice.

Ideologically and in terms of their Judaism, Chabad (or Lubavitcher Chasidim because they were the followers of the Lubavitcher Rebbe) and the religious Zionists of Mizrachi had fundamental disagreements. Most members of Chabad would not consider themselves Zionists. Chabad and other Chasidic sects, as well as non-Chasidic ultra-Orthodox groups like Adass Israel, were always opposed to Zionism and, later, to the state of Israel. Zionism was a movement of non-believers that rejected the teaching of the rabbis over thousands of years that God would ingather the Jews to the Holy Land only with the coming of the Messiah. Nevertheless, the differences between the Chabad and Mizrachi did not seem to cause any rift between the Werdigers, on one hand, and the Blochs and Mark and Rosanna Leibler on the other. They were close, and they were all committed Jews.

At the time that Bloch left ABL, Nechama Werdiger had known that there had been tension between Bloch and Leibler. Of her husband's relationship with the two men, she said:

> Yes, Arnold had been Nathan's lawyer, our lawyer, from the time Nathan went into business. But by the time Arnold left, Nathan had formed a relationship with Mark, too. He considered Mark a very good lawyer. There was never any question of leaving ABL. Never. And I don't know of anyone who did leave, except perhaps members of Arnold's family.

In her 1987 book, *The New Boy Network*, Ruth Ostrow examined the way migrants and refugees, many of them Jewish survivors of the Holocaust, were transforming Australian business. Less than three decades after arriving in Australia, some of them were among the country's richest people. By the time *Business Review Weekly* put out its 1987 Rich 200, the list included Marc Besen, John Gandel, Eddie Kornhauser, Maurice Alter, and the Smorgon, Liberman, Rockman and Werdiger families. All of them, along with non-Jews such as Bruno Grollo, were clients of ABL. Some of those on the *BRW* list—George

Herscu, Abe Goldberg, Larry Adler and his son Rodney—ended up being exposed as crooks and some ended up in jail. Herscu and Goldberg had been ABL clients. The vast majority, however, survived the 1987 stock market crash and went on to accumulate wealth beyond their own imaginings.

In the early 1980s, many of them were the backbone of ABL's client list. The vast majority operated through trusts and private companies and, therefore, the sort of relationship they had with their lawyers was very different from the relationship between lawyers and the boards of public companies. The difference defined the sort of law firm that ABL was from the start and that, to some extent, it remains today. Its clients expected a close relationship with their lawyers. Unlike the boards of public companies, they did not seek only legal advice. They wanted advisers who understood their entrepreneurial dreams and schemes, lawyers who knew the law but who could also advise them on how to maximise their chances of successfully building their businesses. This included advice on how to structure their companies so that they did not pay any more tax than was necessary under the law, including High Court and Tax Office rulings. In the first few decades of ABL's existence, tax advice was a significant, perhaps even central, part of the firm's earnings. Although he was many years Bloch's junior, by the time Bloch left ABL, Leibler was on the road to establishing himself as one of Australia's foremost tax lawyers.

Not long after Bloch's departure, Leibler started to seriously develop his political contacts and political influence. His growing reputation gave him the opportunity to reach out to senior politicians, even to federal Treasurers, who would most likely agree to meet him to discuss a particular tax issue. The tax problems of many of his clients made it urgent for Leibler to do so.

It was not only Leibler's reputation as a tax lawyer that gained him entrée to John Howard when he was Treasurer and, later, to Paul Keating. It was also the fact that some of ABL's clients had relationships with Howard and Keating and other senior politicians, and some donated generously both to the Liberal Party and to the Australian Labor Party.

What occurred during these years can only be described as a time of tax madness. In 1980, Prime Minister Malcolm Fraser set up a Royal Commission, headed by Frank Costigan QC, to investigate the criminal nature of the Federated Ship Painters and Dockers Union. Costigan certainly did that, but, more importantly, uncovered a vast tax avoidance industry that involved some of the country's business leaders and eminent lawyers. The so-called "bottom-of-the-harbour" schemes, in which officials of the Painters and Dockers played a small part, became a symbol of the way the rich and powerful had avoided paying tax. These schemes were helped by a High Court that, under Chief Justice Garfield Barwick in the 1970s, had delivered judgments in landmark cases that made widespread tax avoidance legally acceptable.

Some 7000 companies and 30,000 individuals were involved in the bottom-of-the-harbour schemes. More than $1 billion in tax was avoided, according to most estimates. The schemes were blatant in their intent—to avoid paying what should have been a legitimate tax bill on company profits. At its simplest, it involved a series of paper transactions in which a company was stripped of its assets and accumulated profits, leaving no tax payable. These assets were then transferred to a new company that carried on business as before. The original company was then metaphorically dispatched to the bottom of the harbour through a transfer to someone with no assets and no idea of what was actually happening. Often, the old company's records were simply "lost". Some of the people to whom the assets were transferred were members of the Painters and Dockers Union.

The Costigan Commission revelations reinforced a widespread view in the community that payment of tax by the wealthy and by business had become voluntary. The tax burden fell ever more heavily on pay-as-you-earn (PAYE) taxpayers on modest and low incomes, who could neither take advantage of tax avoidance schemes or afford sharp lawyers to advise on how to get out of paying tax. The whole tax system was in danger of being discredited, and senior ministers in the Fraser government, including Treasurer Howard, knew that, if the government did not act to, at the very least, outlaw these tax avoidance schemes, it would not survive.

Given the nature of ABL's clients and Leibler's developing reputation as one of the smartest tax lawyers around, it was inevitable that the fall-out of the Costigan Commission revelations would affect ABL's clients and, therefore, present Leibler with some serious challenges. Leibler would not tell me how many of ABL's clients had been involved in the bottom-of-the-harbour schemes, but there can be little doubt that the number was significant. They needed his help, especially when it became clear that the Fraser government, with an election due within a year or so, was determined to make the avoidance schemes illegal and perhaps—this was Leibler's big concern—to pass retrospective legislation to recoup tax that had been avoided.

In 1980, before the Costigan Royal Commission had delivered its reports, the federal parliament passed legislation, introduced by Howard and supported by the Labor Opposition, that made it a criminal offence for any person to create a company or trust that was unable to pay tax debts, or to aid or abet a company or person to do so. The new law meant that both those who took up the tax avoidance schemes and their promoters would be criminally liable. There is no doubt that some of ABL's clients would have been targets of this legislation. At that stage, they were in no way liable for tax that had been avoided through the schemes. They were, however, vulnerable to further legislation that would force them retrospectively to pay the tax they had legally avoided.

Through the 1970s and into the early 1980s, Leibler knew about the tax avoidance schemes that some of ABL's clients had signed up to. The schemes were widely advertised, including in the *Australian Financial Review*. It was common knowledge in tax circles and in business that the schemes were operating and that thousands of businesses were involved. Yet the Australian Taxation Office (ATO) never gave any signal that the schemes were not above board. As Leibler commented,

> Garfield Barwick's High Court had handed down literalist inter-pretations of the scope of the anti-avoidance provisions of the tax laws that made it relatively easy to find loopholes. The court looked at the letter not the intent behind the enforcement provisions, which on one reading was to stop blatant tax avoidance schemes.

I asked Leibler what he told his clients when they told him they were signing up for one of the schemes. Did he warn them that there might be problems in the future? Did he say that such avoidance schemes may be legal but might be considered ethically dubious?

Leibler replied that clients came to him armed with legal advice from very eminent QCs that stated, without qualification, that the schemes were legal. He said that tax avoidance was not necessarily illegal at the time. It was different from tax evasion, which was a criminal offence. "Huge numbers" of people were entering into tax avoidance schemes. So, if a client came along, protected by a QC's opinion, and said he wanted to sign up for one of the schemes, Leibler did not advise against it:

It seemed to be an acceptable way, legally, of treating their tax obligations so that, yes, they didn't have to pay tax, but you know, I didn't know in detail how these schemes worked. I did not know how companies were being liquidated, that they were going to the bottom of the harbour. What I did know was that eminent QCs were advising that the promoters of these schemes had a perfectly legal way of dealing with any tax issues that may arise.

What about ethics, even morality? Did these things play any part in the sort of advice that Leibler gave his clients back then, gives his clients now? Is there an ethical imperative for people to pay their fair share of tax and is it in any way—or should it be—part of the advice that a lawyer of Leibler's eminence raises with his clients?

The first time I asked him about ethics and tax, Leibler said that, if you are going to have a modern Western civilised country, then you had to raise revenue for a range of things and paying tax was a necessity, even a duty, you could argue. But few people considered it a duty to pay tax. Few people wanted to pay more in tax than they had to. He then said that he was not sure that there were ethical and moral issues involved in taxation issues.

As a tax lawyer, his duty was to understand not just tax law but the way the ATO operated. In theory, the Commissioner of Taxation was meant to administer the tax system, but, in practice, the ATO was too big for that, so what the Commissioner did was set the culture, set guidelines, and oversee major cases. Leibler continued:

> But they are public servants. The money they raise and the money they don't raise is not coming in or out of their pockets. They will be more concerned with perceptions, rules, regulations, how the government sees things. I have had cases where, at the request of the Tax Office, a client has ended up paying less than we were prepared to pay because that fitted into some paradigm

of theirs. You need to understand all of this if you're going to be good for your clients.

Yet, another time, when he was looking back at those years, he said that, given what he had learnt over time, his advice to clients would now be different. If he had been back then the lawyer that he is today, his advice would have been not to get involved in the schemes. Perhaps, he said, he was just second-guessing himself with the benefit of hindsight, knowing what happened after the Costigan Royal Commission.

Months later, in a further interview, Leibler said again that he was not sure about ethics when it came to tax issues. On the one hand, federal treasurers and tax commissioners gave speeches about doing the right thing and fairness and paying your fair share of tax, because, otherwise, where would we get the money to build schools and hospitals and transport systems. On the other hand, they never talked about all the money going to waste in the bureaucracy and money that goes to things that Leibler said were not necessarily worth spending taxpayers' money on. For the first time, Leibler moved away from a discussion of the ethics of tax minimisation to an ideological position in favour of neo-liberal small government.

He remained adamant that the whole tax avoidance mess of the bottom-of-the-harbour period was the responsibility both of the courts, Barwick's High Court in particular, and of the inaction of the Taxation Office. He did acknowledge that many people, especially PAYE taxpayers, felt that the tax burden was falling so heavily on them because the wealthy had ways of minimising, even avoiding, paying their fair share:

> All the things they say about people needing to pay their fair
> share of tax is negated by the fact that there's nothing fair about
> the tax system in a whole variety of ways. So, it's not as if people

back then, during the bottom-of-the-harbour days, were acting illegally, stashing money away illegally. They were doing something that was advertised in the newspapers and that the High Court and the Commissioner of Taxation knew about and did nothing to stop.

Howard's legislation to outlaw tax avoidance schemes was passed in early 1981. Leibler thought the legislation was inevitable. He understood that the government had to act. But, when Howard introduced further legislation in 1982 designed to retrospectively claw back the tax that many of his clients had avoided through the schemes, Leibler publicly opposed it. For the first time, he resolved to see Howard to urge him to abandon the proposed new law.

Leibler was not alone in his concern. The 1982 Cabinet papers, released in January 2012, revealed that "no issue provoked more anguish than John Howard's move to retrospectively claw back the ill-gotten proceeds of what started out as legal tax avoidance arrangements," according to the *Australian Financial Review*. Some in the Fraser Cabinet opposed retrospective legislation as a matter of principle, and the Cabinet papers show that Howard had sympathy for this position. Indeed, he proposed withdrawing the legislation at one stage, but Fraser insisted it be tabled in the House of Representatives. The House and the Senate passed it in October 1982.

Interviewed in his Sydney office in 2018, John Howard remembered those first meetings with Leibler in Canberra in 1982. He said that their relationship, now decades long, had deepened since then. Howard remembered that the meetings

> were regarding tax matters. Not his tax matters personally, but I understood that he was coming from the position of representing his clients, some very influential clients, though he never said

so. This was at a time when I, as Treasurer, was fairly active in fighting tax avoidance schemes. It was tough. There was hand–to-hand combat. There was a lot of revenue at stake. People like Mark, on behalf of his clients, always think the Tax Office is too aggressive and the Tax Office thinks some clients and lawyers like Mark are too reluctant to pay tax.

Who was right? Howard laughed that loud guffaw laugh that said he was not going to talk about that.

Leibler, Howard said, was highly intelligent and forceful. He called a spade a spade. But Howard wanted to emphasise that Leibler had not convinced him to withdraw the legislation. He said that Leibler must have known that it was politically impossible for him to do so, even if he had wanted to. The decision had had no effect on their relationship. They liked and respected each other, Howard said.

Howard was right. Leibler had known that, in the climate of the time, with the Labor Party accusing the government of being soft on tax cheats, he was not even remotely likely to convince Howard to change his mind. He did, nevertheless, establish a relationship with one of the most important figures in Canberra. In years to come he would build many more.

Far from marking the end of ABL, as Leibler may have feared in his worst nightmares, the 1980s turned out to be a very good decade for the firm, as it was for so many people in business and the law. Victorian Premier John Cain opened ABL's new offices in Lonsdale Street in 1985. As the practice expanded, it entered merger talks with one of Australia's big establishment law firms, Sydney-based Stephen Jaques. A heads of agreement was even signed in 1985, but, in the end, the merger made no sense, according to Leibler and the other long-time partners. They had all decided that it would rob ABL of the strength that had served the firm so well during the bottom-of-the-harbour years—its reputation for advising and supporting high-net-wealth individuals who expected and were given instant access to partners, no matter how trivial their issues seemed.

The decision not to merge meant that, for the time being, ABL would remain an essentially boutique firm of mainly Jewish lawyers servicing Jewish clients. A brochure from 1986 contains short profiles of the six partners; all are men, and five are Jews. A photo in the brochure, taken when ABL's offices were still in Lonsdale Street, shows a rather nondescript foyer with modest couches and a round marble-topped table, on top of which sits a glass vase with a bunch of red tulips, which, frankly, look fake.

Four years later, in 1990, Joe Gersh oversaw what amounted to a takeover of the largely Jewish Melbourne firm, Cooper Korbl. That merger brought another leading lawyer, Philip Chester, to the firm; it also brought Solomon Lew as one of ABL's biggest clients. A year later, hiring Leon Zwier opened a new field for ABL in corporate restructuring and insolvency. The merger also brought in many clients who were not Jewish—organisations such as the big corporate restructuring specialists, Ferrier Hodgson and KordaMentha.

In 1990 the firm relocated to 333 Collins Street, a building that was once the grand headquarters of the Commercial Bank of Australia before it merged with the Bank of New South Wales to form Westpac in 1982. The move from less salubrious Lonsdale Street was a signal that ABL was determined to expand its base into the legal world of listed companies and major corporations that formed the pillars of the Australian business establishment. This was a world that had not always welcomed Jewish lawyers and businessmen with open arms.

CHAPTER 8

In October 1973, when Mark Leibler was just 30 and still a relatively junior Jewish leader, Egyptian and Syrian armies attacked Israel. At the time, Israel was occupying the Egyptian Sinai Peninsula and the Syrian Golan Heights territory it had taken after the 1967 war. The 1973 conflict came to be called the Yom Kippur War, after Judaism's holiest day, when the fighting began. Three days into the war, Israel, with its military totally unprepared, faced the distinct possibility of defeat. Leibler remembered the fear of those days, the feeling that Israel was once again fighting for survival. He also remembered that war as a turning point in the Jewish community's relationship with the Whitlam government and, more broadly, with the Australian Labor Party (ALP). Throughout the post-war years, around 50 per cent of the Jewish community had supported Labor. When Gough Whitlam was elected in 1972, some of the ALP's major donors were Jewish.

Until the election of the Whitlam government, the Liberal and National parties in coalition and the ALP had an almost ironclad consensus to support Israel, just as they shared strong support for the ANZUS Alliance and for the United States as leader of the Free World and as its underwriter and protector in the fight against international communism. In the aftermath of the Six-Day War, when the Soviet Union shifted to a virulently anti-Israel position, support for Israel and for the United States became firmly connected.

Prime Minister Whitlam changed the direction of Australian foreign policy. He asserted Australia's independence, making it clear that his government was not as totally committed to the alliance with the United States as Australian governments had been in the past. On

Israel, he declared that his government would be even-handed. For Jewish community leaders, this meant that Australian government support for Israel could no longer be taken for granted. It put the long association between the ALP and Israeli Labor Party—every Israeli prime minister before 1973 had come from the Israeli Labor Party or affiliated parties—into crisis.

On the fourth day of the war, a delegation of seven Jewish leaders went to Canberra to meet with Whitlam. Isi Leibler was part of the delegation; Mark Leibler was not. It was a dreadful meeting for the Jewish delegation. Whitlam essentially told them that he would not condemn Egypt and Syria for starting the war. More important for the delegation, given that Israel seemed in danger of losing, was Whitlam's refusal to publicly support a ceasefire.

Seven months later, when Whitlam called an early election in May 1974, the ALP was concerned that Jewish donors would abandon Labor because of Whitlam's Middle East policies. As Sam Lipski described it in *Let My People Go*, Labor officials organised a breakfast for a gathering of Jewish leaders at Melbourne's Chevron Hotel, then owned by prominent Jewish businessman Eddie Kornhauser. In an attempt to repair relations with the community, Whitlam would speak at the breakfast. Mark Leibler was there.

It was, in Lipski's words, a disaster. Leibler remembered the impact that breakfast had on him. From the start, Whitlam made it clear that he was not there to apologise for the positions he had taken on the Middle East. Leibler had forgotten much of what Whitlam said, but he did remember as if it happened yesterday that, in response to a question that annoyed Whitlam, the Prime Minister said, "You people need to realise there is a large Arab community in Australia, a Christian Arab community." Leibler was stunned. He thought it was the first time that an Australian prime minister had referred to Jews as "you people," with all that meant in Jewish history. He realised that he could never assume that Australian governments would support Israel. He understood that when he was elected to leadership positions it was vital to make the case for Israel to both sides of politics and to establish better, more professional connections with leaders of both parties.

The meeting marked a profound change for some in the ALP as well. It is now a commonplace accusation that the so-called Jewish Lobby— or Israel Lobby as it is sometimes described—has undue influence on Australian government policies toward the Israeli–Palestinian conflict. It has also become common practice to accuse it of being powerful and bullying. Bob Carr, former Labor premier of New South Wales and Foreign Minister in Julia Gillard's last years as prime minister, is perhaps the most prominent politician to engage in such accusations. Their genesis inside the ALP goes back to that breakfast in Melbourne in 1974. After that event, Lipski said, Whitlam told ALP supporters that he had felt "ambushed". He accused the Jewish leadership of "trying to blackmail him into supporting Israel."

The wariness between Jewish leaders and Labor politicians may still have hung in the air when Mark Leibler first met Bill Hayden, in Hayden's Canberra office in September 1982. Hayden was then Leader of the Opposition in the federal parliament. Leibler was president of the Victorian State Zionist Council, still very much a junior community leader. It was a difficult time to be a Zionist leader. The Israeli invasion of Lebanon had provoked protests around the world. The Fraser government had condemned the invasion, and so had Hayden.

Jewish businessman Saul Same, a long-time ALP supporter and donor, had organised for Leibler to meet with Hayden. Hayden had already rejected a meeting with Isi Leibler, a far more senior Jewish leader than his younger brother. Hayden disliked Isi Leibler. He thought him difficult to deal with, prone to angry outbursts, and quick to make threats. More importantly, Isi Leibler was close to former union chief Bob Hawke, who at the time was stalking Hayden for the Labor leadership.

Hayden may also have been reluctant to see Mark Leibler. Leibler had said some harsh things about Hayden after the Opposition Leader had gone to Israel in 1980 and, despite intense lobbying by Jewish community leaders, had gone to Ramallah in the West Bank to visit Yasser Arafat, leader of the Palestinian Liberation Organisation (PLO), which was committed to Israel's destruction. Indeed, Arafat had publicly restated that position shortly before Hayden's visit. Later, in November 1981, Hayden had made a statement in parliament describing then Israeli Prime Minister Menachem Begin as the biggest threat to world peace. In a confidential briefing paper for Jewish community leaders drafted immediately after his meeting with Hayden on 23 September, Mark Leibler wrote that Hayden had "behaved totally irrationally in relation to issues affecting Israel."

Leibler's paper made only oblique reference to the Israeli invasion of Lebanon just a few months previously and to a shocking event that had profound repercussions for Israel, for Ariel Sharon, then Defence Minister and architect of the Lebanon invasion, and for Jewish communities and leaders around the world. Between 16 and 18 September 1982, a few days before Leibler met Hayden, hundreds of Palestinian men, women and children were massacred in the Sabra neighbourhood of Beirut and in the nearby Shatila Palestinian refugee camp. The massacre was the work of Israel's ally in Lebanon, the Christian Phalangist militia. It generated widespread outrage, and, as the invading force,

Israel was held responsible for the atrocity perpetrated by its allies. There was deep concern at these events in the Australian Jewish community, many of whose members already believed that the Lebanon war had been a disaster. What was supposed to be a limited invasion of Southern Lebanon to push the PLO out of the region had, at Sharon's direction, turned into a full-scale invasion of the entire country.

Leibler's briefing paper bears evidence of the division in the Jewish community and among its leaders over the invasion and the massacre. Leibler was in Canberra with Saul Same, waiting to see Hayden, when Isi called him to say that Dr Joachim Schneeweiss, then president of the Executive Council of Australian Jewry, intended to send a telex to Israeli Prime Minister Begin calling for an immediate and independent inquiry into the Sabra and Shatila massacre. Mark Leibler tried to stop Schneeweiss sending the message to Begin. In his view, it was not for diaspora Jewish leaders to tell the Israeli government what to do. He spoke to the presidents of the New South Wales and Victorian Boards of Deputies and to the president of the Zionist Federation of Australia, urging them to get Schneeweiss to back down. In the end, Schneeweiss did not send the message to Begin. Leibler won, but what could not be papered over was the division among Jewish community leaders over what had happened in Lebanon. In the briefing paper, Leibler conceded that this division existed.

I experienced these tensions and the hard line that the Leiblers and their supporters took against dissent from their position, when I was invited to attend what I was told would be a panel discussion of an article I had written in *The Age* about the divisions in the Jewish community over the Lebanon invasion. This discussion was my first encounter with some of the people who would later work for the Australia/Israel & Jewish Affairs Council, which was to fall foul of politicians like Bob Carr. On this night these people were bruising in their criticism of what I had written, to say the least. I knew nothing of Leibler's meeting with Hayden or with any other member of the Hawke government. At the time I had had almost nothing to do with representatives of Jewish community organisations.

Before he met Hayden, Leibler had met with Barry Cohen, a former Whitlam government minister and staunch Israel supporter. Cohen told Leibler that there should be a "free public interchange of views between Jewish leaders and members of the Jewish community." Leibler had disagreed. "I indicated to Cohen that he would never convince responsible Jewish leaders in Australia that we should indulge in public criticism of Israeli Government policy," he wrote in the briefing paper. "Any justified criticisms were more than adequately articulated by our enemies."

In those days Mark and Isi Leibler saw themselves as policemen of the extent to which members of the Jewish community could be critical of Israel. If anyone crossed the Leibler line, the brothers reacted with the sort of trenchant, even personal, criticism that made enemies of Jews and non-Jews who found themselves on the receiving end of their often vitriolic attacks.

Thirty-six years later, I asked Mark Leibler whether he still believed that no Jewish leader should ever be critical of Israeli government policies. He was silent for a while before he answered that he had changed, mellowed perhaps. He now believed that he had reacted too fiercely to people who said things that he considered to be wrong and even bordering on anti-Semitism. Nevertheless, he still believed that Jews in the diaspora, Jewish leaders in particular, should not make statements that criticised Israel's security positions. "Israel's enemies do that well enough," he said, continuing:

I think that when it comes to domestic policy in Israel, Jewish leaders can be critical and sometimes should be critical. For instance, I opposed publicly the way the Government threatened to treat the 40,000 or so Eritrean and South Sudanese refugees in 2018, just expelling them from the country. That would have been unacceptable, wrong. But when it comes to security issues, I think Jewish leaders can be critical, but privately, with the Israeli leaders. Given that we do not live in Israel and have to deal with the consequences of security decisions, we should not comment publicly on these issues.

If the relationship between Hayden and most of the Jewish community leadership had been frosty for several years, it deteriorated further after the Lebanon invasion and the massacres, just days before Leibler met Hayden. The relationship had also become frostier because of the leadership battle between Hawke and Hayden the same year. The meeting between Leibler and Hayden took place two months after Hawke's first challenge to Hayden. Hawke had lost that ballot, but he had won significant support. After the vote he said he would not challenge for the leadership again. No one believed him.

Leibler believed that Hayden's hostility to Israel and the Jewish community was in large part because Hayden was convinced that the community was working to get Hawke up as Leader of the Opposition. This sounds far-fetched, but some former Jewish leaders and Labor politicians say that Hawke did tell whoever would listen that he was a hero to the Jewish community, that the Jews were on his side and wanted him to lead the ALP in parliament.

In a note, one of many among his voluminous papers that he wrote after meetings with politicians and public servants, Leibler wrote:

Hayden initially made peace overtures to the Jewish community, but when…Bob Hawke moved into the political arena and

threatened Hayden's leadership, Hayden turned bitterly on Israel…
Indeed Israel and the Jewish community frequently assumed the
role of surrogate to Hayden's obsessive fear of Hawke.

It seemed to me to be fairly obvious that the tension which
characterised Bill Hayden's relationship with the Jewish community
was at least in part attributable to the fact that Hayden saw the
Jewish community as being involved in some sort of conspiracy
with Bob Hawke to capture the ALP leadership from Hayden.

Hayden had agreed to meet Mark Leibler, but had insisted that his
brother could not be there under any circumstance. At the beginning
of the meeting, Mark Leibler told Hayden that the meeting was off
the record as far as he was concerned. He said that since it was not an
official meeting between Hayden and the Jewish community leadership,
he felt that he could be "brutally frank" in his views to Hayden and
he hoped that Hayden would not be offended. Leibler then proceeded
to speak uninterrupted for close to half an hour.

According to Leibler's notes, he began by apologising for the things
he had said about Hayden when the Opposition Leader had gone
to Israel and the West Bank in 1980. He then proceeded to give
Hayden a rather blunt lecture about the way factional politics and the
leadership issue between Hayden and Hawke had "infected Labor's
policies towards Israel, with the consequence that ALP spokesmen
were taking up positions which were totally unrelated to the merits
of Israel's case." Leibler went on to write that Hayden's difficulties
with the Jewish community were due in part to Hayden's "paranoia"
over the relationship between Hawke and the Jews. "The point that I
sought to get across, arising from all of this, was just how regrettable
it was that neither Hayden nor the ALP had been able to really deal
with the issues affecting Israel on their merits."

It is remarkable that Hayden, in response, was apparently prepared to concede that he was annoyed by Hawke's self-description as a hero of the Jewish community, who thought he had Jewish support in his pocket. It is remarkable, too, that Hayden did not raise the Lebanon war and the massacres, although according to Leibler, he did say that "you should be grateful at the Labor Party's muted response to Israel's action in Lebanon." Hayden said that he had been under pressure from the ALP Executive to be more critical of Israel but he had resisted that pressure.

This was probably an understatement. The condemnation of Israel's invasion of Lebanon was intense, not just in Australia but around the world; and that was before the massacres at Sabra and Shatila, which many saw as war crimes. A United Nations commission concluded in 1983 that Israel bore responsibility for what the Phalangists had perpetrated. Several months later, a commission of inquiry set up by the Begin government found that the Israeli military had been aware that a massacre was in progress and had failed to take serious steps to stop it. The commission found that Israel was indirectly responsible, and that Ariel Sharon bore personal responsibility for "ignoring the danger of bloodshed and revenge." Sharon was forced to resign as Defence Minister as a result.

Hayden spoke only briefly about any of this, saying it was increasingly difficult for him, a member of the ALP Left, to resist the widespread conviction among his colleagues that the government was being too soft in its criticism of Israel.

When the meeting ended, Leibler asked Hayden whether he could have a minute alone with him. Saul Same left the room. Leibler told Hayden that he had been surprised to hear that he had refused to see Isi Leibler. He asked why. Hayden said that, in a phone call in 1980,

Isi Leibler had threatened to urge Jews to vote Liberal if Hayden went ahead and visited Yasser Arafat, and that Isi had improperly recorded that telephone call. Mark Leibler replied that he knew for a fact that the phone call had not been recorded. Moreover, he had seen notes of what Isi had said and that he had not threatened to urge Jews to vote Liberal. His brother, he said, would never do that. Hayden, according to Leibler, accepted these assurances, and agreed to see Isi in future, although it is not clear that they did ever meet, because four months after Mark's meeting with Hayden, Hawke replaced him as Labor leader shortly before the 1983 federal election.

In the notes he wrote after his meeting with Hayden, Mark Leibler said that he believed Hayden was "amenable to building a closer relationship between himself and the Jewish community."

> It is my view that this initial contact should be followed up with further informal meetings and discussions in the not too distant future. Although Hawke's personal support for Israel is beyond question, as he continues to strive to become leader and ultimately Prime Minister, there is very little doubt that his public statements in support of Israel will become less frequent and more muted...Above all I believe in the importance of frequent informal contacts between Jewish community and Zionist leaders and the top leadership of the ALP.

This is how Leibler was to develop his political networks over the years— with informal meetings and contacts, and, in some cases, by developing friendships. As for Hawke, Mark Leibler, unlike Isi, was never close to him. In this record he was implying that it was a mistake for Jews to see Hawke as "their" leader. He felt uncomfortable with Hawke's professed love for Israel and the Jews; such love, he believed, is almost always disappointed.

And so it turned out: Hawke became a critic of Israel and, in 2018, urged the ALP to support the campaign to recognise Palestine at the United Nations. A few months later, the ALP was to adopt this position at its annual conference, but when Hawke had spoken out, it was not Labor policy. Mark Leibler has told people that he never trusted Hawke. But he grew to trust Hayden and, later, he became a fierce supporter of Paul Keating. This was to have serious repercussions for his relationship with his brother, who was not close to Hayden and had virtually no relationship with Keating. It was Bob Hawke who had been his friend and supporter.

That meeting between Leibler and Hayden was the beginning of a relationship that became a close and warm friendship spanning decades. Leibler commiserated with Hayden when he lost the leadership to Hawke. The former Queensland policeman, a committed atheist and member of the Labor Left, and the religious Zionist who probably voted Liberal—certainly during the Whitlam years—formed a bond that Leibler said transcended differences about politics, the Middle East and the policies of the Israeli government.

"I liked him from the start," Leibler told me in an interview in his Caulfield home. Among the photographs in his study is one of Bill Hayden and his wife Dallas, when Hayden was Governor-General, at the bar mitzvah of Leibler's son, Jeremy, in 1992. "He is a decent man. He was the best minister in the Whitlam government. I always enjoyed being with him and I think he enjoyed it too. We connected."

After a Labor government was elected in March 1983, Hawke agreed to Hayden's request to be Foreign Minister, a job that Hayden felt might salve his bitterness at losing the leadership by allowing him to spend a lot of time out of the country. Hawke also promised not to interfere with Hayden's work on foreign policy, including, explicitly, policy on Israel and the Palestinians. Hawke said this, even though in his days as president of the ACTU, he had publicly said that his contacts with Israeli trade unions and with Israeli politicians like Shimon Peres meant that he could play a role in helping to bring about peace between Israel and the Palestinians. For some time, he was in regular contact with Peres and other Israeli Labor Party figures, but, sadly, did not bring about peace in the Middle East.

In early 1984, Mark Leibler was elected president of the Zionist Federation of Australia, the youngest person ever to hold the post. It was a significant step for him. He was determined to transform the organisation from a community body that ran Zionist educational programs and youth groups and funded gap years and study tours in Israel for young Jews, into a professional lobbying outfit that put Israel's case to Australian politicians in Canberra.

Leibler's friendship with Hayden was the beginning of his successful cultivation of senior government figures of both political persuasions. The friendship meant that, when Hayden became Australia's Foreign Minister, Leibler had access to the cabinet minister who was in a position to determine Australia's stance on the conflict between Israel and the Palestinians. No other Jewish leader had this sort of access, not even his brother.

Two years later Leibler was to achieve his greatest result as a Jewish leader, one that led to international recognition in the Jewish and Zionist worlds. Ironically, it was not Bob Hawke, the self-proclaimed best friend of the Jews, whom many Jews did indeed love, but Bill Hayden, with his reputation as a sometimes trenchant critic of Israel, who made this achievement possible.

CHAPTER 9

From the time he was elected president of the Zionist Federation of Australia (ZFA) in 1984, Mark Leibler started to think about how he might play a role in rescinding the United Nations resolution, passed by the General Assembly in 1975, that stated that Zionism was a form of racism. UN Resolution 3379 was the result of a campaign by the Arab states, with the critical support of the Soviet Union, to transform Zionism from a movement for Jewish self-determination that had culminated in the establishment of the state of Israel, into a colonialist racist enterprise. The Soviet Union's position had profoundly influenced large sections of the left in Europe and, to a lesser extent, in the United States and Australia.

For a decade after the resolution was passed, there had been no attempt to organise an international campaign to rescind it. At the height of the Cold War, there was virtually no chance of the General Assembly overturning the resolution, given the implacable position of the Soviet Union and its satellite states, of the Arab Bloc, and of most nations in what was then called the Third World. For most Jews, this resolution was a travesty. Israel, which had given many thousands of Holocaust survivors a reason to go on living, had been labeled a racist state by the United Nations; in just three decades the victims of the most murderous form of racism had been turned into racists.

The resolution marked the end of the period after World War 2, when much of the West, including the left, considered Israel to be a consolation prize for the Jews for what they had suffered. For much of the left, led by the Soviet Union, Israel had been a sort of socialist experiment in collective living, evidenced in the scores of *kibbutzim* across the country. Yet by 1975, whatever guilt there may have been, especially in Europe, over what had been done to the Jews had dissipated. And anyway, the Israel that the old left had felt so connected to, the Israel whose founders and first generation of political leaders had all been socialists or social democrats, no longer existed.

By the time UN Resolution 3379 was passed, more than 700,000 Jews from Arab countries in the Middle East and North Africa had settled in Israel. Most had been expelled from countries where they had lived for a millennium or more, in large part as punishment for the creation of Israel. They transformed Israel's demographics and, eventually, its politics. In June 1977, they helped to elect Israel's first right-wing government, led by Menachem Begin, former leader of the Irgun, the right-wing terrorist group that operated in Palestine during British rule between the world wars. With Begin's election, the socialist experiment conducted by the early Zionist leaders was effectively dead.

For Leibler, the resolution was an outrage. From the time it was passed, whatever faith he might have once had in the United Nations—which had, after all, voted to establish the state of Israel—was gone for good. For years it frustrated him that nothing could be done to overturn the resolution, but he always believed that, in time, it would be.

In November 1984, a few months after Leibler had become ZFA president, Israel's President, Chaim Herzog, launched an international campaign to annul UN Resolution 3379. The campaign would be led by the World Zionist Organisation and the Israeli Foreign Ministry. Mark Leibler would run the Australian campaign through the ZFA. Now that the professional crisis that had consumed so much of his time after Arnold Bloch's departure from ABL had passed, he threw himself into the campaign.

Leibler has always compartmentalised his days. Since he was a young man, he has written daily "to do" lists and his diary has mapped out virtually every hour of the day. He is obsessive about recording in contemporaneous notes the substance of his meetings with political leaders and his planning and execution of major campaigns. The campaign to rescind the Zionism-is-racism resolution is recorded in two thick, bound volumes of notes of meetings, transcripts of interviews, and newspaper cuttings. These volumes, one from 1986 and the other from 1988, detail the role of Australia, and of Leibler, in the worldwide campaign to rescind the UN resolution.

That Australia played a significant role is clear, but what is truly remarkable is the role played in the campaign by Bill Hayden, formerly a trenchant critic of the Israeli government, especially after the 1982 Lebanon invasion. For Hayden the politics of the campaign inside the ALP were risky. Significant figures in his own Left faction were likely to oppose any government move to get involved. Hayden also knew that, if Bob Hawke were to take charge of moves to get the resolution rescinded, he would face fierce opposition from the Left faction, who regarded Hawke as too close to the Jewish community.

In the 1986 volume of notes on the campaign, Leibler describes how Hayden became critical to its success in Australia. What is not in the notes is the role played by his developing friendship with Hayden, the discussions they had about Israel and the Palestinians, the way Hayden became more and more interested in the history of the conflict and in Israel's history. He studied it all, changed his mind about some things, and worked out a position that was entirely consistent with his views as a social democrat.

From the start, when Zionism became a movement in the late 1880s, the international socialist movement had supported Zionism's goal of

Jewish self-determination. It had seen Zionism and democratic social-ism, in the words of Israel's first Prime Minister, David Ben-Gurion, as "two sides of the same coin." Decades before the United Nations voted in 1948 to partition Palestine into a Palestinian state and a Jewish state, the ALP and the Australian trade union movement had developed ties with the fledgling trade unions in British-controlled Palestine and with the leaders of the emerging Israeli Labor Party, including Ben-Gurion.

For Hayden, as he made clear in a keynote address he gave to the ZFA Biennial Conference in April 1986—the first by a Foreign Minister—this old connection between the Labor Party in Israel and the ALP formed the basis for his support for the Jewish state. The close fraternal relationship between the two social democratic parties had led Herbert Vere ("Doc") Evatt, the former Australian foreign minister elected president of the United Nations General Assembly in 1948, to enthusiastically support the resolution that partitioned Palestine into two states.

In the middle of 1985, Leibler, as ZFA President, wrote to polit-icians, public figures and leading journalists arguing that the Zionism-equals-racism resolution had contributed to both anti-Zionism and anti-Semitism worldwide. He asked them to support the campaign for the resolution's annulment. The response, according to Leibler's notes was overwhelming; there were letters of support from church leaders, academics, people in the arts and politicians from both sides of politics. Bob Hawke wrote a letter of support; so, too, did Opposition Leader Andrew Peacock. Hayden was the first politician to write to Leibler supporting the campaign, noting that

> the policy of successive Australian governments has been and
> continues to be absolute opposition to any attempt to declare that

Zionism is a form of racism…The government will continue to adhere to this position. I wish you well in your campaign and would be glad to keep in contact with you as it proceeds.

Leibler noted Hayden's offer. Clearly he thought it important, as it indeed turned out to be. In August 1985, the United States Congress passed a motion denouncing UN Resolution 3379, but stopped short of calling for it to be rescinded. Leibler noted: "It immediately occurred to me that perhaps the principal objective of the Australian campaign should be to bring about a similar result, a resolution of both houses of parliament denouncing resolution 3379 but more than that, calling for its rescission."

He went to Hayden, not Hawke, with the proposal. Apart from having the relationship with Hayden, Leibler knew that Hayden had the best chance of convincing the ALP Left to support such a move. He wrote to Hayden's principal private secretary, Michael Costello, enclosing a copy of the motion passed by the United States Congress and asking him to explore with Hayden the possibility of Australia doing something similar. Such resolutions were relatively common in the United States Congress but rare in the Australian parliament. Indeed, Leibler could find no record of such a resolution ever being passed on a foreign affairs issue.

Over the next few months, Leibler met Hayden several times. From the first of these meetings, in October 1985, Hayden was sympathetic to the proposal, but indicated, according to Leibler's notes, that "he might have reservations about proceeding if this was likely to cause severe strains within the ALP." Hayden raised the ZFA's long-standing invitation to address its executive on the subject of Zionism. He wanted to take up the invitation but wanted to "do the necessary reading" over the summer break.

CHAPTER 9

Leibler immediately invited Hayden to be keynote speaker at the ZFA's Biennial Conference in April 1986. Hayden accepted, and told Leibler that he would announce his support for a joint parliamentary resolution in his speech. But this was not in the speech he gave. As Hayden later told Leibler, his draft had referred to it, but that a staffer had removed it. Clearly, there was some level of disagreement, even in Hayden's office, about whether he should lead the charge on Leibler's proposed resolution. Nevertheless, when Hayden was asked after his speech whether he would support a resolution by parliament condemning the Zionism-is-racism resolution, he said that he would.

Leibler, meanwhile, in the early months of 1986, met with Opposition Leader John Howard, Nationals leader Ian Sinclair, and Don Chipp, leader of the Australian Democrats. All three said they would support a joint parliamentary resolution along the lines proposed by Leibler. He then wrote to Hayden enclosing a draft resolution for him to consider and asked whether he could meet relevant members of Hayden's staff to discuss the final form of the resolution.

On 14 July 1986, Hayden wrote to tell Leibler that he had "initiated moves for a resolution to be introduced into both houses of parliament dealing with this matter." Two weeks later, a senior Foreign Affairs official sent Leibler the text that Hayden had approved. It set out the "evils of the 1975 resolution and then put the resolution: This House recommends that the Government of Australia lend support to efforts to overturn resolution 3379 in the United Nations." Leibler recorded in his notes that he found the proposed resolution "more than satisfactory." No wonder; it went further than the motion passed by the United States Congress because it actually called for the UN resolution to be rescinded.

Over the next four months, Hayden worked to get his colleagues in the Socialist Left to sign on to the proposed resolution. He addressed meetings of the faction on the issue, he called in favours from some of his factional colleagues, he made some minor changes to some sentences to ease concerns expressed by several members of the Socialist Left. It is clear from Leibler's detailed notes that Hayden took considerable political risks to get the resolution approved, first by the Socialist Left and then by the ALP parliamentary caucus. He did all this without any involvement by Hawke, who had been little more than lukewarm about his government pushing the joint parliamentary resolution. Leibler recorded his communication with Hayden's office:

> At 11.45 a.m. on Tuesday 21st October 1986, I received a telephone call from Jill Courtney [a Hayden staffer] on behalf of Bill Hayden to inform me that the proposed joint parliamentary resolution went through Caucus unanimously. However, she told me that Bill Hayden wanted me to know that "questions were asked" and that just for the moment, I shouldn't "crow too much about it." The resolution would be put to the House of Representatives on Thursday afternoon.

In a subsequent telephone call, Hayden asked Leibler not to make too much of his role in the press release that Leibler intended to put out.

> Hayden told me that we would be creating difficulties for him if we made too much of a fuss or if we placed too much emphasis on his role in relation to the introduction of the joint parliamentary resolution. He maintained that such a course of action would "detrimentally affect his credibility in certain circles." I explained that we very much appreciated his personal role but that we were anxious not to cause him any embarrassment.

Leibler was in the House of Representatives when the resolution calling for the rescinding of UN Resolution 3379 was passed. Hayden did not speak to the resolution. Bob Hawke had decided that he would be the only speaker on the Government side. John Howard spoke for the Opposition. The resolution was carried unanimously in the House and the Senate at the same time. Hayden left the House just before the speeches started. As he passed Leibler, he said: "Mark, I hope you don't mind me leaving, but I have already read the Prime Minister's speech."

Hayden's role and the risks he took were never publicised. But in *Bill Hayden: An Autobiography*, published in 1996, he writes about how his attitude to Israel had changed:

> When I was Foreign Minister, Mark Leibler, a leader of the Australian Jewish community with whom I became friendly, suggested my criticism of Israel may have owed something to my earlier competitive hostility towards Hawke. I think Leibler was partly correct...I am certain that a large part of my attitude was learnt at my mother's knee, listening to her talk about the mystical cause of Ireland...From such values the cause of the Palestinian people was warmly embraced to the point of gross simplification of Israel's situation.

Hayden describes how he had been unenthusiastic when Leibler first came to him with the proposal, but had become convinced, over time, that he should take charge of framing the joint parliamentary resolution on UN Resolution 3379. He also writes that in doing so, he had done Hawke a big favour:

> I saw Hawke and proposed I should act on this matter. He was, understandably, a little uncertain of the political wisdom of such a move from Australia, fearing it would have international repercussions and cause internal party dissension. I quickly persuaded him that the risk was all mine...To Hawke's surprise and delight, I delivered Party endorsement for the initiative...

Because of the importance of the resolution, he explained, he would move it in Parliament. I replied that I would be happy to speak after him. He suggested it was better to restrict the speakers to one from the Government and one from the Opposition and so it proceeded.

The joint parliamentary resolution was passed two weeks before Israel's president, Chaim Herzog, came to Australia on a state visit. It had been Leibler's plan for the resolution to be passed before Herzog's visit. He had worked for months to make it happen.

The United States Congress passed a resolution virtually identical to the Australian one; indeed, its sponsor, Senator Patrick Moynihan, called it the Australian resolution. Both the French and European parliaments eventually passed resolutions similar to the Australian one. During debate about the United Nations' Zionism-is-racism resolution, members of both parliaments pointed to the Australian joint parliamentary resolution as a model.

In November 1987, Hawke wrote to Leibler about the resolution in the United States Congress: "It was with great pride and pleasure that we learnt that the US Congress passed the 'Australian Resolution'... and that Israeli president Chaim Herzog had referred to the Australian Resolution in a speech to a joint session of the United States Congress."

For Leibler, this was all proof that Australia could play a significant role in the Middle East and that the Australian Jewish community could have influence in international Jewish affairs way beyond its small size. His brother, Isi, was already a significant figure in international Jewish affairs through his role in the Soviet Jewry movement. Now Mark, nine years younger than his brother, had become a leader of significant international standing, both in Israel and in the wider Jewish world.

Over the years, Leibler said, his friendship with Hayden continued to become more intimate. Shortly after Hayden was appointed
Governor-General in 1989, he gave his first major speech in the new
role at a function in Melbourne hosted by ABL. During visits to
Melbourne, Hayden would sometimes dine at the Leibler home. Of
their friendship, Leibler says:

> I think our friendship was based on mutual respect and on the fact
> that we had, from the start liked each other and had an affinity
> for each other despite our very different backgrounds. Yes, we
> had differences about the Middle East, but they were ones we
> could each accept. And really, what he did on that infamous UN
> resolution was just so politically brave and principled.

On 8 January 1996, Hayden wrote to Mark and Rosanna Leibler
to tell them that "at midnight on February 15, Dallas and I cease
occupying the office. In other words, at that bewitching hour, I turn
into a pumpkin." Hayden wrote that, as was usually the case, a farewell function would be held at Parliament House hosted by the Prime
Minister, to which the outgoing Governor-General could invite a
limited number of private guests: "As Dallas and I have regarded you
as long-standing close friends, I was wondering if you could check
your diaries to see if you would be able to attend this function."

Rosanna and Mark Leibler were there for Hayden's farewell. By then,
more than four years had passed since the United Nations General
Assembly had voted, on 16 December 1991, to revoke the 1975 resolution
stating that Zionism was a form of racism. The vote was overwhelming:
111 nations for its revocation, 25 against, with 13 abstentions.

Twenty-two years later, in August 2018, when Bill Hayden was 85
years old, Leibler received an email from Daphne McKenzie, Hayden's
executive assistant:

Dear Mr Leibler,

Bill Hayden has asked me to send this invitation and letter to you
and Rosanna. He doesn't expect either of you would be able to
attend due to the shortness of notice for which he apologises but
is sending just in case. To save time with postage, I have scanned
and attached the four pages which make up the invitation.

He is feeling a bit down today. He was watching on the history
channel a series of commentaries on how Jewish people were
treated at Auschwitz where he and Dallas visited, you may recall.

He and Dallas send their best wishes.

On the first page of the four-page invitation was a rather ornate cross;
on the second, was a letter from Hayden:

Dear family and friends

This news and invitation may come as a surprise to you. After years
as a professed atheist and much contemplation, I will be baptised
at St Mary's Catholic Church in Ipswich on 9 September 2018. I
should explain a little of what brought me to this major decision.

Hayden then set out how, over the years, he had come to appreciate
the friendliness towards him of people in Church orders.

After my stroke, I spent seven months in hospital which meant
I had a lot of time to think about matters. I thought about my
conviction in public life to try to serve the needy and the vulnerable. I concluded it was largely the influence of my own mother
who was a Catholic and the influence of the nuns of the Ursuline
Order who taught me at primary school…So after dwelling on
these things, I found my way back to the core of those beliefs—the
Church. I suddenly realised something I had not considered in
this way before, ironically by reading a book on Shia Islam which
pointed out that Christianity was a religion not of rules but of love.

After he read the email, Leibler sat in silence for some time at his office table, where he sometimes ate lunch alone. He was surprised, and moved. He had not heard from Hayden for some time. He had not known about the stroke that had rendered Hayden unable to speak or write. Leibler replied:

Dear Bill,

Thank you so much for the kind invitation to your forthcoming Baptism. Had it not been scheduled on the eve of the Jewish New Year, I can assure you that both myself and Rosanna would have travelled to Brisbane to be with you and Dallas on this special occasion which we appreciate, is so meaningful to you...

Over the years, in conversations with various people both within and outside the Jewish community, I often reflect on the many constructive interactions which I had with you over a long period of time, particularly in your capacity as Foreign Minister and Governor-General. I always found you to be an astute and strategic person to deal with and, of course, a person of the utmost integrity.

Rosanna joins me in conveying to you and Dallas our warmest regards

Mark

They had spoken about many things over the years, but not about faith. Hayden was a committed atheist and Leibler a religious Jew. He would have liked to have spoken about his faith, but Hayden had not once asked him about it. Now it was too late.

CHAPTER 10

By the mid-1980s Mark Leibler had begun to establish the Zionist Federation of Australia as a political lobbying powerhouse. He had expanded the organisation's base to include representatives of the Liberal congregations, which had never been part of the ZFA because, historically, many of their members had been lukewarm Zionists. Leibler was determined to make the ZFA as representative of the Jewish community as possible. The Liberals, he decided, had to be represented, even if some people in the Orthodox congregations would not support this move.

In his mid-40s, Leibler was full of restless energy, a driven man. He devoted several nights a week to ZFA business, even as he put in 12-hour days at ABL. Many nights, he would come home from a meeting and immediately go to his study to finish ABL work, often working until the early hours of the morning, his study filled with cigar smoke.

Leibler's transformation of the ZFA into an organisation with great political clout is illustrated by the controversy over the citizenship status of 7000 Australians who had made Aliyah. Becoming a citizen of another country when you were an Australian citizen was not possible until 2002, when the Howard government amended the Citizenship Act. If you were already a citizen of another country, as were the many hundreds of thousands of post-war migrants, you could retain that citizenship when you became naturalised as an Australian. But Australian citizens could not become citizens of another country unless they gave up their Australian citizenship, as Rupert Murdoch had to do when he chose to become an American citizen.

There had long been confusion about whether the more than 7000 Australians who had settled in Israel were a special case. Israel's Law of Return, a foundational law of the state when it was established in 1948, automatically made Jews who came to settle in Israel Israeli citizens. On the face of it, that would mean that Australian Jews who had settled in Israel had implicitly renounced their Australian citizenship. But it had long been assumed that, as long as Australians who settled in Israel had not renounced their Australian citizenship or formally taken up Israeli citizenship, their Australian citizenship would not be taken from them. This assumption proved to be questionable.

In February 1986, the Labor government introduced legislation to amend the Australian Citizenship Act in order to clarify the Act's prohibition on dual citizenship. It seemed like non-controversial legislation to the government, but, even before it was passed, the Immigration Department delivered rulings through its officials at the Australian Embassy in Tel Aviv that Australians who had settled in Israel before 1981 and had become Israeli citizens would have their Australian citizenship revoked and their passports cancelled. So, too, would Australians who had come to Israel after 1981 and had not taken out Israeli citizenship but had been granted permanent residency through special visas for Jews who came to settle in the country and automatically became citizens under the Law of Return. Until 1986, the embassy had told these people that their Australian citizenship would not be affected by their becoming Israeli citizens.

There was outrage and panic. Hundreds of Australians protested outside the embassy in Tel Aviv. In Australia, the ZFA was inundated with demands for help. Contrary to what Australian immigration officials had always told them, not only would adult Australians in Israel lose their citizenship, but so would their children who had been born in Israel. These children had not chosen to settle in Israel, yet their ability to return to Australia as citizens was to be denied them. This was not what Immigration Minister Chris Hurford had intended.

One of the ZFA's core missions is to promote and foster the in-gathering to Israel of Jews from the diaspora. The 7000 Australian Jews who had settled in Israel represented a Zionist success story. The ZFA boasted that a larger proportion of Australian Jews had settled in Israel than from any other Western country. But most of these people had continued to consider themselves Australians, fulfilling the Zionist dream but not giving up their connections to the country where they had either been born or had grown up and, in most cases, still had family.

In some countries, this situation might have raised the old charge of dual loyalties, a long-standing anti-Semitic trope in which Jews are a sort of fifth column, with greater loyalty to their fellow Jews than to the country in which they live and are citizens. Here were Jews, committed to Israel, living and raising children there, even serving in the Israeli army, and yet determined to hang on to their Australian citizenship. But there is no evidence that this charge of dual loyalties was raised by members of the Liberal and National parties in coalition and the ALP. Australia did not have a history of this sort of anti-Semitism.

After 2002, when dual citizenship became legal, partly in recognition of Australia's diversity and multiculturalism, the issue lost all of its heat. Australians who make Aliyah retain their Australian citizenship, as do their offspring. But in 1986, when Australians could not take out citizenship of another country without renouncing their Australian citizenship, the idea that Jews, given their history and the unique status of Israel's Law of Return, should be granted an exception to the dual citizenship laws was problematic for some people.

There is a fat volume of notes, press releases, and letters between Mark Leibler and senior immigration officials, Coalition leaders, senior officials of the Israeli government, and Australia's then Immigration Minister, Chris Hurford, about the status of Australians who had made Aliyah. What is clear from the notes, letters, phone calls, and flights to Canberra to meet with officials and politicians, is the sense of urgency that gripped Leibler, the pressure he was under to fix this issue for those thousands of Australians in Israel and their families in Australia. From January until April 1986 Leibler was a man possessed, furiously working on this issue, and sometimes furious when he didn't get his way, as, for instance, when an Immigration Department official refused to see the logic and force of the case Leibler was putting to him.

A note dated 18 February 1986 records a meeting with the Permanent Head of the Immigration Department, Bill McKinnon. According to the notes, McKinnon had previously promised Leibler that he would urge Hurford to further amend legislation designed to clarify aspects of the Immigration Act. The proposed amendment would specifically address the issues facing Australian Jews living in Israel, making it easier for them to regain and retain their Australian citizenship, as long as they expressed an intention to permanently return to Australia within three years.

Hurford had agreed to this amendment. Leibler thought that McKinnon had also agreed to urge Hurford to remove the word "permanently" from the amendment. In other words, expressing an intention to simply visit Australia would have been enough to enable Australians in Israel to regain their citizenship. Leibler's note states:

> McKinnon arrived and we found an empty conference room in which to talk. The conversation was very heated and I was quite abusive. I pointed out that my own credibility and that of the

Zionist Federation had been destroyed because, on the basis of our discussions on 11th of February, I had given assurances that the problem of the "need to intend to return to live permanently in Australia" had been resolved. The word permanently was to be removed. McKinnon became quite irritated and said that he had only committed to trying to get the legislation altered.

At that point, Leibler noted, they had both "calmed down", but Leibler had remained adamant that "this problem would have to be resolved even if it meant I had to go and see the Prime Minister for the second time that day." Leibler had met with Bob Hawke that morning as part of a delegation organised by the Executive Council of Australian Jewry:

> I insisted on seeing Chris Hurford…who interrupted a lengthy meeting with a rather important lobby group in order to see me… It was a very friendly and relaxed meeting. We were drinking scotch together…Hurford agreed that he would be putting to cabinet an amendment to the legislation which would delete the reference to "permanently" as originally agreed between McKinnon and myself.

By April 1986, Hurford, with the support of the Opposition, particularly from Shadow Immigration Minister Ian McPhee, and from Don Chipp's Democrats in the Senate, announced amendments to his proposed citizenship legislation. These amendments, which Leibler had advocated for so strenuously, restored the citizenship of all Australian Jews living in Israel who had had their citizenship revoked, whether they had arrived in Israel before or after 1981. All they had to do to retain their restored Australian citizenship was declare that they intended to visit Australia sometime within the next three years.

Even that requirement was softened before the legislation was passed; all that these people had to do in order to retain their citizenship was be in regular contact with people—most likely, family members—in Australia. Even this was not spelt out and contact with friends would in all probability have been sufficient. Leibler's victory was complete. A press release from Hurford about the amendments praised Leibler for the way he had informed the debate over the legislation. Hurford sent him a handwritten note in March 1986:

Dear Mark

I attach the entire committee stage debate [on the legislation]. The Jewish News might be interested...Please let me know if the outcome is not satisfactory.

Sincerely
Chris

Nine months later, in the January 1987 Australia Day awards, Leibler was made an Officer in the General Division of the Order of Australia for his service to the community, especially the Jewish community. He was the first Zionist leader to receive such an award.

The citizenship campaign yielded another dividend for Leibler, one that would be central to his work for the next seven years. On one of his trips to Canberra he met Helene Teichmann. Don Chipp's senior adviser, who had very good contacts in the ALP. Her former husband, Max Teichmann, had been a renowned lecturer in politics at Monash University—they had met when Helene had been his student—and a widely published columnist. Max Teichmann was close to a number of senior figures in the ALP, including Bill Hayden and Jim Cairns, so that, from her student days onwards, Helene had formed long-standing friendships with Labor people, including John Button, who became a highly respected Industry Minister in the Hawke government.

Leibler knew from their first meetings that Teichmann was the sort of person he was looking for, not only to get him access to politicians in Canberra, but to help with his transformation of the ZFA. At first, he knew nothing of her background. He didn't even think she was Jewish until after he had hired her. Instead, he had thought that Max Teichmann, who had been close to some organisations in the Jewish community and had written a column for the *Australian Jewish News*, was Jewish. He wasn't. Helene Teichmann, however, was a child of Holocaust survivors, but had had little to do with the Jewish community. She told me that being Jewish had always been fundamental to her identity, but she was not religious and not a committed Zionist like Leibler. She had grown up in a more secular, non-Jewish world.

Teichmann is a striking, handsome woman, always elegantly dressed and immaculately groomed in a European style, always alert to what is going on around her. She runs her own consulting business. Her son, Zac, was in business with her but left to practise as a psychologist, though he still looks after her books. She has clients in federal and state politics, as well as several overseas political clients. Some of Australia's leading business people use her services. In her seven years at the ZFA, no one was closer to Leibler. They remain close and she gives him advice from time to time.

I have known Helene Teichmann since childhood; our families were close. We did not see much of each other over the years, but I had fond memories of her and of her parents. When we spoke, Teichmann, like all good political consultants, was nevertheless careful about what she had to say. She remembered coming to Melbourne from Canberra to talk to Leibler about working for the ZFA:

> I said to him "You have to understand I'm not your average Jewish girl." I said, "What are you going to do when someone

rings you and they say they saw your right-hand person driving a Mercedes on Shabbat past a *shul* and maybe there's someone non-Jewish in the car with me, a non-Jewish gentleman," and he said: "I don't care what you drive and I don't care what you eat and I certainly don't care who you make love with, but you know, maybe you could not drive past a *shul* on Shabbat." I knew then we could work together.

He told me that the Jewish community had businessmen and lawyers and doctors by the thousands "but we really don't have people who understand how the Australian political system works and how you can get the best out of it and that's what I want you to give back to the community, that knowledge and expertise." I was impressed, yes, I was.

When Leibler offered Teichmann the job of communications director at the ZFA, with the promise that she would be executive director within months, she accepted immediately. She started in August 1987. She hired several bright university students to work part-time at the ZFA, ostensibly to make the office more professional, but in fact, she admits, to tutor her in Israeli politics, about which she knew very little. What she knew about was lobbying and making and maintaining networks in politics, the arts, and business.

With Teichmann's contacts book, smarts and indefatigable energy, the ZFA became ever stronger as a rival to the Executive Council of Australian Jewry for influence in Canberra and in the community. The seeds of the brutal conflict between Australia's two most significant Jewish organisations and between its leaders, the brothers Isi and Mark Leibler, had been sown.

CHAPTER 11

Dressed in one of his trademark Italian charcoal suits, with a grey cardigan, white shirt and red silk tie, his black loafers polished, Paul Keating had arrived early, and had sat down on a dark leather couch in the large high-domed foyer of 333 Collins Street. The Commercial Bank of Australia for whom the grand building was built has long gone, but its marble floors, ceiling frescoes and wide-arched entry with its polished wooden doors all remain.

Keating had asked to meet at ABL, which he said was conveniently located near his hotel. He was wearing a green soft peaked cap and looked like an Irish businessman, sitting there with earphones in his ears and looking down at his phone, oblivious to the people walking past, some of whom stopped and looked to make sure that they had seen right—that this was indeed Paul Keating.

His handshake was soft and he spoke so quietly that I had to concentrate to hear what he was saying. He seemed contained, within himself, in the way he had sometimes been when he was Treasurer and Prime Minister but not performing in the House of Representatives, where his words were like daggers and his voice rasped, and sometimes snarled and mocked, as he displayed smiling contempt for his opponents and their works.

We took the lift to ABL's foyer on the 21st floor. Mark Leibler was waiting by the long desk in front of Daphne Stamkos, ABL's long-serving receptionist. She had seen Keating at ABL several times when he was Prime Minister, and now Keating greeted her with a smile and a nod of recognition. Leibler and Keating shook hands. Leibler said that Keating was not there to see him and that he had organised one of the boardrooms for our meeting; with that, he showed the way and disappeared into his office.

Keating said he remembered well the first time he met Leibler, in Sydney, on 15 April 1988. From the start, he found Leibler very intelligent and in his relationships with people, intelligence was "a very high mark."

> So if you are dealing with someone who is very intelligent and who is well motivated as well, then you are already feeling comfortable with them and being prepared to listen to them, what they have to say to you. Listen for the value, the bits of value. In public life you always have to listen for the little chips of value, you know. [With Leibler] I was always aware of the fact that this is a very smart guy who would say things of value, who was not there for talking's sake.

The reason for the meeting between Leibler and Keating in 1988 dated back to the bottom-of-the-harbour arguments of the early 1980s. John Howard's legislation had not been tough enough for the Labor Opposition. In parliament, Keating, then Shadow Treasurer, had described Howard as a supporter and facilitator of tax avoidance by the wealthy. After the Hawke government was elected in March 1983, it introduced legislation that, in essence, retrospectively gave the Commissioner of Taxation the power to treat a company's income and capital reserves as dividends and, therefore to tax these reserves. Such reserves had never been taxed in the past, but the legislation was in large part the new government's attempt to recoup the tax it felt it had lost from companies and individuals involved in bottom-of-the-harbour schemes.

Leibler thought the legislation was appalling. In his view, it was not only retrospective, but it overturned the settled position that a company's income and capital reserves were not subject to tax unless paid out as dividends. He knew that if the legislation was to pass, some of his wealthiest clients would be liable for many millions of dollars in tax. Some could be bankrupted. Leibler tried to set up meetings with John Dawkins, the Finance Minister, who had carriage of the legislation, but Dawkins, to Leibler's frustration and anger, refused to see him. The legislation passed the House of Representatives in June 1983.

The Coalition in Opposition had opposed the legislation and would oppose it in the Senate. One vote, that of independent Senator Brian Harradine, would determine whether the legislation would pass or fail. While the legislation was being debated in the House of Representatives, Leibler began an intense lobbying campaign to convince Harradine to vote against the legislation when it came to the Senate. He flew to Canberra to see him. He sent Harradine notes that explained why the legislation was bad law, would cause major business failures, and might even lead to an economic downturn and a significant increase in unemployment. Leibler knew that Harradine was inclined to support the legislation. He was in many ways an old-style Labor man who was not naturally inclined to support wealthy businessmen, even if he felt the proposed law was unfair. Politically, there was nothing in it for Harradine to vote against the legislation; in fact, he was likely to be accused of being on the side of business and the wealthy. He wavered, torn between following his political interest and his understanding, shaped by Leibler's lobbying, that it was bad legislation. In the end, he voted against it. The legislation did not pass.

It was a major victory for Leibler and for his clients. But it was not the end of the matter. A few years later, the High Court of Australia, in a high-profile tax case, ruled that the legislation that Leibler had helped to block was not needed. The Commissioner of Taxation could apply section 260 of the Taxation Act to tax the revenue and capital reserves of companies that had been involved in the bottom-of-the-harbour schemes and other forms of tax avoidance. It was this ruling that led Leibler to seek a meeting with Keating.

Helene Teichmann said that it was relatively easy for a tax lawyer of Leibler's reputation, who represented so many wealthy clients, to organise meetings with senior politicians on both sides of politics:

> The door will be opened. If it's to stay open, it will only stay open if you have something to offer, something to say, bring something to the table. In other words, the door will stay open for a millisecond and if you come with something meaningful, good; but if you don't, if you come just to bellyache for instance, the door will close, close irrevocably.

In a confidential memorandum about his first meeting with Keating, Leibler starts with the Gregrhon Investments Case of March 1988. In its decision in that case, the High Court refused to hear an appeal against a 1986 Federal Court judgment that had, in essence, expanded the anti-avoidance provisions of section 260 of the Taxation Act. In other words, the Federal Court, backed by the High Court, had made legally possible what the Labor government's proposed legislation had been designed to do two years earlier—make company income and capital reserves liable for taxation if these companies had structured their affairs to avoid paying tax. Harradine's single vote in the Senate had blocked that legislation.

The High Court ruling meant that Leibler was once again faced with the prospect of having many of his clients subjected to what he thought were iniquitous tax assessments on capital and income reserves that they, and he, never expected to be taxed. Within days of the ruling, Leibler called the Commissioner of Taxation, Trevor Boucher. By then, such was his reputation that Leibler could call the Commissioner and know that his call would be answered. He asked Boucher what he intended to do in light of the decision. Boucher told Leibler that the ATO was still considering its position, and would take a few more weeks to do so. Leibler told Boucher that "some urgent remedial action was required" and that it was open to the Commissioner to make a ruling that would, in essence, ignore the Federal Court decision.

According to Leibler's notes of the conversation, Boucher was sympathetic but "it was apparent to me that he would not act without the concurrence of the Treasurer Paul Keating." Leibler then called Ken Henry, Keating's adviser on tax and, later, Secretary of Treasury for 10 years. Leibler sent Henry a summary of the issues he wanted to discuss with Keating. Two weeks later, Henry called Leibler to say that Keating had agreed to see him; but first Leibler was to meet with Henry. At this meeting, Leibler gave Henry a collection of summaries of some of Leibler's cases, in which new section 260 assessments had been issued to his clients. The summaries, he said, would illustrate "the gross inequities" of these assessments. File numbers of cases were included so that Keating could verify the facts with Boucher without disclosing the identity of Leibler's clients.

Leibler made sure to keep Boucher informed of his dealings with Henry and with Keating. They were done in strict confidence, because they were fraught both for the government and for the Commissioner of Taxation, who was independent and did not answer to the Treasurer. Keating could not officially instruct Boucher to do anything about the issues that Leibler wanted to raise with him. It was within Boucher's powers to issue an administrative order that would nullify the contentious assessments already issued, but he had to be seen to be acting independently, not on Keating's orders.

For Keating the political risks were substantial, if it became known that he had met with Leibler to discuss specific 260 assessments, even if Leibler's clients were anonymous. Gareth Evans, then Attorney-General, had urged the Federal Court to rule the way it did in the Gregrhon case and had supported the High Court's refusal to hear an appeal against the Federal Court's ruling. Most of the Hawke cabinet would probably have supported Evans. The political imperative remained what it had been since the bottom-of-the-harbour revelations—the government had to be seen to be tough on tax avoidance.

At the meeting in Sydney with Keating and Henry, Leibler outlined what he saw as the "iniquity" of the tax assessments that had been issued after the Federal Court's decision in the Gregrhon case. He argued that legislation was not necessary and that Boucher could act administratively without legislative backing. Henry had told him that Keating was unlikely to do any more than politely listen to his presentation, but in his notes of the meeting, Leibler writes: "In fact, Keating did respond and very positively. He said quite specifically that he was in agreement with the line I was putting and that he would take the matter up with Boucher" with a view to achieving a solution along the lines Leibler recommended. His notes continued:

> He showed me a letter from Boucher which said Boucher needed legislative backing to do anything along the lines I had been suggesting. Whilst Keating did not rule out the possibility of legislative action, it was apparent to both of us that such a course of action could be politically very difficult indeed.

What Leibler does not convey in his notes is the respect he had for Keating from almost the moment they met. Far from being non-committal in order to buy time during which he could simply forget about Leibler's proposed action, Keating had made commitments that illustrated that he had personally read the documents and case studies that Leibler had sent to Henry and was ready to respond. He was, Leibler thought, a special politician.

During the meeting, Leibler noted, Keating said that he disagreed with Dawkins on the tax bill that had ultimately failed in the Senate on Harradine's vote, but could not argue against it when the political climate was so anxious about tax avoidance. He also criticised the way Evans had supported the Federal Court's decision on the Gregrhon case.

It took several meetings with Boucher and several conversations with Henry, who had become the conduit for exchanges between Keating and Leibler, before the Commissioner of Taxation agreed to issue an administrative order that would deal with most of Leibler's problems with the section 260 assessments. Leibler did not get his way entirely, but, overall, the financial threat to his clients was significantly diminished. None of this was made public, and Leibler was adamant that he did not tell a single client of his dealings with Keating over the section 260 assessments. It would have been improper to do so, he said. He was only now prepared to talk about what happened because so many years had passed since his first interaction with Keating.

I asked Leibler about what other specific tax matters he had gone to Keating with after the successful resolution of the section 260 issue. Leibler said he could not be specific because any disclosure might breach client confidentiality. So, he went to Keating on behalf of clients? "I am not going to discuss this at all. These things have to remain confidential." But most of the contact with him was over tax matters? "That's right."

Sitting in the boardroom at ABL just two doors down from Leibler's office, Keating said that he had been lukewarm about Evans urging the Federal Court and High Court to rule in favour of expanded powers for the Tax Commissioner under section 260. He thought the Howard legislation had made the necessary changes after the revelations of the Royal Commission on the Activities of the Federated Ship Painters and Dockers Union. But he said there had been a prevailing view that previous High Court rulings under Garfield Barwick as Chief Justice had diminished the Taxation Commissioner's powers under section 260. Evans wanted the new court to re-examine those powers. Keating, as Treasurer, could hardly say "Oh, no, the Commissioner doesn't want those extra powers." Keating recollected,

> So Mark came to see me on behalf of his obviously great body of clients. I think he wanted the government to legislate some clarity about these assessments, which he saw as iniquitous. These people had already been issued with assessments for unpaid company tax [under the Howard legislation] and now they were being issued with another set of assessments for the same taxation offence. But the government would have found it politically very difficult to legislate a diminution of the power which the High Court had given the Commissioner.

It was clear that Keating had gone back and refreshed his memory about the tax issues. More than that, it seemed probable that Leibler, perhaps at Keating's request, had sent him his notes about their interaction in early 1988. Keating continued,

> I took the view during Mark's first meeting with me that it is a minister's job to resolve problems—not make them, but to resolve them. And the real question was, would I just sit and say "Oh well, it's not for me, it's a matter for the Commissioner and if he thinks we need to legislate we will consider it?" Or do I say, "Well, look, there is a problem as you identify and therefore it is a problem that could seek an administrative solution in which case, on that basis, I could talk to the Commissioner." Boucher

sent me a minute saying that he could see a way of dealing with it administratively if I agreed as Treasurer. So that's what we did.

Keating paused, as if he was remembering what he had achieved as Treasurer:

> You see, in my view, most of Australia's tax avoidance problems were due to the absence of capital taxation. People could simply turn income into capital and avoid paying tax. The capital gains tax [introduced by the Hawke Government in 1985] changed that fundamentally. The Commissioner had legislative power and a statute behind him. When people were turning income into capital he was able to tax them under that power.

I asked whether he knew that Leibler did not initially support a capital gains tax. "I didn't know that but it does not surprise me", he replied. "He had to represent the interests, as he saw them, of his clients. But I bet he understood that a capital gains tax was fundamentally important if we were to deal with tax avoidance."

Did he know some of Leibler's clients? To which he responded:

> Yes I did. You know, I have always been somewhat critical of members of the Jewish community, for two reasons. I mean Richard Pratt, who I had a really great relationship with, used to say to me, "You know, you are one of the great entrepreneurs of public life, you changed the way the country functions," and I said to Richard that it was his great fortune that he started growing his business when there was a great deal of money around because I had opened up the economy, opened markets, and of course his business grew rapidly. He was a very clever man, a great entrepreneur, and I said to him, "Well, Richard, for a rationalist why then don't you perpetually support the Labor Party, why on earth are you trying to join the Melbourne Club, be respectable among people who, if not anti-Semitic, have discriminatory views

about people like you?" I said, "Better wish them good luck as you wave them goodbye, move off, continue to grow your fortune but remember the antecedents of the growth were the big reforms of the Labor Government in the 1980s." He used to laugh at that because he knew I was right.

So, I asked him whether the Jewish community, at least people like Pratt, should have followed the money, so to speak, seen the reforms to the economy that had allowed their businesses to thrive and voted Labor? Keating replied, "Well, after all that to vote for the Coalition out of old habits—you know, I thought that was pretty dumb and most Jewish entrepreneurs were never dumb so I could never quite work out why this is where they were stuck."

Was there anything else that puzzled him about the way some members of the Jewish community voted? Keating replied:

> The other thing is that the Labor Party—me particularly, but the Labor Party in general—believed in a cosmopolitan Australia. I remember a speech I made attacking Howard. I made the point about the difference between patriotism and nationalism. All these nationalists like Howard and Hanson have one thing in common. Their question is always who's in and who's out. They are not Hitler, of course not, but it's the question that obsessed him. We know the consequences. Patriotism…a patriot is happy in a cosmopolitan setting. That's where the Labor Party was and that's where I was.

> So why would Jewish people ever vote for someone like Howard? Immediately after he was elected, he enabled and legitimised Pauline Hanson through the confected notion of political correctness. In other words, the whole notion of reasonableness and decency was thrown out the window on the basis that she had the right to say those things. Then when she started taking votes from them, Howard shifted the whole outfit in her direction. I told Beazley in the Tampa election, called him from Vietnam,

told him "You have to get out in front of Howard, not just follow, because Howard will pull the race card on you and there's no point in trying to be Howard and assuage the concerns of those lowest common denominator people Howard was talking to."

Did he listen? "Well, the answer is obvious." Did Keating ever discuss this with Leibler?

I must have done so. Really, I can't remember. But I could never understand the Jewish community, you know. It was always somewhat of a mystery to me that the Jewish community here could ever vote for the Coalition whilst Howard-type views abounded. The conservatives have moved even further down that path, so that fellow in Queensland, [Peter] Dutton, could seriously be considered by the conservatives as a possible prime minister. So I got a bit short with them [the Jewish community], still am I suppose. I tell them that "the one party that would actually stick with you through thick and thin on the question of identity, your identity, is the Labor Party. And by the way, who helped you make all the money."

Did Leibler agree with him? "You have to ask him. But if you see how involved he is in Indigenous issues, for instance, how he has publicly disagreed with Howard and all the rest of them, that tells you something I think." A few days later, when I put Keating's views to him, Leibler said he wasn't sure whether Keating was right that the Jewish community voted overwhelmingly for the Coalition. He said he was unaware of any polls or surveys that have been taken on Jewish community voting in Australian elections.

Keating was right about Jewish support for the Coalition parties. Surveys of Jewish voting intentions taken as far back as 1966 show a steep decline over the past five decades in support for the ALP. There are no surveys for the whole community in 1966, as far as I can tell, but a Jewish community survey in Victoria before the 1963 election showed 39 per cent support for the ALP and 40 per cent support for the Liberal Party. By 2017, support for the ALP, according to comprehensive survey of Australian Jews undertaken in the Gen17 report, was at 19 per cent, compared with 50 per cent support for the Liberal Party. Around 10 per cent said they supported the Greens.

As for Jewish business people, Leibler said that some have had close relationships with prime ministers on both sides of politics. "John Howard certainly, and Bob Hawke of course, and yes, Paul Keating, and so too Malcolm Turnbull...well he held the seat with the largest Jewish population in the country."

So, I asked him, Jewish business people had played some part in the lives and political destiny of Australian prime ministers? To which he replied:

> I'm not going to go there and name names. But, you know, when I was president of the ZFA, sometimes I would call one of these business people who I knew had a close relationship with politicians on both sides of politics. I would ring up and explain that there was a problem and that they needed to sit down with the PM and explain the problem. They would always be very helpful doing that.

Asked why they did that, he replied:

> I mean, they were close to these prime ministers in all sorts of ways. But they did feel strongly about some issues, particularly support for Israel, you know, partly because they had backgrounds or their parents did, in the Holocaust, and they knew where they had come from. They weren't into issuing public statements but they had the sort of relationships with prime ministers and foreign ministers, too, that allowed them to intervene.

While Leibler would not name these business people, an educated guess would be that they included Frank Lowy, Dick Pratt and, today, his son Anthony, Saul Same and, to a certain extent, Solomon Lew. Going back to the 1970s and 1980s, they would have included property developer Eddie Kornhauser, who was very close to Hawke, and Peter Abeles, then head of the transport conglomerate, TNT, whom Hawke described as one of his closest friends and mentors. I asked whether that was a unique situation for a Jewish community of such small size. "The answer is, yes," Leibler replied.

Asked about Keating's view of John Howard as an enabler of Pauline Hanson and of an exclusionary form of nationalism, Leibler said that he had publicly criticised Howard over the way he had dealt with the Pauline Hanson issue. Did he support Keating on the republic? "Yes, I did. I am a supporter of Australia becoming a republic."

Asked whether the Jewish community would have voted for Hawke in greater numbers than they voted for Keating, Leibler said he thought it might have. "Hawke was considered particularly close to the Jewish community. And close to Israel. He often said so. He sort of thought he knew everything about the Jews and Israel. He even thought he could go there and solve all the problems. Keating was never like that."

What about John Howard? "I think he understood the Jewish community. I think he really did." He had empathy for the Jews? "I have a huge amount of respect and affection for Howard, who was unshakeable in his support for the Jewish community and Israel." Did he ever talk to Keating about Howard's closeness to the Jewish community? "I don't think so. There would have been no reason to do so."

When the interview with Keating was over, Leibler was waiting for him in the ABL foyer. He had thought that perhaps Keating would have a few minutes on this Friday afternoon to spend with him before his next appointment. They set off down the corridor to Leibler's office. Two hours later they were still there, sitting together at Leibler's table.

CHAPTER 12

When his first challenge to Prime Minister Bob Hawke for the leadership of the Labor Party was unsuccessful, Paul Keating resigned as Treasurer and moved to the backbench. The vote in caucus on 3 June 1991 was 64 for Hawke and 44 for Keating. Given that Hawke had been Prime Minister for more than eight years, had led the ALP to an unprecedented four election victories, and had been a hugely popular politician for a long time, the caucus vote represented the beginning of the end for Hawke.

Two days after the vote, Mark Leibler sent a handwritten letter to Keating:

> Dear Paul
>
> Strange isn't it that the loser on the votes emerges looking very much the winner in all other respects. But then perhaps not surprising at all!
>
> Congratulations on the performance. I look forward in anticipation to the Second Act—its final and successful completion.
>
> Wishing you much luck
>
> With best wishes
> One of your many admirers
> Mark

Keating wrote back, thanking Leibler for his note, and for his "words of encouragement and support," appending a PS: "Not sure about the second act!"

Five months later, the second act duly arrived. In late December, Keating launched a second attempt to defeat Hawke; this time 56 Labor MPs voted for him to replace Hawke as their leader, and 51 voted against him. Hawke immediately quit parliament and Keating became Prime Minister. Australia was still in the throes of a recession—the recession that Keating had famously said "we had to have." Could he reinvigorate a government that had been in power for eight years? Could he possibly win an election in 1993 against the Coalition parties with John Hewson as their new leader?

In the Jewish community, there was apprehension about Keating. On 27 December 1991, the veteran Canberra correspondent for the *Australian Jewish News*, Bernard Freedman, wrote that, while Jewish community leaders were taking an optimistic view about future Australian government policy on Israel under Keating, "their optimism seems to be founded more on hope than any publicly known facts. Unlike former Prime Minister Bob Hawke, warmly praised by community leaders for his unwavering support for Israel, there is little in Mr Keating's career to indicate any special sympathy towards Israel." Freedman went on to say that Keating had "very limited connections with Australia's Jewish community" and that, in 1990, he had successfully lobbied the Immigration Department's senior officials to allow the controversial Muslim religious leader, Sheikh Taj Eldine el-Hilaly, to stay in Australia after his visitor's visa had expired; this was despite the protests from Jewish leaders, who alleged that Hilaly had made anti-Semitic statements.

At the time, there was a wave of grief through some sections of the Jewish community at Hawke's departure. In another article on the same page as Freedman's, entitled "Tributes to Bob Hawke", numerous Jewish leaders effusively praised the former prime minister. Leslie Caplan, president of the ECAJ, described Hawke as a man of "extraordinary ability, intellect, compassion and charm who had a special relationship with the Jewish community." Leibler, then president of the ZFA, was quoted as saying that Hawke was "a giant among men, a great prime minister, a close friend of the Jewish people and a constant supporter of the security and integrity of Israel."

Asked about his effusive praise of Hawke in light of his letter to Keating two days after Keating's unsuccessful tilt at the Labor leadership, Leibler said there was nothing contradictory about praising Hawke and having not long before written to Keating, more or less urging him to have another go at the ALP leadership. Hawke's time was up. Leibler had long believed that Keating would be a great prime minister.

I asked Helene Teichmann about Leibler's relationship with Hawke. Were they close? "Well they had a working relationship," she replied. But he didn't like him? "No, he didn't like him." But he really liked Keating? "Yes, there was bromance between them."

Keating's defeat of Hawke had significant consequences for the senior leaders of the Jewish community. Almost all of them had developed a relationship with Hawke, whom they considered the community's and Israel's greatest friend in the Labor government. Isi Leibler was particularly close to Hawke, who had long played such a prominent and active role in the Soviet Jewry movement, even after he became Prime Minister. In 1978, as president of the Australian Council of Trade Unions (ACTU), Hawke had travelled to the Soviet Union to plead with Soviet officials to allow Jews to leave if that's what they wanted. He came back to Australia and announced that he had secured an agreement. It turned out to be a false promise. Soviet officials announced there had been no agreement; Hawke felt humiliated and was distraught.

Hawke's defeat by Keating was particularly hard for Isi Leibler to handle. Hawke had been a close ally, not just on the Soviet Jewry issue but on Israel as well. Isi Leibler was soon to assume the ECAJ presidency again when it moved to Melbourne after Leslie Caplan's two-year term in Sydney ended. Even without the ECAJ presidency, Leibler was widely recognised as the most prominent and powerful leader in the Jewish community, but with Hawke gone his contacts in and access to the government were severely diminished. He had no real relationship with Keating, and developing one would be difficult, given his well-known closeness to Hawke.

His brother Mark was really the only Jewish leader with a significant relationship with the new prime minister. He said as much in his praise of Hawke published in the 27 December 1991 issue of the *Australian Jewish News*:

> It is true that Mr Keating is regarded as somewhat of an enigma. He would be the first to concede that he has very limited knowledge of Jewish affairs and the complexities of the Middle East.
>
> I can certainly say that he is certainly not an unknown quantity to me…In the light of my contacts with Paul Keating over many years…there is no reason to believe that there will be any shifts in government policy which would be adverse to the interests and concerns of the Australian Jewish community.

These words signalled to his fellow community leaders, especially his brother, that he, Mark Leibler, had a relationship with Keating that none of them enjoyed. He would be uniquely placed to make the case to Keating on any issue that concerned the Jewish community. He would not restrict himself and the ZFA to issues that pertained only to the government's Middle East policies.

CHAPTER 12

In fact his relationship with Keating to that date, while warm and friendly, had mainly involved issues of tax and taxation policy. By the time Keating became Prime Minister, Leibler was unassailably the most prominent and widely known tax lawyer in Australia. He had been a member of the Commissioner of Taxation's Advisory Panel and was known to have the ear of the Treasurer and senior officials in the Australian Taxation Office, including the Commissioner.

When Keating became Prime Minister in late 1991, although Mark Leibler was not yet a match for his brother in terms of his standing as a Jewish leader in Australia and overseas, as the only Jewish leader to have a relationship with Keating, it was inevitable that, sooner or later, the Leibler brothers would be at each other's throats.

Despite Mark Leibler's connection to the new prime minister, there was widespread concern, even alarm, among community leaders about the position of the Keating government's position on the conflict between Israel and the Palestinians, especially that of Foreign Minister Gareth Evans. Many Jews had been alarmed by the Scud missiles that Saddam Hussein had rained down on Israel during the Gulf War and by the sight of Israelis wearing gas masks out of fear that the missiles would be armed with poison gas. Many Australian Jews were concerned about the safety of relatives in Israel.

The Palestinian Liberation Organisation (PLO) organised mass demonstrations in the West Bank and in Gaza in support of Saddam Hussein and the Scud attacks. In doing so, the PLO leadership made a strategic mistake, given that most of the Arab world considered Saddam Hussein's invasion of Kuwait an act of war. All the countries that were part of the coalition that went to war with Iraq to liberate Kuwait cut contact with the PLO, which found itself isolated at the end of the first Gulf War.

In April 1992, 13 months after the end of the war, Evans decided that the Australian government should restore ministerial contact with the PLO. Keating publicly supported the decision, but there is little doubt that he was ambivalent about it. Keating, unlike Evans and other Labor politicians, such as Bob Hawke, Bob Carr and several senior figures in the New South Wales Labor Right, had never had a great interest in the conflict between Israel and the Palestinians, or any feeling that Australia had a significant role to play in resolving it. Keating accepted that Evans did not share this view and allowed Foreign Minister Evans to make the running on the government's position.

During a trip to the Middle East in May 1992, Evans visited a Palestinian refugee camp in the West Bank and, in a speech, severely criticised Israel's expansion of what he said were illegal settlements. He expressed support for United Nations Resolution 194, passed at the end of the 1948 war, which called for the right of return for Palestinians who had fled or been forced out of their homes by the war. This position was controversial because, interpreted one way, it could result in the return of all Palestinians and their descendants displaced by the war, which would have meant the end of Israel as a Jewish state. In the main, both the Coalition parties and the ALP had followed the United States position on the resolution, as meaning that an unspecified number of Palestinian refugees, perhaps a token number, would be granted the right of return in any peace settlement. Evans had not been clear what he meant when he said he supported Resolution 194.

The context of Evans' criticism of Israel is important. At the end of the Gulf War, the United States and the Soviet Union agreed to sponsor a peace conference on the Middle East. At the Madrid conference of 30 October–1 November 1991, Israelis and Palestinians (although not the PLO officially) met with representatives of the Arab states, the United States, the Soviet Union and the European Union to put in place a process to revive negotiations between Israel and the Palestinians. In the lead-up to the conference, American President George Bush and his Secretary of State, James Baker, had to more or less force the right-wing Israeli Prime Minister, Yitzhak Shamir, who had encouraged the growth of settlements in the West Bank, to attend. Shamir refused to stop settlement development in the West Bank and made it clear that he would take part only with great reluctance in the bilateral negotiations with the Palestinians that had been agreed to at Madrid. The negotiations quickly went nowhere, and it was in this context that Evans decided to re-establish ministerial contacts with the PLO and to criticise Israel, and Shamir in particular, during his Middle East trip.

Nevertheless, many Jews were disturbed by Evans' statement; Mark Leibler was enraged. When the Foreign Minister returned to Australia, Leibler met him before Evans was to meet a delegation of Jewish community leaders. According to people with knowledge of the meeting, Leibler and Evans exchanged views in a very robust fashion. Insults were exchanged.

There was disquiet among some Labor MPs as well. The veteran Whitlam and Hawke government minister, Barry Cohen, told *The Australian* in June 1992 that the Jewish community in Melbourne and Sydney had always been a source of ideological and financial support for the ALP, noting, "That will be weakened whenever a government appears to be antagonistic towards the state of Israel". To some, Cohen's statement was troubling. There was, and still is, great sensitivity in the Jewish community about any threat, overt or implied, that leading Jewish businessmen who were known to be major donors to the ALP—as they were to the Liberal Party too—were likely to curtail their donations because of the position a government took on Israel and the Palestinians. Jewish leaders did not want to be seen to be suggesting in any way that they could tell Jews how to vote. They couldn't and everyone knew it.

The minutes of meetings of the ZFA executive in late May 1992 show that Leibler, while fiercely critical of Evans, was adamant that Jewish leaders should not make any threats about donations to political parties or threaten to urge the Jewish community to vote against the government because of its policies on the Middle East. At the same time, Leibler consistently defended Keating, who had come under some attack by Jewish leaders for not repudiating Evans' statements about the PLO and Israel. One ZFA executive member said that, if Hawke had still been prime minister, Evans would not have been allowed to go to the West Bank and take the positions he had taken. Leibler disagreed.

He argued that Evans had made it very difficult for Keating, who was to speak at the ZFA's biennial conference in Melbourne in May 1992, just before Evans' visit to the West Bank. At the ZFA executive meeting Leibler insisted that Keating was the right speaker for the conference despite the fact that he had not publicly criticised Evans. He was Prime Minister, after all. It was Leibler who had convinced Keating to speak at the conference. Opposition Leader John Hewson, who had criticised Evans for his position on the PLO, had also agreed to speak at the conference. When he introduced Keating at the conference, Leibler was scathing about Evans:

> The decision by Foreign Minister Gareth Evans, on the eve of the 44th anniversary of Israel's independence, just one week prior

to his visit to Israel, to upgrade contacts with the PLO came as a bolt from the blue to the Australian Jewish community.

> I have already spoken to Senator Evans and explained why the Government's action has caused so much distress within the Jewish community...I hope that you, Prime Minister, will agree to personally reconsider the Government's position on this issue which is of such vital concern to the Jewish community.

Leibler knew that Keating would not repudiate Evans in his speech. He had discussed the speech with Keating, who had agreed to some adjustments but no major concessions.

However, while Keating did not in any way criticise his Foreign Minister, his speech focused on the ALP's historic commitment to Israel and emphasised his government's unwavering commitment to Israel's security. Keating spoke of his optimism that, after the Madrid conference, the peace process would be reinvigorated and that negotiations between Israel and the Palestinians would be about issues of substance:

> As we see it, Israel's independence and security are ultimately dependent on its being able to find a stable accommodation, a modus vivendi, with its Arab neighbours...The restoration of our earlier policy on contact with the PLO is consistent with our long-established aim of encouraging the forces of moderation rather than extremism within the PLO.

Keating foreshadowed what Evans would say at the refugee camp in the West Bank, though without the sort of rhetoric that Evans was to use:

> Along with many other countries, including the United States, Australia has long expressed its opposition to Israel's continued settlement activity in the Occupied Territories. As friends of Israel, we have to say that we regard such activity as an obstacle to

peace…Australia urges Israel's Arab neighbours to come to terms with Israel and recognize its right to exist as an independent state.

The audience at the ZFA conference did not greet Keating's speech with enthusiasm. At the end, some did not applaud at all. Prime Minister Keating did not receive a standing ovation, as Opposition Leader John Hewson did the next day when, in his speech, he criticised Evans for the decision to resume ministerial contacts with the PLO.

Yet Leibler went in to bat for Keating, not just at the conference but in the Jewish community in general. He described the speech as balanced and argued that it in no way endorsed the way Evans had expressed himself about the PLO and the settlements issue. Leibler's view was not widely held among other Jewish community leaders.

During our interview at ABL, Keating remembered this issue only vaguely. He recalled that he had discussed the Middle East with Leibler and that Mark probably did influence him in some ways, but not so that the Middle East became one of his major foreign policy concerns. He told me:

> There were many people in the Labor Party, like Hawke and Carr and the Jewish MPs like Barry Cohen and others, who were very interested in Israel. They went there, they knew all the personalities; there was fraternal contact between the Israeli Labor Party and our Labor Party. But that wasn't my interest and so I left all that to them. And when I became Prime Minister, broadly speaking, I left all that with Gareth Evans.

Keating agreed that the Jewish community had been critical of his position on the settlements and the PLO, remembering "once meeting Mark and his brother. It got a bit heated." Asked whether Mark Leibler was critical, he replied: "Maybe. But my natural interest in foreign policy devolved to Asia not the Middle East. I would look at the Middle East forensically, not emotionally. Unlike some, I did not think Australia had a significant role to play in the Middle East."

I asked Keating whether, despite disagreements over Israel, Leibler remained close to him. "I think that's right, yes", he replied. "I hope Mark thought I was an earnest soul, that I tried to take on issues with an open mind, without prejudices, just like I took on the tax issues with Mark."

Asked whether he knew that Leibler had supported him at the 1993 election when most Jewish leaders supported the Coalition and John Hewson, Keating replied: "Yes, I do know that. I do know that." Did Leibler raise donations from Jewish businessmen for Keating and the ALP in 1993? "I don't know about that. You should ask Mark about it." Leibler would not say whether he had raised donations in the Jewish community for Keating and the ALP before the 1993 election when he was asked about it, but I have confirmed from other sources that he did indeed raise more than $1 million from 12 donors, not all of them ALP supporters.

Shortly after Evans returned from the Middle East and Keating had spoken at the ZFA conference, the whole issue of Evans' comments suddenly became irrelevant. In the Israeli election in mid-June 1992, the Shamir government was defeated. Yitzhak Rabin led the Israeli Labor Party to victory and became Prime Minister.

Many senior figures in the Keating government had ties to Israel's Labor Party and its trade union movement. Many knew Rabin and other members of his government, including Shimon Peres. The sharp criticism of Israel's settlement policies was significantly toned down. The secret negotiations between Palestinian and Israeli officials in Oslo became public and, when the Oslo Accords between Rabin and Yasser Arafat were signed on the White House lawn on 13 September

1993, it seemed as if, for the first time, peace between Israel and the Palestinians was a real prospect.

On 25 November 1995, however, Rabin was assassinated by Yigal Amir, a right-wing extremist virulently opposed to the Oslo process. The Likud Opposition led by Benjamin Netanyahu was bitterly opposed to Oslo and criticised Rabin in language that many thought had encouraged the deranged Amir to kill him. Netanyahu was there at the right-wing rallies and, when speakers called Rabin a traitor, he remained silent. He had remained silent when members of his party described Rabin as a betrayer of the Jewish people and of Israel.

Asked about Oslo, Leibler said he had been a supporter of the process and of Rabin. He was devastated when he learnt of Rabin's assassination. He had hoped that it would not stop the Oslo process but feared that Rabin's death would encourage extremists bent on violence in order to destroy Oslo. And so it turned out. Keating also remembers how upset he was at Rabin's assassination:

> I had to go to the funeral. I had to show my respect and support for what Rabin had stood for. Yes, I knew how difficult that time was for Mark because we had talked about the hope in Oslo, the chance for a real peace. We both thought that Rabin was a leader of real stature. He was a former soldier with a distinguished military career, he was a long-time Labor politician, a social democrat and he had the courage to make concessions for a real peace with the Palestinians. His death was such a blow.

Three months after Rabin's death, on 2 March 1996, Australia went to an election. No-one except Keating believed that the ALP would win. For months, all the polls had pointed to a landslide win for the Liberal–National Coalition. Keating could not bring himself to believe that he would be defeated by John Howard, whom he saw as a reactionary whose politics were stuck in the 1950s and would take Australia back to being an outpost of Britain, tied ever more closely to the mother country and the British monarchy. Although Keating had pulled off an almost miraculous win in the 1993 election, there would be no miracles for him this time. The ALP was defeated in a landslide.

The day after the election, knowing that Keating would be devastated, Mark Leibler sent a handwritten letter:

Dear Paul

To say I am disappointed is somewhat of an understatement. In my books you go down as the greatest PM. this country has ever had. We could certainly have done with a few more years of your leadership.

You have unquestionably more than made your mark on Australia. You have led this country with breathtaking vision and never shied away from tackling the difficult issues...I believe that in the course of time this will also be the verdict of history. Looking back at your role over the last 13 years, both as Treasurer and as PM, I believe it is accurate to say that the impact you made on the Australian people...is unmatched. You have changed this country and the Australian people very much for the better—and in these respects, there can be no turning back the clock...

On a personal level, I consider it a real privilege to have been able to get to know the real Paul Keating as distinct from his public persona. I am generally not given to hero worship...Suffice it to say that I have really enjoyed our association—more so than any other association which I have had in the world of politics.

Rosanna joins me in wishing you and Anita every joy, satisfaction and success in whatever you decide to do in the future...We would also like to keep in touch, something that should be easier in the future than it was in the past because of your very heavy responsibilities.

When you're next in Melbourne, please give me a call. We'd love
to get together for lunch or dinner if you can spare the time…

Warmest regards and best wishes
Mark Leibler

Most people who have worked with Mark Leibler, or have known
him as a Jewish community leader, would be surprised by this letter to
Keating, which was never made public. Most would have assumed that
Leibler was a rusted-on supporter of the Liberal Party—a reasonable
assumption given Leibler's public support for small government and low
taxes. And, given his prominence as a Zionist leader, it was reasonable
to assume that he would be closer to conservatives like Howard, whose
views on the Middle East were unquestionably more in line with the
views of the majority of the Jewish community than those of the ALP.

Mark Dreyfus, Labor frontbencher and Attorney-General in the
Gillard government, has had a relationship with Leibler for almost 20
years, from when Dreyfus was on the editorial board of the *Australia/
Israel Review*, a monthly publication distributed to politicians, public
servants, journalists and subscribers, still published by the Australia/
Israel & Jewish Affairs Council. Dreyfus spoke of when he, as a QC,
had once been in a professional relationship with Leibler and had been
briefed regularly by ABL lawyers, although not, as he remembered,
by Leibler himself. He said that his views on the Middle East were
often at odds with Leibler's, but that they both believed that only a
two-state solution would have a chance of bringing peace between
Israel and the Palestinians.

He said that, although he had never asked, he had always assumed
Leibler to be a Liberal voter and, in all probability, a financial supporter
of the Liberal Party too. Leibler was a neo-liberal on economics and a

social conservative. It was probably also true that the Liberal Party's position on Israel was more congenial to Leibler than that of the ALP. Dreyfus said he had never known about Leibler's relationships with Keating and Hayden. Clearly, he said, Leibler's politics were more nuanced than he had imagined.

On 22 July 1996, Keating wrote back to Leibler. In a covering note, he apologised for not having written earlier, but said that he had only recently managed to go through the letters he had received after his defeat:

Dear Mark

When I met you in Melbourne after the election, I didn't know that you had written me such a nice letter where you said so many complimentary things; I couldn't let it pass without acknowledgement and returning the compliment.

I was very flattered by you saying that my years as Treasurer and Prime Minister have played a substantial role in defining Australia's place in the world and that the country has changed for the better. I assure you that in a public life, this can be the only real reward, for when it's over, one can only look back and ask the question, has it changed and is it a better place and if the answer is genuinely in the affirmative, it is recompense enough.

Part of the joys of a long public career is getting to know people and getting to know some well. I feel this happened with you—I got to know you, to respect you, to understand how seriously you took your responsibilities and of course, to like you...

Rosanna and you have been good friends to Anita and me and I am sure the friendship will endure. I should be very pleased if it did.

Warmest best wishes
P.J. Keating

CHAPTER 13

Mark Leibler was 48 when he had his first experience of anti-Semitism. On a Monday evening in 1991, he went to Brighton Grammar School to watch his 14-year-old daughter, Ilana, take part in an inter-school debating competition. Ilana, then in Year 10, attended Leibler Yavneh College. Her family's name was now part of her school's name, because in 1988 the family matriarch, Rachel Leibler, and her three sons had donated a million dollars to the school, the largest donation to an Australian Jewish school at the time. In 2020 Leibler Yavneh College describes itself as a "Modern Orthodox Zionist school, with over 700 students from Crèche to Year 12." It believes in reaching out beyond the Jewish community, which was why Ilana and her father found themselves that evening in a classroom at an Anglican school, Brighton Grammar.

As he sat with other parents and listened to the debate, Leibler began to read on the blackboard what appeared to be notes for a lesson. Its subject was "The first Christian martyr—Stephen the Deacon". In essence, the notes appeared to summarise the New Testament's teaching about Stephen and his fate. Stephen believed that the new law of Jesus was to take the place of the old law of Moses. When he told the Jewish Council that they had rejected and killed Jesus, God's promised Messiah, the Jewish authorities were so angered that they killed Stephen in "an act of mob violence".

Christian theology was not an area about which Leibler knew much, if anything. He knew broadly that the Second Vatican Council had, in the early 1960s, repudiated the Catholic teaching that the Jews were eternally responsible for the crucifixion of Jesus—a teaching that had caused countless pogroms against Jews, in which thousands were murdered. But he knew little else. He had not read the New Testament.

Discussing the event many years later, he could not recall whether his daughter sitting in front of that blackboard with other Yavneh students made it personal, or whether he worried that Ilana would be wounded by the anti-Semitism in this classroom. Whatever triggered his reaction, two days later Leibler wrote to the headmaster of Brighton Grammar, describing what he had read on the blackboard:

> It seems to me quite shocking and nothing short of remarkable that in this day and age, a school under the auspices of the Anglican Church should have chosen this method of imparting Christian teaching to young children. If this represents the norm, then none of us ought to be surprised at the incidents of anti-Semitism and other forms of prejudice which appear to be becoming much more commonplace...

> I would be grateful if you would let me know what steps you propose to undertake in the future to bring to an end...a situation in which teachers (or at least one teacher) at Brighton Grammar School transmit knowledge in a way that can only be calculated to stir up anti-Semitism and prejudice against Jewish people.

Responding to Leibler, the Brighton Grammar headmaster, Robert Rofe, wrote a letter that, 28 years later, no headmaster of any Anglican or Christian denomination school would write. Rofe rejected out of hand the suggestion that any teaching by Anglican priests drawing on the New Testament could ever lead to prejudice against Jews, let alone anti-Semitism. The school chaplain whose notes were on the blackboard was

> doing as he was commanded to do, and in turn promised to do, when he was ordained...

I regret that you were upset…however, if you go into a classroom in an Anglican school, you cannot be surprised to see reference made to orthodox Anglican religious teaching.

In response, Leibler did not hold back. Rofe's response was "outrageous," he wrote. People like him who "persist in poisoning the minds of young children with hatred and prejudice" meant that the work of those dedicated to improving relations between Christians and Jews could have only limited impact. He went on to say that he would take his complaint to the Anglican Archbishop of Melbourne, Keith Rayner, and to the Council of Christians and Jews, a body set up in the 1980s to foster understanding and build bridges between people of the two faiths. He told Rofe that he would also inform those Jewish parents "misguided enough to send their children to Brighton Grammar of the poisonous atmosphere which is being created with your support and blessing."

Leibler sent Rayner copies of his letters to Rofe. On 8 July, Rayner wrote back a letter that is also remarkable. In summary, Rayner writes that it is not possible, from reading the blackboard notes, to conclude that teaching was conducted in a way that would foster prejudice. He writes that he therefore "sees no just cause for complaint." Rayner goes on to defend the teaching of "Stephen's martyrdom" and says that he was taught it when he was young and that it did not make him in any way prejudiced against Jews.

By the time Leibler wrote back eight days later, he had clearly armed himself with an overview of Christian teachings against Jews and their appalling consequences. He had studied the reports of the 1988 Lambeth Conference of the worldwide Anglican church and quoted sections of a report that acknowledged there had been "systemic dissemination of anti-Jewish propaganda against Jews by church leaders," and that through "catechism, teaching of school children and Christian preaching, the Jewish people have been misrepresented and caricatured."

Leibler went on to say that the notes on the blackboard state that Stephen had accused the Jews of rejecting and killing "God's promised Messiah" and that this false charge of deicide had caused the murder of countless numbers of Jews over the centuries. Vatican II had righted this egregious charge against the Jews, so had leaders of the Anglican church in England and elsewhere, but not, apparently, in Australia, he wrote. He asked Rayner to set up a commission to examine the church's teachings about Jews. He finished his long letter:

> Your Grace, I have written with more passion than is usual because I fear for my people, but also because my people have a stake in Christianity being the positive moral force in the world that we need...for God's sake, stop it now [this maligning of the Jews]. Nineteen hundred years is enough and too much.

Rayner's response to this long, detailed and impassioned letter from Leibler was abrupt and unapologetic. In the end, he said, he saw no evidence at all for the need for a commission to examine the teachings of his church about the Jews. What's more, he wrote, dialogue between Christians and Jews, which he favoured, was not encouraged by the "aggressiveness and general tone of your letter. I believe real dialogue will only be practicable, however, in a climate different from that which is reflected in your letter."

The battle and exchange of letters between Leibler and Rayner made the front page of the *Australian Jewish News*. An editorial came out in strong support of Leibler. The conflict was covered in *The Australian* and *The Sunday Age*. Several leading academic theologians wrote letters in support of Leibler. There was almost no support for Rayner's position or for the way the New Testament's story of Stephen was apparently being taught in Anglican schools.

On 11 September 1991, Mary Lotton, Secretary of the Council of Christians and Jews, wrote to Leibler to "inform you of our actions in response to the copies of correspondence between yourself, the Anglican Archbishop of Melbourne... and the headmaster of Brighton Grammar school." After examining the exchange of letters, she wrote, four members of the executive met with Rayner to

> discuss the issues raised in the correspondence. On Thursday September 5, these representatives met with Archbishop Rayner, who accepted the desirability of setting up a special committee of the Council for the purpose of identifying areas in the New Testament, the teaching of which, without appropriate explanations and cautions, are capable of provoking hostility towards Jews...The special committee will draft guidelines for clergy and teachers for the purposes of avoiding such consequences.

The result of the special committee's work was a book-length examination of the way Christian teachers and clergy should examine the relationship between Christians and Jews. Its guidelines, entitled *Rightly Explaining the Word of Truth,* cover all the issues that Leibler raised in his correspondence with Rayner and more.

Leibler launched the book, which was to be distributed to clergy and teachers across Australia, at a function organised by the Council of Christians and Jews on 11 November 1991. In his speech, Leibler said that he was just a practising Orthodox Jew with little knowledge of the area and that it "would never have occurred to me that a person in my position would one day have the privilege of having a positive impact on the course of interfaith relations in this country." He recalled the inter-school debate he had attended to see his daughter perform. The father and the Jewish leader had intersected in a profound way:

> The fact that this had come about as a direct consequence of my visit to Brighton Grammar School and my subsequent correspondence with the Anglican Archbishop the Most Reverend Keith Rayner, is a source of considerable personal satisfaction. It demonstrates the importance of "speaking one's mind" and being forthright and tenacious when faced with teachings or conduct which have the potential to cause anti-Semitism.

Ilana also remembers that evening when her father came to watch her debate and saw the notes on the blackboard. She remembers the accusation that the Jews had killed Jesus, and that her father gave no indication during the debate that he had seen what was written on the blackboard. He was concentrating on her performance. On the way home, they discussed what had happened. Her father explained what had so upset him and why it was so wrong and why it was necessary to not let things like that go. He said that he was going to try and do something about it. Knowing her father well, she knew that he would.

CHAPTER 14

The photographs of Mark Leibler displayed in his study show his round full face, pencil-thin moustache and thinning black hair. Taken perhaps 30 years ago, they are of a man both well pleased with what he has achieved and anxious to achieve more in the future. Back then, Leibler smoked cigars, in his office as well as at home, and was more than partial to a good Scotch whisky. Anyone who knew him back then says that he was often arrogant, often angry, and that he would regularly swear during arguments with opponents.

Leibler reluctantly gave up cigars a few years ago, but he still likes a whisky or two and is still prone to using robust language. In the many hours we spoke together, Leibler did his best to be calm, precise in his answers and patient, even when it was clear that he considered some questions ignorant or foolish. But every now and then, a question would so exasperate him that he would become red-faced, swear and let his anger flare for a moment or two. He let it be known that he was not happy with the line of questioning to which he was being subjected. At these moments, it was possible to see why some of the politicians he had dealt with, and some in the Jewish community who had opposed him politically, might have felt that Leibler was brash, arrogant, a bully.

None of his opponents or critics in the Jewish community were prepared to put their names to their sometimes scathing criticism of Leibler's behaviour—or of his brother Isi's behaviour, for that matter. Some of the politicians who felt bullied by Leibler—Kevin Rudd in the last months as Prime Minister and later Foreign Minister, and Bob Carr when he replaced Rudd as Foreign Minister in the Gillard government—have publicly accused Leibler of threatening and trying to intimidate them, although the idea that a Jewish leader, even a tough one like Leibler, could intimidate or seriously threaten politicians like Rudd or Carr seems far-fetched.

It would be unfair to quote anonymous critics, but, given that the Jewish community is in some respects still like an Eastern European *shtetl*—insular, gossip-prone, where politics are played hard and people have long memories and extract revenge against their opponents when they can—it is not surprising that critics of Leibler would speak only on condition they remained anonymous. One of his critics is considered, even by his opponents, to be a person of integrity, who has no revenge agenda against Leibler and has not been involved in community politics for a long time. This critic commented:

> The Leibler brothers are brilliant, no doubt about it, and there is no doubting their contribution to the Australian Jewish community. Mark has an incredible intellect, with the ability to immediately recognise the substantive issues. He was a brilliant leader, responsible for building the ZFA into the pre-eminent Jewish organisation in Australia. There is, however, a massive vicious streak running through the genes of both brothers.

Isi would sometimes be open to reconciliation after he had attacked someone, if it was politically expedient. Mark is a much more uncompromising and dangerous foe. I once witnessed Isi and Mark savaging Arnold Bloch at a Victorian Board of Deputies meeting. Mark really put the boots in. He was clearly enjoying himself. Arnold was a brilliant man and he was no wilting lily but he was no match for Mark in terms of viciousness. No-one was.

When I put this view to him, Leibler conceded that he might have been angry at times when he was younger and that he had sometimes played community politics hard, perhaps brutally. But he insisted that he had never "put the boot in" when he had argued with Bloch. It was never personal. It was always about policy differences or conflicts over power, over which organisation spoke for the Jewish community. He said he had never worried about what people thought of him, whether he was stepping on toes. He had always believed that any organisation was only as good as its leader: "If people were pissed off, too bad. Mind you, I do think I am less angry nowadays. I don't go after people as hard as I used to. It can be counter-productive, make enemies of people for no good reason."

By the early 1990s, Isi and Mark Leibler, both battle-scarred after decades of Jewish community struggles, were senior leaders not only in Australia's Jewish community, but also in the organisations of world Jewry. Isi had served several terms as President of the Executive Council of Australian Jewry and was co-chairman of the World Jewish Congress. He had been a major player in the successful Free Soviet Jewry movement.

No-one doubted Isi Leibler's commitment to the Jewish community or his contribution to its health and to its future. But he made enemies. He was a passionate and often volatile leader, ruthless when he felt that his leadership and authority to speak for the community was challenged. His attacks on opponents, or people he considered opponents, were legendary for their bluntness and vitriol.

A letter he sent to the much-loved Jewish community activist, Johnny Baker, at the time a former president of the Victorian State Zionist Council and a member of the executive of the Zionist Federation of Australia, is a good illustration of the way Isi Leibler responded when he felt challenged. It no longer matters what the dispute with Baker was about, except that it involved the perennial question of who

spoke for the Jews. The first and last paragraphs of the letter, dated
2 October 1995, read:

Dear Johnny

I don't wish to impose upon you the obligation of writing me
yet another tortuous rationalisation of your hang-ups, so I will
be brief....

For a New Year resolution, you might endeavour to generate a
little more humility and try to exhibit less bitterness. It would
do you good.

Gmar Tov [good ending on Yom Kippur]
Isi

By the early 1990s, meanwhile, Mark Leibler had been president
of the Zionist Federation of Australia for more than eight years. He
had transformed the organisation with the help of Helene Teichmann,
the ZFA's Executive Director. He had unmatched political contacts
in Canberra and a record of getting things done. Less volatile in per-
sonality than his brother, Mark could also be scathing in his criticism
of perceived opponents, especially Jews who challenged his right as
ZFA president to speak on behalf of Australian Jewry, not just on
Australia–Israel relations, but on anti-Semitism and, in reality, on
any issue that he decided was important.

In a dispute with Leslie Caplan when he was President of the
Executive Council of Australian Jewry, Mark Leibler wrote Caplan
a letter that, in some ways at least, Isi could have written. Predictably,
the letter was about a dispute between the ECAJ and the ZFA, about
which organisation spoke for the Jews. Leibler was prompted to write
it by a letter to the editor in *The Age* in July 1992 by an ECAJ official
who wanted to point out that his organisation was the "peak body of

the Australian Jewish community" and that readers of *The Age* should not be under the impression that the ZFA was the only body with concerns about Australia's policies on the Middle East.

On the surface, the letter seems fairly inoffensive, but it enraged Leibler because it suggested that the ZFA had been trying for some time to undermine the ECAJ. Just a small part of Leibler's long response, also written in July 1992, is enough to establish the similarities between the two brothers:

> Dear Leslie
>
> I am writing to communicate just how appalled both my colleagues and I were when we read the letter published in the Melbourne Age on 17 July 1992 under the signature of Jeremy Jones in his capacity as Honorary Secretary of the Executive Council of Australian Jewry...
>
> Leslie, do you realise that your colleagues at the ECAJ have effectively succeeded in making a very public distinction between Jews and Zionists?
>
> Congratulations to the ECAJ! Its little public outburst has succeeded in getting across the very message that the enemies of the Jewish people have been promoting for so long.

Those "enemies of the Jewish people," according to Leibler's letter, included Larry Stillman, a long-time activist in the left-wing Jewish Democratic Society, who had also written a letter to the editor of *The Age*, published on the same day as the ECAJ letter. Stillman wanted to point out that neither the ZFA nor the ECAJ spoke for all Australian Jews. This was undoubtedly true. Small but vocal Jewish groups, such as the Jewish Democratic Society, were bitter opponents of the Leiblers and the way they played their community politics. The Jewish Democratic Society leadership hated what they saw as the Leiblers' stifling of free speech in the community and the way the Leiblers invariably referred to those who questioned their right to speak for all Australian Jews as enemies of the Jewish people, or even self-hating Jews. In the early 1990s, however, these groups represented only a very small number of Australian Jews.

In a sense, silencing their critics on the left was not the main game for the Leibler brothers. Perhaps it had been in the past, but no longer. The main game was the battle between the ECAJ and the ZFA. The two peak Jewish community bodies had a history of seemingly petty conflicts over which organisation spoke for Australian Jews, but, in the main, these rifts were healed without any long-term consequences. That was because the ZFA never matched Isi Leibler's standing, influence and power—until Mark Leibler became its president.

By the time Isi Leibler returned to the presidency of the ECAJ, when its headquarters returned to Melbourne in 1992 after a two-year rotation in Sydney, Mark Leibler was becoming a match for his brother. There was no way, however, that Isi would accept that his brother, nine years younger than him, could take on the role of spokesman for the Australian Jewish community. That was his role.

In January 1993, Isi Leibler visited Israel. Several months earlier, the Israeli Labor Party leader, Yitzhak Rabin, had been elected Prime Minister. The defeat of the right-wing, Likud-led coalition of Prime Minister Yitzhak Shamir had been something of a political earthquake in Israel and, therefore, in diaspora Jewish communities. It was the beginning of a shift in Israel that would lead to the Oslo process and the handshake on the lawns of the White House between Yasser Arafat and a reluctant Rabin, urged on by a beaming president Bill Clinton. For Zionist movements and Jewish organisations around the world, the shift in Israel was a challenge. Most of them had supported the policies of the right-wing Shamir government; they now had to adjust to the positions taken by the new Rabin administration, and that adjustment was not always easy.

One of the most powerful lobbying organisations in Washington is the privately funded American Israel Public Affairs Committee (AIPAC), which is perhaps the most professional and powerful Jewish body advocating for Israel in the United States. AIPAC's annual conference attracts scores of members of Congress, the Secretary of State, and if not the President, then at least the Vice President. Shortly after he was elected, Rabin told American Jewish leaders, including AIPAC officials, that they needed to modify their lobbying for Israel. That was code for his view that their lobbying was counter-productive and that Israel was perfectly capable of developing its own relationship with Congress and the President without their interventions. Rabin's message was a stunning repudiation of the work of AIPAC. An Israeli prime minister was telling the most influential Jewish lobby group—perhaps the most influential lobby group in Washington—to back off, that he did not need their help.

When Isi Leibler returned from Israel, where he met with Rabin and a score of other Israeli politicians, including Foreign Minister Shimon Peres, an article by Bernard Freedman and Sam Lipski in the *Australian Jewish News* in January 1993 quoted Leibler as declaring that Rabin had asked him to inform Jewish organisations in Australia, including the ZFA, that they should "drop the quasi-diplomatic role they have adopted in Australia–Israel affairs of state." Instead, government-to-government relations should be left to the Israeli Embassy in Canberra, and Jewish organisations should concentrate on trade with Israel, fighting anti-Semitism, and urging Jews to make Aliyah.

For those people not engaged in Jewish community politics, Leibler's comments seemed to do no more than convey Rabin's view, already expressed to AIPAC in the United States, to the leadership of Australian Jewish organisations, including the ZFA. For Mark Leibler, however, the remarks were a repudiation of his life's work, of the years he had spent building up his political contacts in Canberra so that he could put the best case for Israel to whatever government was in power. This was an attack not by Rabin, but by his brother. It could not go unanswered.

In a furious piece in the *Australian Jewish News* the following week, Mark Leibler said that he had spoken to his brother, who had assured him that "in neither his discussions with Prime Minister Yitzhak Rabin nor with the *Jewish News* were the activities of Australian community organisations on issues related to Israel ever mentioned." In other words, Leibler was accusing the two journalists who had written the story about Isi Leibler's meeting with Rabin not only of misquoting his brother but of virtually fabricating some of what was attributed to him. Leibler went on to say that after the AIPAC controversy, he had written a letter to Rabin in which he had set out the "full gamut" of work by the ZFA, including its political lobbying. Rabin had written back stating that he had "no reservations", only praise, for the activities of the ZFA.

This was not the most consequential part of Leibler's article, however. Of greater significance was the suggestion that his brother, when asked by Mark, had denied saying anything to Freedman and Lipski about what Rabin had said, anything that could be construed as criticism of the work of the ZFA, and of Mark Leibler, its president. So, what was the truth? The journalists were well-known and respected in the Jewish community; Lipski was Editor-in-Chief of the *Australian Jewish*

News and a long-time friend of Isi Leibler. Had they misquoted the ECAJ president, or even fabricated some of his quotes? Or had Isi Leibler, when confronted by his brother, done what politicians often do when they feel cornered—blamed the journalists for his problems?

At the bottom of Mark Leibler's piece, one of the journalists, Bernard Freedman, wrote that Isi Leibler had "volunteered the information about Mr Rabin's views on the role of Jewish communal organisations" in two conversations Freedman had had with him: one when Leibler was in London on his way back to Australia and the other by phone on 17 January, after Leibler had returned home. A postscript stated: "The AJN stands by its report—The Editor."

Most people who knew the brothers understood what was going on. In all probability, most community leaders did not believe that Freedman and Lipski had so egregiously misquoted Isi Leibler. What was clear was that the battle between the brothers had been joined. Whatever Isi Leibler had actually said about Rabin, the fact was that he had come back to Australia and had challenged his younger brother's often-declared position that he could speak for the Jewish community on issues that affected Australia's relations with Israel and on any other issue that affected Australian Jews.

It is also unlikely that Mark Leibler believed that Freedman and Lipski had misquoted his brother. In recent months his relationship with his brother had become tense. Isi had become more and more emphatic about the supremacy of the ECAJ over any other community organisation, including the ZFA. He knew that Mark had better contacts in Canberra, especially with Paul Keating, than he had. Indeed, when Bob Hawke had left politics after his defeat by Keating, Isi Leibler lost much of his access to the Labor government—access that Hawke, his friend over many years, had always facilitated.

Much of Isi Leibler's anger about what he saw as his brother's challenge to his leadership of the Jewish community became focused on Helene Teichmann, by then seen as a lobbyist with unmatched access to government. Teichmann had been ZFA Executive Director for more than five years. She was totally loyal to Mark Leibler and thought that Isi's attempt to rein in his brother, to shut down his political work, which she had helped to develop on a wide range of issues, was laughable. Isi Leibler and Helene Teichmann did not like each other, to say the least. According to Sam Lipski, Teichmann had helped Mark Leibler transform the ZFA into a lobbying powerhouse. In the battle with his brother, she would play a key role. Isi also had someone working for him, but Lipski described Teichmann as unique—the best networker and lobbyist he had ever met.

Teichmann was not prepared to talk to me about Isi Leibler, at least not on the record. They were bitter enemies when the rift between the two brothers was at its height and, at one stage, Isi Leibler said wounding and ugly personal things about Teichmann, for which he was forced to apologise when she threatened to sue for defamation. After her initial refusal to revisit the dispute, Teichmann gradually opened up a little. After I noted that the two brothers were different, she replied:

> The difference between Mark and Isi when it came to political associations was that there were two strings to Mark's bow, so to speak. There was the professional thing, the fact that he was a renowned tax lawyer, which meant he could make contacts with Treasurers and Finance Ministers and he was a Jewish leader of standing at the same time. Isi had no professional expertise to offer.

I asked what her relationship with Isi was like when Keating became Prime Minister? "I am not going to talk about Mark's relationship with Isi." Your relationship with Isi Leibler? "My relationship with Isi Leibler was toxic."

The brawl between the brothers erupted publicly in April 1993, ostensibly over a meeting Teichmann had organised for Mark Leibler and a delegation of ZFA officials with her good friend, the newly appointed Immigration Minister, Nick Bolkus. By then, Leibler had attended meetings of ethnic community leaders that Teichmann had organised. The Keating government was considering the introduction of racial vilification legislation into the federal parliament and had circulated draft legislation for comment from interested groups. At public meetings, officials from the Attorney-General's department explained and discussed the proposed legislation.

The ECAJ and the ZFA made virtually identical submissions to the government. Both organisations had long advocated for such legislation; both urged the government to include criminal sanctions for extreme forms of racial vilification. But what mattered for Isi Leibler was not that he and his brother held virtually the same positions on the legislation; what mattered was that this was an issue for him to deal with, not his brother. The ECAJ, not the ZFA, spoke for the Jewish community on racial vilification and on anti-Semitism. He was now being cut out of lobbying on the legislation, actively undermined.

The Racial Hatred Act was passed in 1995, adding to the Racial Discrimination Act of 1975 its contentious Section 18C, which made it unlawful to offend, insult and humiliate or intimidate a person or group on the basis of colour, race or ethnic origin. (It was Section 18C that Prime Minister Tony Abbott sought to repeal in 2014 at the urging of conservative commentators, including Andrew Bolt who had fallen foul of the law for several columns he had written questioning the Aboriginality of a number of Indigenous activists. When Bolt asked Leibler to support the elimination of Section 18C, he of course declined. Bolt seemed unaware that Leibler had played an important role in getting the 1995 legislation passed and would never support the repeal of Section 18C, not even to support Bolt, who had always seen himself as a strong supporter of Israel, unlike the left-wingers who opposed any change to 18C.)

The 1995 legislation did not have criminal sanctions, as both the ZFA and the ECAJ had demanded; it was, nevertheless, a victory for Teichmann, who had organised the meetings of leaders of several ethnic communities—Greek, Italian, Chinese and Vietnamese, among others—that led to a unified position on the need for racial vilification legislation. Teichmann had also organised for these leaders to meet with Bolkus and with Opposition Leader Alexander Downer. At the meeting with Downer was one of his senior advisers, Graham Morris, who later became a key adviser to John Howard. At one stage, according to people who were there, the representative of the Vietnamese community spoke. No sooner had he started saying that the Vietnamese community was grateful for what Australia had given them than Morris interrupted him to ask why, if the Vietnamese were so grateful, was their leader there criticising Australia.

Helene Teichmann described what happened next: "Mark stood up, angry, furious really, and said 'what you have just said is disgraceful. This meeting will not go ahead until Graham Morris leaves the room.' He left the room." Asked about this, Leibler said that he clearly remembered how furious he was with Morris. He could not remember whether he had asked Morris to leave the room, but this was probably true, given how angry he was.

He had always made it clear, and he wanted it to be clear now, that Helene Teichmann had organised the meetings with ethnic community leaders in her own time and not as an official of the ZFA. Teichmann, when asked, confirmed that she had not sought her boss's permission to organise the meetings, nor had he driven the process in any way. He was invited simply as a Jewish leader and was happy to attend. It was in this context that Teichmann organised for the ZFA delegation to meet Bolkus in April 1993.

Whether or not Teichmann had acted for Leibler in organising the meeting with the ethnic community leaders really did not matter. Everyone, including Bolkus, knew how close she was to the ZFA president. When Bolkus met Leibler and two other ZFA executive members, she was there. It was clear to Bolkus that Leibler had been more active than any other Jewish community leader in the campaign for the proposed extension of the Racial Discrimination Act.

Immediately after the meeting, Leibler issued a press release declaring that the meeting with Bolkus had been warm and friendly, and that they had covered "areas of concern to the Australian Jewish community relevant to Senator Bolkus as Minister for Immigration and Ethnic Affairs and a member of the Cabinet." Leibler went on to say that Bolkus had expressed his support for the proposed racial vilification legislation and that he was "interested in the Zionist Federation of Australia's submission."

Leibler surely must have known how his brother would react to this. But Leibler had more to say about the meeting. In his media release, he said that he had discussed with Bolkus the problems with family reunification for Jews in distress, an issue that had been raised with Bolkus by the Jewish Welfare Society. Leibler had also raised the Jewish community's concern that the Holocaust denier, David Irving, would be granted a visa to come to Australia. Finally, "republicanism and the services to migrant communities were also raised."

CHAPTER 14

It did not take Isi Leibler long to respond to his brother's press release. More surprising were the public nature and vehemence of his response. In a press release from the ECAJ, Isi wrote that the ZFA had invited the ECAJ to join the delegation for the meeting with Bolkus, but that the ECAJ had, of course, refused; it could not be the junior partner in such a delegation and, anyway, on such issues the ECAJ preferred to deal with the government in its own right. The ECAJ would not "dilute its role as spokesman for the Jewish Community," Isi Leibler wrote. He went on to deplore what he described as "the politics of prestige," a barb clearly directed at his brother. "Now the Australian Zionist agenda has been broadened to include anti-Semitism, multiculturalism, welfare and immigration." However, the ECAJ would not endorse "public Zionist initiatives in the domestic arena which overlapped or conflicted with the primary role of the ECAJ nor would it accept invitations to join the ZFA when it unilaterally set up appointments with government ministers without prior consultations."

Mark Leibler's reply, published in the *Australian Jewish News* on 14 May 1993, significantly escalated the conflict: "Nothing could be more insulting, hurtful and personally offensive to a Jewish community leader than an allegation accusing him of engaging in 'the politics of prestige.' This is precisely the allegation levelled at me in the public statement issued by the ECAJ."

A separate letter signed by members of the ZFA executive, including Mark Leibler, accused the ECAJ—Isi Leibler, in other words—of sending the ZFA a number of

> extraordinary letters...sometimes letters of complaint; sometimes letters of demand; sometimes letters that were just plain sour grapes...We are deeply saddened by the fact that the ECAJ appears to have lost sight of its purpose which we assumed was to

advance the interests of the Jewish community...Whatever else, those interests cannot be served by petty sniping and griping over "form" rather than "substance"...Of one thing we can be certain—the enemies of Israel, Zionism and the Jewish people will be rejoicing at the ECAJ's embarking on this time-consuming, childish debate over who is and who is not, doing what.

In a letter published on 21 May in the *Australian Jewish News*, Isi Leibler said he would "disregard totally the hostility and personal abuse levelled against me." He went on to say that he had the support of every major community body in his fight with the ZFA, and that he took great umbrage at the suggestion that under his leadership the ECAJ had "lost its ability to act or speak on behalf of the Jewish people."

Inevitably, the dispute grew even more personal. Isi Leibler wrote at least two private letters to Mark that could not be found among his papers. When asked about the letters, Mark Leibler said only that he had not kept them and that he did not want to talk about them.

In response to Isi's letters to the *Australian Jewish News*, and perhaps also to the private ones, Mark Leibler wrote another letter to the *News*. He was "personally sickened, not only emotionally but also physically by the events of the last few weeks." He went on to accuse the ECAJ—meaning his brother—of embarking on a "public campaign to destroy the ZFA's standing and integrity simply because our record of constructive achievement was too good. The ECAJ's attempt to discredit the ZFA will not succeed."

Sam Lipski, Editor-in-Chief of the *Australian Jewish News* throughout the conflict, said that everyone knew that Helene Teichmann was advising Mark and that a former *News* journalist was writing the letters and press releases for Isi Leibler. Lipski said that both of them were very good at their jobs and that they, especially Teichmann, had become targets of the brothers' anger with each other. The increasingly ugly dispute dominated the letters' pages of the *News* for weeks. Most letters supported the ECAJ's claim that it, not the ZFA, spoke for Australian Jewry. In all probability, many of the letters were organised by the brothers. Asked about the fact that most letters favoured his brother, Mark Leibler said it did not worry him. He had the support of the ZFA executive and the officials of every state Zionist body.

Most of the letters were not personal attacks on either brother, with one notable exception. It came from Joe Gersh, then a senior partner at ABL and immediate past president of the Victorian Jewish Board of Deputies. According to Gersh, he lost the presidency because Isi Leibler, his long-time mentor and friend, had secretly withdrawn his support and backed another candidate when Gersh came up for re-election. In our interview, Gersh said he was so wounded by what he considered to be Isi Leibler's betrayal of him that he decided never again to be involved in Jewish community politics, or to put himself in a position that made him a target for what he saw as Isi Leibler's duplicity. In his "Open Letter to Isi Leibler", Gersh wrote:

> This public sniping has to stop. You were the one who started it. And you have to be the one to bring it to an end…
>
> What you must now admit is that despite your past achievements, many of which were extraordinary, and despite your own very considerable talents, you may not be the best person to resolve this impasse. In fact you may be the very worst…
>
> Admit it Isi, you set this agenda. You have always believed that government representation and media access are the be-all and end-all of Jewish public life…What is enraging you now is that you have been beaten at your own game. There is no question today that the ZFA's access and entree to the highest levels of government far exceed yours…Your belated decision to stand

for ECAJ president was the result of the fact that you could not otherwise gain access to Prime Minister Keating.

There is no room for your opponent-smashing confrontationist style. Our community is strewn with the lay and professional communal colleagues who have crossed your path and have been discarded by you.

You may not like it Isi, but the only obvious solution in the community's interest is for you to stand aside as ECAJ President.

Gersh's letter was personal, and brutal. Even Mark Leibler would have been made uncomfortable by it. Nevertheless, it spelt out what Mark Leibler's supporters believed—that this was a battle over access to government, for recognition as the main spokesman for the Jewish community, as well as a personal battle for power between the brothers. It was so fierce in part because Mark had surpassed his brother as a Jewish leader with access to the political class. It was Mark and not Isi who could talk to the Prime Minister and to several members of his Cabinet. And his confidante, Helene Teichmann, had helped open the doors for him to cabinet ministers such as Nick Bolkus.

The fight was bound to attract general media attention. The *Sydney Morning Herald* and *The Australian* published substantial feature articles on the warring brothers who were leaders in the Jewish community. Even the *Herald Sun*, in the paper's "Insider" column, written by the well-known business reporter Christopher Webb, noted:

Millionaire businessmen Mark and Isi Leibler are engaged in an extremely bitter struggle over which of the organisations they head represents the Australian Jewish Community…Some observers see the brawl as a classic example of sibling rivalry between the brothers who hold positions of great power within the Jewish community and, as well, operate their own very successful businesses.

Mark reckons he has been physically sick at the way the dirty linen of the ECAJ and the ZFA has been publicly aired.

When I interviewed him 25 years later, Sam Lipski agreed that the dispute had been particularly bitter because they were brothers and highly combative people. But Lipski said there was also a substantial issue at stake. It was about who speaks for the Jewish community. That question, he said, has never been resolved. In none of the several editorials Lipski wrote about the dispute did he refer to sibling rivalry. He saw the dispute as one of substance. There were real issues involved, even issues of principle. In one editorial, he wrote:

> The clash between the ECAJ and the ZFA is the most significant community clash within Australian Jewry for more than four decades. It must be resolved...There is much more to the dispute than the politics of personality. There are basic issues of community structure and leadership in the balance.

Lipski went on to write that "if you happen to believe in the idea of an Australian Jewish community" the structure mattered. In that case, you had to support the position that the ECAJ, as the organised peak body of Australian Jewry, spoke for the community on issues from welfare to education to issues about anti-Semitism and multiculturalism and immigration, "while maintaining a sympathetic and balanced attitude to Israel." The ZFA, he wrote, could and should not purport to speak for the Jewish community.

Twenty-five years later, Lipski said that he was more convinced than ever that the ZFA, or any Zionist organisation, should not speak for Australian Jewry:

> The basic principle remains and perhaps is even more important than ever: When it comes to lobbying government, it is not

Zionists who are doing the lobbying but Australian Jews, represented by a roof body that is not a Zionist organisation but a community-wide body that feels accountable to its constituents. I am happy with it to be called the Australian Jewish Lobby. It is not the Zionist Lobby. They are not there to lobby for a Zionist agenda. The Zionist Federation should be about education within the Jewish community, to bind the Jews in Australia to Israel through cultural activity and educational activity.

In today's world, if we want to defend and support Israel, we are strengthened by going as Australian Jews, not as extensions of the worldwide Zionist movement.

Asked what he meant by "today's world", Lipski said it was not about being ashamed of being a Zionist, but about the basis on which you are lobbying government, and representing whom, exactly? The Jewish Lobby, if that's what you wanted to call it, had to represent Australian Jewry, including Jews who may or may not define themselves as Zionists. In "today's world", conflating the words Zionist and Jew is problematic. The meaning of Zionist and Zionism is unclear and contested and, for some people, especially on the left, these are terms of abuse. For many people, the word, Zionist, is now synonymous with the word, Jew. And for many Jews, anti-Zionism is a euphemism for anti-Semitism. Given all this, Lipski argued, would it not be both more accurate and more in the interests of Australian Jews for bodies like the ZFA not to assert a right to speak for the Australian Jewish community, especially on issues that have no connection with Israel or Zionism? Even on Israel, Lipski said, a Zionist organisation should not speak on behalf of the whole Jewish community. The ZFA should confine itself to supporting the Zionist youth groups, organising Zionist education in the day schools and organising and funding the "birthright" visits to Israel by young Australian Jews.

When Lipski's views were put to him, Mark Leibler would have none of it, not even today, when he no longer occupies any leadership position in the Jewish community. For Leibler to accept Lipski's position, or his brother's position, would mean repudiating the years he had spent building up the lobbying muscle of the ZFA. More than that, to accept the Lipski position would mean, in his view, accepting the appalling notion that the word Zionist is a term of abuse and not to be used by Jews and Jewish organisations. That he will never do.

By the end of May 1993, the brothers had stopped talking to each other. At the time, they were neighbours, with only a fence separating their back yards. They still went to their mother's house for Shabbat lunch most Saturdays and sat in their reserved seats together for Sabbath services at the Mizrachi Synagogue, a short walk from their homes. No doubt these lunches and Saturday morning services were tense—not only for the brothers.

Rosanna Leibler had been close to Isi Leibler's wife, Naomi, but the dispute made it impossible to continue their friendship. The women stopped seeing each other. Rosanna spoke of the impact on family life:

> It was very upsetting for all of us, for Mark's mother in particular. She was a very powerful personality and she was very proud of her sons and what they had achieved and here they were fighting and fighting in public. For me, I was there for Mark and I suppose Naomi was there for Isi. It made it very hard for us.

She remembered the falling out between Mark and Isi as lasting for "a couple of years, maybe longer."

It lasted until Rachel Leibler intervened. At a Sabbath lunch, with the brothers there with their wives and children, Rachel called Isi and Mark away from the table and into her study. She told them that the fighting, at least the public fighting, had to stop. The Leibler name was being damaged. And above all, they were brothers and there could be no *broyges* (a Yiddish word that is hard to translate but means something like a serious falling out) between brothers. In front of their mother, Isi and Mark promised to stop their public conflict. Rosanna said that they did stop, "but it took time for them to get over what had happened. It took time for all of us."

Leibler did not enjoy talking about his falling out with his brother. He was worried how it would affect Isi, now in his 80s and living in Israel. And anyway, he and Isi were close, and their families were close, and whatever problems they had had in the past had long ago been resolved. I asked him whether he thought the issues they had fought over were resolved, to which he replied: "No. I mean our personal issues, they were resolved. We got over it. We were always close, and we were close again. And we are close to this day."

But what about the issues, were they resolved? "Well, I did not change my position. The ZFA continued to work the way it always worked when I was president. Nothing changed. I guess you could say that it was not formally resolved, but in practice, I did not change the way I worked as a Jewish leader."

When asked who won the fight, whether there was a clear winner, Mark answered, "I don't want to comment on this other than to say that in a sense, we were both losers and also winners. But however bitter the arguments, at no stage did they threaten our relationship as a family. On personal and family issues, we always had each other's back." I pointed out that some people say that he won simply because he, the younger brother, was the junior leader, and that, by Isi taking him on the way he did, Isi elevated Mark to an equal, but he would not comment on that.

In a phone call with Isi Leibler in Jerusalem, he told me that, at the time of the conflict with his brother, he was already occupied with international Jewish issues, principally with the Soviet Jewry movement, so he wasn't fully engaged with what was happening with his brother in the lead-up to the dispute between them:

> Frankly, I couldn't think too much about Mark or anything local. My business was in some stress and that too was taking up my time. I should have seen it coming. Mark and I always had this fundamental disagreement about the respective roles of the ZFA and the ECAJ. It became bitter because I had enemies, people I had ridden roughshod over on particular issues.

I asked him whether Helene Teichmann was important in the dispute. He replied, "Mark had one great lobbyist." He said that the falling out with his brother was "not one of the proudest moments of my life." Nor was it, he said, the proudest moment in his brother's life. He agreed that it could, however, be seen as the making of Mark as a national leader: "We were both losers, but he probably gained more because in the process he became a national leader more quickly than otherwise would have been the case."

In 1998, Isi Leibler made Aliyah, thus fulfilling what he saw as his destiny as a Jew and a Zionist, and settled with his family in Israel. By then his younger brother, now aged 55, was no longer president of the ZFA. He was president of the United Israel Appeal and chairman of a new body, the Australia/Israel & Jewish Affairs Council (AIJAC). He was unassailably the senior Jewish community leader in Australia, and increasingly important and active internationally as a Jewish leader. He was also one of the country's leading tax lawyers.

By this time Leibler had also embarked on a new path. He was becoming active in the fight for recognition and justice for Indigenous

Australians. The involvement was to grow over time and would transform him from a parochial Jewish politician into a more complex public figure, with reach and influence in Australian life that no other Australian Jewish leader, not even his brother Isi, has ever matched.

CHAPTER 15

In 1993, the human rights lawyer, Ron Castan QC, came to see Mark Leibler to ask whether ABL would take on an Indigenous land rights claim. It had been a year or so since Castan had led the legal team that had successfully argued the Mabo case before the High Court. The court's majority ruling had repudiated the long-held notion of Australia as *terra nullius*—a country with no law, or even people, before Europeans arrived in 1788—and had established native title based on the relationship of Indigenous people to their land. It was a landmark decision and Castan was advising the Keating government on its proposed native title legislation in response to it.

The Yorta Yorta people of north-central Victoria were the first to launch a native title claim, even before the Native Title Act was passed. In a report on racism in Australia that Castan had written for the Australian Human Rights Commission in 1990, he found that racism against Indigenous Australians was most virulent in the mid-Murray River region in northern Victoria and southern New South Wales. That area included Yorta Yorta country.

When Castan came to see him, Leibler knew virtually nothing about the Yorta Yorta case, or about Mabo and the Native Title legislation. He was aware that Castan, Ron Merkel and other Jewish lawyers had helped set up the Victorian Aboriginal Legal Service and were heavily involved in Indigenous legal battles, but he had no detailed knowledge of the issues. He had not given them much thought. Although he had developed a friendship with Prime Minister Paul Keating, Indigenous issues had not been a big part of it. Instead, they often discussed

Keating's push for a republic, his focus on the Asia–Pacific region and, from time to time, the state of Australian politics.

Castan asked Leibler and ABL to take on the Yorta Yorta case pro bono. He told him that the case might go for years, with appeals all the way to the High Court. Some of the firm's partners were concerned about the open-ended nature of the commitment and the likely cost; ABL was a commercial law firm, so what did it know about Indigenous people or constitutional law? Nevertheless, Leibler told Castan that ABL would take on the case and that ABL would stay with it, no matter how long it took to be resolved.

Leibler cannot remember why he agreed to this. Perhaps he had not truly appreciated what the commitment would mean. Around that time, Castan also proposed that ABL take on a young Indigenous lawyer, Noel Pearson, to do his articles at the firm. Leibler agreed to that as well. These two decisions were to have a profound effect on ABL and on the course of Leibler's life.

From the time Arnold Bloch first hung out his shingle in the early 1950s, ABL had always done extensive pro-bono work, nearly all of it for Jewish institutions, from schools to welfare bodies to community bodies like the ZFA. Leibler's commitment to Castan would change how lawyers who worked there regarded the firm; it would change the way some of the best and brightest young lawyers of the day came to see ABL as a firm for which they wanted to work.

In November 1993, ABL hired a young lawyer called Peter Seidel to lead preparation of the Yorta Yorta case. For the preceding three years, Seidel had been the associate of the acting Chief Justice of the Federal Court, Charles Sweeney. Seidel said that Sweeney had hired him because they had both been students at Christian Brothers colleges—Seidel in Box Hill and Sweeney in St Kilda. Seidel had always been passionate about Indigenous issues, especially in the law. In several interviews we conducted in an ABL boardroom, its walls hung with Indigenous art, Seidel was both self-deprecating and brimming with enthusiasm, so that it was easy to miss the evidence of his sharp mind:

> A Franciscan priest taught us Australian history at school in 1977 and I recall it was like a light bulb went off in my head. I remember he read us a chapter from a book about Captain Cook discovering Australia and he told us that this was a lie, this was not how Australia started, Australia started 40,000 years ago. I still remember him saying that. I wanted to be involved in some way, in my professional life, working with Aboriginal people.

Seidel heard about the position at ABL from a friend at the Aboriginal Legal Service in Victoria. He got the job and started work at ABL in November 1993. Some time passed before he actually met Leibler. When they met, Leibler said at the start that ABL was committed to the Yorta Yorta case and would provide whatever resources were needed, for as long as they were needed. Seidel's youth and relative inexperience seemed to be no issue.

The Yorta Yorta claim was lodged on 21 February 1994, one of the first lodged under the new Native Title regime. The excitement, the daunting challenges, the thrill of being given the work when he was so young, were still in Seidel's voice as he spoke of that time. He said that Leibler, never asked why the case was going so long or talked about costs; instead, "if I needed to talk to him, get some advice, he was always there."

The case dragged through the courts for five years. At first Seidel worked alone, then two junior lawyers were hired to join his team. At times, Castan gave Seidel advice on the law and on legal tactics. As it was one of the first native title claims under the Native Title Act passed by the Keating government in 1993, it was highly contentious. Interests opposed to the granting of native title ran scare campaigns suggesting that court decisions could lead to most of Victoria being handed over to Aborigines. At a press conference, Premier Jeff Kennett showed a map of Victoria with shaded areas that he said would be the subject of native title claims; they covered half the state.

In the end, over 500 parties registered their opposition to the Yorta Yorta claim. Seidel said that Leibler, nevertheless, maintained his commitment, even when it was clear that the Kennett government was furiously working to ensure the claim failed, and when it became clear that the case was likely to be lost in the first instance and would then have to be appealed, perhaps all the way to the High Court.

The Yorta Yorta claim was dismissed by Justice Howard Olney in the Federal Court on 18 December 1998. Famously, Justice Olney ruled that "the tide of history" had washed away any evidence that the claimants had an unbroken connection with traditional laws or observed traditional customs. In the appeal to the full bench of the court, Castan, briefed by Seidel, appeared for the Yorta Yorta claimants. The hearings were held over two days in August 1999. The court's decision to reject the appeal by a 2–1 majority was handed down on 8 February 2001. Ron Castan did not live to see the outcome of the appeal, having died in hospital from a golden staph infection following back surgery in October 1999. An appeal to the High Court was heard in May 2002 and dismissed by a 5–2 majority on 12 December of that year. The Yorta Yorta people had lost their almost decade-long battle to be granted native title over their traditional lands.

There was, however, one consolation. In May 2004, Victorian Premier Steve Bracks signed a co-operative management agreement with the Yorta Yorta elders that covered public land, rivers and lakes in north-central Victoria. The agreement gave the Yorta Yorta a say in the management of traditional country, including public land along the Murray and Goulburn rivers.

By 2004, Leibler was already committed to devoting significant time and resources to Indigenous issues. Among Indigenous leaders ABL was now widely recognised as a go-to firm. Seidel had been a partner for three years, in charge of the burgeoning pro-bono work, making him the first pro-bono partner at any Australian law firm. Some of the pro-bono work involved dealing with the legal affairs of Jewish organisations, such as the day schools and Jewish Care, which runs Jewish aged care homes. Some included legal work for the Zionist Federation of Australia and for the Australia/Israel & Jewish Affairs Council (AIJAC), the powerful lobbying group for Israel that Leibler chairs.

Over time, Indigenous rather than Jewish work has come to be the largest part of ABL's pro-bono commitments. Moreover, the work for Indigenous organisations led ABL to take on pro-bono work for environmental groups, such as the Australian Conservation Foundation and Greenpeace, and a range of charitable trusts and organisations. Today ABL is believed to do more pro-bono work as a percentage of its fee revenue than any other Australian firm. In 2018, ABL had revenue approaching $100 million and set aside about $4 million for pro-bono work. These pro-bono commitments give it a dimension far beyond its reputation as a commercial legal firm.

In 2008 ABL, in conjunction with the Kensington Community Legal Centre, lodged a racial discrimination claim on behalf of six young South Sudanese Australians who alleged that, over three years, police officers in the Melbourne suburb of Flemington had breached the Racial Discrimination Act by stopping and searching them because of their ethnicity. It took four years for the case to be settled, with Victoria Police admitting no wrongdoing, but agreeing to examine and change its procedures where necessary. Seidel said it had been a major test case. The racism that the young men had been subjected to was shocking. Racism against the South Sudanese was pervasive, he said. ABL, which was committed to fighting racism, had to take the case; "The outcome was important. The Victoria police did outlaw racial profiling and made changes to its police training. There are still problems of course. Look at how federal government ministers have sown fear in the general community about young Sudanese people."

Seidel, who has been with ABL for more than a quarter of a century, believes the pro-bono work brings "massive benefits" for the firm. As he put it,

> It's not so much about bringing us clients who like what we do, though that does happen. It's more that we attract outstanding young lawyers who want to work for a firm that does this sort of work. And I think our work permeates the whole culture of the place. People are proud to be working here.

One of these young lawyers is Nyadol Nyuon. She grew up in the huge Kakuma refugee camp in Kenya after her family fled Sudan during the civil war in the mid-1980s. The family spent almost 10 years in the camp. Nyuon had gone to primary school in Nairobi and was doing the final year of high school when the news came through that Australia had accepted them as refugees. She was 18 when she arrived with her mother and six brothers and sisters. The family lived in Dandenong, a suburb in Melbourne's outer southeast, and Nyadol, the eldest child, had to care for her siblings while she completed Victorian Certificate of Education at Hallam Secondary College. She completed an arts degree at Victoria University before she was accepted into the

Law School at Melbourne University. In 2013, she was the first South Sudanese woman to graduate in law from the university. She did a clerkship at ABL in 2014 and accepted a position the following year. Other firms had made offers, but a barrister who had mentored her during her study suggested she choose ABL, where she would work with some of Melbourne's best commercial lawyers. "I liked the ethos of ABL," Nyuon said. "It was a place where people understood that my background was different and that the challenges faced by South Sudanese Australians were big ones. I felt from the start that there was a lot of empathy."

No doubt one day Nyuon will write the story of her life: how her family escaped the fighting in Sudan, the horrors she witnessed, the trek for weeks to Kenya, her first experiences of Australia, the challenges she faced as a student and looking after her siblings while her mother went back to South Sudan for a long stay. It is clear that she is a remarkable figure. She is increasingly invited to appear in the media, an advocate for her community and fearless in calling out the racism that the South Sudanese community is forced to confront. She is articulate, passionate, yet measured, and smart, and if she wants it, she could be on the road to a political career.

However, as her public profile has grown, so has abuse on social media, some of it physically threatening, much of it misogynistic and racist. At times she has had to shut down her Twitter or Facebook account; at other times she has wondered whether she should just shut up. Once when she was having family problems and struggling to focus at work, her supervisor told her to go and see Leibler. Of that encounter, Nyuon said:

> I was initially concerned about what I was going to say when I first went to see Mark because we were not on the same platform

in terms of power. But he told me to not give up, to decide what I wanted to do, how much I wanted to be involved in the community aspect of things, and he said the firm would support me, whatever I decided. But he said "I hope your decision will not be influenced by the fact that people try and intimidate you. I know it's hard but we will be here for you." That mattered a lot to me.

In early 2018, after she had been on the ABC television program *The Drum*, she received an email from Mark's son, Jeremy, an ABL partner. He was in Israel at the time. She had been fiercely critical of the federal government, especially Home Affairs Minister Peter Dutton, who had made the implausible claim that people in Melbourne were frightened to go out to dinner because of violence by African youth. Jeremy Leibler praised her performance on TV and told her to hold the line. That email, Nyuon said, was "really good." In September 2019, she made *Australian Financial Review*'s list of the 100 most influential women.

CHAPTER 16

In 2000, Prime Minister John Howard asked Mark Leibler to become a director of the newly established Reconciliation Australia, which was to replace the Council for Aboriginal Reconciliation, created in 1991 by the Hawke government with cross-party support. When Howard made his offer, Leibler had given up his leadership of the major Jewish community organisations that had been such an integral part of his life. He had grown tired of the long, frequent and often boring meetings he had to attend as a leader in Jewish representative organisations, such as the Zionist Federation of Australia. He had completed six years as president of the United Israel Appeal. He was chairman of the Australia/Israel & Jewish Affairs Council (AIJAC), a position he had held since 1996 and still holds today. But apart from AIJAC, his leadership commitments were increasingly in international Jewish and Zionist organisations.

Howard's offer changed his life. Leibler had come to know several Indigenous leaders, Noel Pearson in particular, and, for a decade, he had encouraged and supported Peter Seidel's team at ABL, but he had never really thought about playing an active role in the Indigenous peoples' battle for recognition and justice.

Howard had known Leibler since they had first discussed the bottom-of-the-harbour tax issue in the early 1980s, when Howard was Treasurer. At the centre of their relationship was Howard's committed support for Israel, which he invariably described as the only democracy in the Middle East and a country that shared Australia's values. His government was probably Australia's most pro-Israel government in a long time. The two men's closeness is best illustrated by the fact that, on 14 April 2003, less than two weeks after the start of the second Iraq war, with Australian troops on the ground, Prime Minister Howard gave the keynote speech at the 50th anniversary celebrations of the establishment of ABL.

Howard's speech highlighted the way Leibler had been able to compartmentalise his public life. All his different roles, as a lawyer, Jewish leader and developing activist on Indigenous matters overlapped, fed into, and strengthened each other. In his speech, he said:

> I have known Mark Leibler for more than 20 years. I don't think in my life I have met a person with a keener intellect, a sharper sense of advocacy for the causes in which he believes…Mark has of course been strongly identified with the causes that are dear to Australian Jews. I have had a long association with the Jewish community of Australia of which I am unapologetically proud. I have found Mark a good counsellor…Also, I share a great admiration for the stoic way in which Israel has defended itself against constant attack and constant harassment.

Howard went on to praise ABL as a major Australian success story. Leibler had built a "very fine firm" that boasted a variety of clients and had made its mark not just in Melbourne but throughout Australia: "Can I thank you, Mark, and your firm, for the contribution that you have made to Australia. We are all more than anything else united by that great bond of affection for a very remarkable country."

When I spoke to him, Howard said that he, personally, had chosen Leibler to be a director of Reconciliation Australia because he thought Leibler would be a good fit for the organisation. He said he knew that Leibler had a commitment to "practical reconciliation", and that this was what Reconciliation Australia was all about. "I think Mark and I had broadly the same views—well, exactly the same views—about enhancing the opportunities and status of Aboriginal and Torres Strait Islander people. I was about getting a reconciliation process going to do practical things."

Leibler was to spend 10 years on the board of Reconciliation Australia, the last five as a co-chair with the Indigenous leader, Mick Dodson. If he and Howard had held, in Howard's words, the same views on Indigenous issues—that what was needed was "practical reconciliation", and that there was no need for an apology to the Stolen Generations—that was certainly not true by the end of Leibler's time at Reconciliation Australia. By then, he believed strongly in the rightness of an apology to the Stolen Generations and in constitutional recognition of the place of Indigenous people in Australian history. Howard's assumption was probably never true. He had simply made it based on what he thought was Leibler's politics.

Everyone who worked with Leibler on Indigenous issues agreed that his views were deeply held and uncompromising. Seidel said that, as long as he had known him, Leibler had never sought to minimise the impact of European settlement on Australia's Indigenous peoples. Unlike Howard, he had never believed that there was a misguided, "black armband" view of history. Seidel believed that Leibler, from the time ABL had got involved in the Yorta Yorta case, had always argued that history had to be acknowledged, and the injustices suffered by Indigenous Australians had to be urgently addressed.

People who worked with him at Reconciliation Australia, later on Gillard's Expert Panel, and even later when he co-chaired the Referendum Council, all described Leibler as blunt, impatient to get things done and determined not to waste time on trivial issues. He could be fierce when he thought someone had said something foolish. He never wanted public acknowledgement for his work; that should go to the Indigenous people who worked with him. These people all agreed that Leibler's political advice and contacts on both sides of politics were crucial to the workings of the bodies that he co-chaired.

Barbara Livesey, CEO of Reconciliation Australia from 2005 until 2010, the period that Leibler co-chaired the body with Mick Dodson, has fond memories of working with Leibler:

> I felt intimidated I suppose at first by Mark. He was forceful, clear, direct. Always wanted to get to the important stuff we had to deal with. His way was so different to Mick Dodson's way, which was slower. Mick liked to use silences. He wanted time to ruminate on things.

Livesey said that it took time for Leibler to understand that Dodson and the other Indigenous board members were not like him when it came to running meetings. He adjusted and worked closely with Dodson, and a friendship grew that lasted long after Leibler left Reconciliation Australia. Livesey soon lost the feeling that Leibler was intimidating. She said he was a listener, and very generous with his time:

> I could call Mark any time and no matter where he was—in the car, interstate, even in Israel—he would take the call or call me straight back. He was totally dedicated and passionate about the work we were doing. But what I saw was that he wanted no praise and no recognition. He used his connections to advance our agenda but he never made a big deal of it.

Leah Armstrong replaced Barbara Livesey as CEO in 2010, a few months before Leibler left to take up his appointment as co-chair, with Pat Dodson, of the Expert Panel on Constitutional Recognition of Indigenous Australians. Armstrong was well-known as an Indigenous leader when she took the job. Her family came from Boigu Island in the Torres Strait. She grew up in Mackay and later moved to Newcastle, where she worked for the Awabakal cooperative, which provides a sort of safety net of services for local Indigenous people. She helped to set up the Yarnteen Aboriginal and Torres Strait Islanders Corporation in Newcastle, running it for 19 years before joining Reconciliation Australia. She is now Director of the Wollotuka Institute at the University of Newcastle, which focuses on expanding and developing Indigenous education.

When Armstrong came to Reconciliation Australia in 2010, she had never met Leibler, but she knew Seidel. ABL had done the legal work for one of the businesses developed by the Yarnteen Aboriginal and Torres Strait Islanders Corporation. Armstrong said that, while Leibler and Mick Dodson were different in some ways, they were both very direct, blunt, people who said things straight. They set the agenda for the organisation. They wanted to engage the nation in a conversation about reconciliation, but they also wanted to turn good intentions into practical outcomes. Of the two men, she said:

> They had different perspectives I suppose. Mick Dodson was an Aboriginal man and he had first-hand experience of the things we were trying to address. And Mark had his perspective. There were great intellectual arguments at board meetings sometimes.

> But someone like Mark, who relates his experiences of being Jewish to the experiences of Indigenous people, could come close to being able to feel what Indigenous people were feeling.

Perhaps the organisation's greatest achievement during Leibler's decade as a director and co-chair were the Reconciliation Action Plans (RAPs), launched in 2008. The RAPs provide a framework for business, community organisations and schools, to help them participate in a practical way in the reconciliation process. Each organisation devises its own RAP and sets different goals. It might get involved with local Indigenous groups, provide services and funding for specific reconciliation projects, educate its workforce about reconciliation, or develop a program to provide employment opportunities for Indigenous people. Hundreds of businesses have signed on to RAPs, including the major banks and multinationals such as BHP. Leibler used his business contacts to approach big and small companies to sign on. Hardly any refused him. Leibler said it was not difficult to get business to sign on to a RAP; business in the main was ready to get involved in reconciliation.

When the RAPs were first launched, ABL was one of the first to sign on. Since then it has employed 10 Indigenous people—lawyers, paralegals and cadets—as part of its RAP commitment. Seidel said that, at any one time, two or three Indigenous people are working at ABL. Asked whether the decade that he spent as a director and a co-chair of Reconciliation Australia had changed him, Leibler said that it did not change his understanding of the injustices and racism that blighted the lives of Indigenous people. That understanding had developed after ABL took on the Yorta Yorta case and after Pearson joined the firm.

How was it, then, that until he was 50, Leibler had never thought much about Australia's Indigenous people? In their own country, where they had lived for thousands of years, they had been treated as strangers, outcasts, subjected to virulent—at times elimination-ist—racism. Leibler said that he was like many Australians of his generation; Indigenous Australia had been remote from his life. Like most Australians, he had never been forced to confront the destructive consequences of European settlement. He had not had to do so until relatively late in his life:

You know, we never learnt anything at school about Indigenous people and their history. I do remember reading books, which I found quite fascinating, about Dreamtime and that sort of thing, but I was just not conscious of, you know, Indigenous Australians.

I met people involved in the Yorta Yorta case and in other cases that Peter Seidel was running. They were people of great character and passion. I came to realise the extent of the injustice Indigenous people had suffered, how they had been scarred by racism and how they were still suffering. We were still failing them.

In 2010, Prime Minister Julia Gillard appointed Leibler to co-chair the Expert Panel on Constitutional Recognition of Indigenous Australians. Over time, they became friends, but when she appointed him, their relationship was in its infancy. Gillard had met Leibler at Jewish community functions over the years, but that was all. Gillard told me in an interview:

Obviously I knew that he was a senior leader in the Jewish Community. But I do very clearly remember Mark being in [Melbourne's] western suburbs, probably in my electorate, for the launch of a Reconciliation Action Plan at, I think, David Smorgon's business. I wasn't on the top of the Labor tree. I was there as the local member.

Gillard said that they sat together at the event and that, talking to him, she saw how committed he was to reconciliation. It was separate, she said, from anything to do with advocacy for the Jewish community.

The Expert Panel's members included Leibler's co-chair, Pat Dodson, brother of Mick Dodson, academic and writer Marcia Langton, leading Indigenous human rights lawyer Megan Davis and Noel Pearson. Shireen Morris, a constitutional lawyer and adviser to Pearson, describes a meeting of the Expert Panel in her 2018 book, *Radical Heart*, which focuses on the Indigenous battle for constitutional recognition:

> Noel would often arrive late for meetings, like a grumpy rock star. When Pearson talked, the room fell silent. The panel members strained to hear him…Even Leibler—who generally bossed everyone around, who barked orders at the bureaucrats and who many years prior, was mentor and teacher to the young Pearson who had done his articles at ABL—deferred to Pearson's superior intellect.

When the Expert Panel was formed, Pearson had had very little to do with Reconciliation Australia. Without spelling it out, Pearson indicated that it was not work that particularly interested him. Barbara Livesey recalled a rather heated argument between Leibler and Pearson about some aspect of Reconciliation Australia's work. Pearson, she said, had argued that reconciliation was not the main game for Indigenous people. What was needed was constitutional change—not just some token preamble to the document recognising that Indigenous Australians were the nation's first people, but a genuine voice, enshrined in the Australian Constitution, that would give them some control over their destiny. After a decade with Reconciliation Australia, Leibler had moved a long way towards Pearson's position. He had come to believe that the Constitution had to be changed in a substantive way.

In 2013 the Expert Panel produced a report that set out a number of possible changes to the Constitution that would, in the panel's view, not only recognise the place of Indigenous people in Australian history and their special needs in contemporary Australia, but would remove clauses from the Constitution that some legal experts considered racist. Within days of the panel handing its report to Gillard, she was replaced as Prime Minister by Kevin Rudd, whose government lost the 2013 election. Despite the new prime minister's professed friendship with Pearson over many years, Tony Abbott's government never considered the report.

In December 2015, under a new prime minister, Malcolm Turnbull, the idea of constitutional change was revived. Leibler was appointed co-chair, with Pat Dodson, of the Referendum Council on Constitutional Recognition of Aboriginal and Torres Strait Islander People. It was set up jointly by Turnbull and Opposition Leader Bill Shorten, in a bid to achieve bipartisan support and given the task of coming up with constitutional amendments that could be put to the people in a referendum.

Pearson was appointed a member of the Referendum Council. He had never been an easy member of any organisation, as he could be volatile and passionate, and sometimes very angry. Pearson and Pat Dodson were not best friends; at times Leibler, who was close to both men, had to mediate between them, both on the Expert Panel and on the Referendum Council. Pearson had concluded that no tinkering with the Constitution would meet the needs of Indigenous people. Instead, he and other Indigenous people developed the idea of an Indigenous advisory body that would be secured through a constitutional amendment. The body would examine and advise federal parliament on any legislation and other decisions that affected Indigenous people. Embedding such a body in the Constitution would mean that no government could abolish it.

Some members of the Referendum Council did not immediately warm to Pearson's idea, and Pat Dodson was one of them. Leibler did warm to the idea, however. He quickly concluded that Pearson's plan was superior to any of the proposed constitutional amendments being considered by the Referendum Council, or to any that had been recommended by the Expert Panel that Leibler had co-chaired with Pat Dodson.

Marcia Langton had worked closely with Leibler on the Expert Panel. She had known him before that, when ABL had done legal work for Indigenous projects in which she had some involvement. Like Leibler, Langton eventually came to support the idea of a constitutionally mandated body that would advise the national parliament on Indigenous issues. Asked about her experience of working with Leibler, Langton said that he had been a terrific supporter of a number of Aboriginal artist groups and other projects with which she had been involved:

> He was very kind, always. He hosted a number of fundraising lunches and he would bring influential people in so that they could begin to understand what we were trying to achieve. He would always get straight down to business. With the Expert Panel, he would put on a lunch, chair the meeting, guide the meeting, ask pointed, critical questions. He was businesslike, supportive, immensely understanding and, you know, always well briefed on the issues. But he was always so humble, never asking for anything for himself, for acknowledgement for what he was doing.

Asked whether she ever wondered where his commitment to Indigenous issues had come from, Langton replied:

> Well he did say to me once and sadly I disagreed with him, but I later realised that he was right, that his own history, being Jewish, gave him a great understanding of the genocide of Indigenous people and you know, there's no question that it did. When I was younger, I thought nobody else could really understand the Aboriginal predicament, but, you know, I've changed my mind about that. Mark understood.

He had sympathy for Indigenous people? "Sympathy is the wrong word to describe his engagement. I learnt something about Jewish… let's not call it philanthropy, but you know willingness to contribute to Australian social and cultural life." Leibler's Jewishness, she said, had informed and inspired his commitment to the work of transforming the lives of Indigenous Australians.

In 2016 and 2017, the proposal for an Indigenous advisory body to be included in the Australian Constitution was endorsed at meetings of Aboriginal people across the country. It was the biggest consultation process ever undertaken in Indigenous communities. Leibler was at Uluru in central Australia in May 2017, when Indigenous represent- atives overwhelmingly adopted the Uluru Statement from the Heart, which called for the establishment of an Indigenous advisory body in the Constitution. He was very moved and proud of Pearson and of the other Indigenous leaders he had worked with over the years. It had taken him some time to come on board with the idea at the centre of the Uluru Statement, but, once he concluded that it was the genuine expression of the hopes and demands of Indigenous Australia, he became one of its most ardent supporters.

Leibler is a pragmatist, not a dreamer. He thought that the advisory body proposal, which had been developed with the advice of conserv- ative constitutional lawyers such as the federal Liberal MP, Julian Leeser, was not radical and had the best chance of receiving bipartisan support—essential for the constitutional referendum to succeed. In this matter, however, he was to be proved wrong.

In late October 2017, Indigenous leaders presented Prime Minister Turnbull with the Uluru Statement from the Heart and the proposal for a constitutionally mandated Indigenous advisory body. Almost immediately, Turnbull rejected the proposal for an advisory body.

He argued that the proposed Indigenous body would become a "third chamber" of parliament and that a referendum to amend the Constitution to establish such a third chamber could never succeed. He did so in spite of the fact that former High Court Chief Justice Murray Gleeson was on the Referendum Council and supported the Uluru Statement, as had a number of conservative constitutional lawyers that Pearson had consulted. Many Canberra observers considered Turnbull's decision to be a desperate attempt to appease his conservative opponents in the government. Leibler was disappointed. He was furious. The idea that the Uluru Statement was about creating a third chamber of parliament for Indigenous people was, to use Leibler's word, "ridiculous".

I spoke to John Howard after the Turnbull government had rejected the Expert Panel's report. I asked him when he realised that he and Leibler did not share identical views about Indigenous issues. He replied:

> Over time, there wasn't one moment. His position on many issues probably changed over time. I think he always supported practical reconciliation. Still does I am sure. But on other things—the need for an apology, what constitutional recognition should entail—we are not on the same page. He has gone further on these issues than I was prepared to go. We talked about it often and we talked about Noel Pearson and Pearson's approach to me to see whether we could agree about constitutional recognition for Aboriginal people. Mark had input on that. It did not work out for various reasons.

I asked Howard whether he was surprised how far from his position Leibler had travelled. "When it comes to respect for minorities," he replied, "it is very understandable that a Jewish person of high intellect like Mark should always be alive to the needs of Aboriginal people, so in that sense, it does not surprise me." Howard recollected a lunch he had with Leibler when he was no longer prime minister. Leibler had tried to persuade Howard to make a statement on the need for constitutional recognition for Indigenous Australia beyond a preamble to the Constitution. Howard was not keen on going beyond a preamble, which remains his position. He had supported Turnbull's rejection of the Uluru Statement, and said that he expected that Leibler was very disappointed with Turnbull. Leibler would never say so, but perhaps he was disappointed with John Howard as well.

CHAPTER 17

He spoke for an hour with no notes at all. At times he spoke so quietly it was hard to hear what he was saying; at other times his voice soared, angry, accusing, and then less angry, as he exhorted his listeners again to act, not just be bystanders. The speech was not linear in structure but moved in loops, backwards and forwards, pausing to tell an anecdote and then soaring rhetorically, demanding, pleading, almost praying. The audience listened in absolute silence. Noel Pearson was mesmerising.

About 250 people were in the hall on the campus of Methodist Ladies College in the middle-class Melbourne suburb of Kew on this October night in 2018. Perhaps half of them were young members of the Australasian Union of Jewish Students; the rest were mostly older people, many of them Jews, who had come to hear Pearson speak. Pearson set out what Indigenous people had decided almost unanimously at Uluru in May 2017. Their call to the rest of Australia is recorded in the Uluru Statement from the Heart—proclaim an Indigenous advisory body through an amendment to the Constitution.

Pearson described how, within hours of the Statement being delivered to him, Prime Minister Malcolm Turnbull summarily dismissed it as creating a third chamber of parliament specifically for Indigenous people, and how Turnbull's successor, Prime Minister Scott Morrison said that he could not support it for exactly the same reason. Former prime minister Tony Abbott had also rejected the proposed Indigenous body.

Pearson said that the time had come for everyone in the hall and outside who believed that these things were important to go beyond verbal support and to demand change. He pleaded for Indigenous people not to be forgotten. Australia, he said, had been built on three things: its Indigenous foundation, its British institutions, and its multicultural present and future. He illustrated his point with three hand gestures that he said his young son had given him. Pearson's fists then joined to form the Indigenous foundation of the country. His fingers made a roof to show the British institutions on which the society was based. Finally, he gently interlaced his fingers to show a multicultural nation coming together. Not a soul in the hall stirred.

On a stand a few metres away from where Pearson delivered the Zelman Cowen Oration was a poster, at the top of which was a photograph of a grey-haired Indigenous man, a Yorta Yorta man. Below the photograph was a timeline of William Cooper's life and struggles as a leader of his Indigenous community. Below the large photograph of Cooper was another of him in front of the German Consulate in Melbourne on 6 December 1938. He is with a group of Indigenous men and women, holding in his hand a petition bearing signatures he had collected from Indigenous and non-Indigenous people. The petition condemned the "cruel persecution of the Jewish people by the Nazi Government of Germany" and demanded that the Nazis stop persecuting the Jews of Germany. It was a month after Kristallnacht—the Night of Broken Glass—during which scores of Jews across Germany were murdered and hundreds of Jewish businesses were vandalised. This Indigenous protest, led by 77-year-old Cooper, was the only private protest anywhere in the world against what the Nazis perpetrated on Kristallnacht.

During his oration, Pearson referred often to the Yorta Yorta elder, whose traditional land straddled the Murray River, who in 1887, at the age of 27, was one of the first Indigenous leaders to campaign for land rights and for recognition of Aborigines as the former occupiers of the land. While he spoke of Cooper's life and leadership and of how he had inspired generations of Indigenous leaders, Pearson referred to Cooper's protest outside the German Consulate only in passing. There was no need to dwell on it; much of his audience knew what Cooper had done.

In 2002, a plaque had been unveiled at the Holocaust Museum in Melbourne in honour of Cooper and his fellow protesters from the Australian Aboriginal League. Six years later, the Israeli Ambassador to Australia had presented Cooper's grandson, Uncle Alf (Boydie) Turner, with a framed certificate to mark the planting of 70 Australian trees in Israel in Cooper's honour. In 2009, five more trees were planted at the Forest of the Martyrs near Jerusalem in Cooper's honour and 12 members of his family were there for the planting. And in 2010, the Chair of Resistance Studies at the research centre of Yad Vashem, the Holocaust museum in Jerusalem, was named the William Cooper Chair.

The text on the poster beside Pearson recorded that, in 2012, Turner led a re-enactment of the 1938 Indigenous protest. In 1938, the German Consul General had refused to accept the petition from Cooper; this time, the Consul General was waiting outside the consulate to invite the delegation in. He accepted the copy of the original petition and apologised for the treatment of Cooper and his delegation. The protest outside the German Consulate in 1938 and its re-enactment in 2012 was a redemption story. It expressed a faith that, even in the darkest times, there were people who acted with courage, and with a sense of shared humanity with those whose humanity had been denied. Pearson did not need to spell this out. The connection between the Jews and Cooper's people was implicit in everything that he said.

Pearson also described how Cooper had continued his struggle for Indigenous rights, even when it was clear that no state or federal government would contemplate transferring land to Indigenous communities. For all his tireless advocacy, Cooper had achieved nothing concrete when he died in 1941. In June 2018, the Australian Electoral Commission announced that the Victorian federal seat of Batman would be renamed Cooper. This was a fitting recognition of Cooper and his struggle for Indigenous rights, yet the long campaign for Indigenous recognition in the Australian Constitution had not yet been won.

Pearson said that when he became downhearted about the campaign for Indigenous recognition, as he often did, he would remember Cooper's struggle, how hard and long it had been. He also acknowledged the presence at the oration of Boydie Turner, who stood and raised an arm as the audience stood and applauded at length.

Towards the end of the oration, Pearson said that he wanted to acknowledge the presence that evening of the family of the late Ron Castan, who had been involved in every significant Indigenous land rights case through the 1990s until his death in 1998. Pearson met Castan when he was a law student at Sydney University and had created the Cape York Land Council in his rented room in Balmain. Castan, Pearson said, had been one of two mentors who had significantly influenced the direction of his life. He had been profoundly influenced by Castan, not just as far as the law was concerned, but about how to live a good and ethical life. He said that not a day passed when he did not think about Ron Castan.

The other mentor Pearson wanted to acknowledge was Mark Leibler, who was in Israel and couldn't attend the oration. Pearson spoke of how much Leibler had influenced the trajectory of his life, from the time he had done his articles at ABL at the prompting of both Castan and Paul Keating. Castan saw ABL as a reasonably conservative firm that would offer Pearson a good grounding in various areas of the law.

He was concerned that Pearson have the option of making his way as a lawyer, earning decent money and able to make a comfortable life for himself, if that was what he wanted. Leibler, Pearson said in his speech, had taught him many things, too many to list, but the one he wanted to acknowledge was about power. Lowering his voice to a whisper, as if he was letting the audience in on a secret, he said, "Power, he taught me about power. How to get it and how to use it."

When I met Pearson at his Melbourne hotel the day after he gave the Zelman Cowen Oration, he was sitting at a table by the window of the hotel's foyer with Shireen Morris. A constitutional lawyer, Morris later ran in the 2019 federal election as the Australian Labor Party's candidate for Deakin in Melbourne's outer eastern suburbs, but failed to defeat the sitting member, Michael Sukkar. In her 2018 book, *Radical Heart*, Morris writes about how her family's Indian and Fijian background shaped her life and played a part in her role as an advocate for Indigenous recognition in the Constitution. She also writes about Melissa Castan, Ron's daughter, who had been her constitutional law lecturer at Monash and was deputy director of Monash University's Castan Centre for Human Rights Law, named after her father. Morris describes Melissa as "a human rights guru" who had taught her about Indigenous rights and had encouraged her to apply for a fellowship at the Cape York Institute, where she has now been a policy advocate for seven years and has become one of Pearson's closest associates. Pearson, who helped establish the Institute, became her mentor, although he has said that he learnt more from Morris than she learnt from him.

After Morris left, we moved to a small table near a window in the hotel's coffee shop. Morris would make a great member of parliament, he said. The ALP was lucky to have her as a candidate. There was a sadness in his voice. Pearson had wanted pre-selection as an ALP candidate for a seat in Victoria, and if not in Victoria, somewhere in New South Wales, but apparently ALP leader Bill Shorten had not been keen on the idea.

Pearson spoke for some time, first about Leibler, then about Jews and the Jewish community. He measured his words carefully. As in his speech the night before, his voice rose and fell depending on what he was saying, on whether he was describing a memory, elucidating a position on the Jews and what Indigenous communities could learn from the Jewish community, or what he had learnt from Leibler. Pearson spent three years at ABL, before leaving in 1998. He smiled when he said that he never actually practised law when he was at the firm, that Leibler had known from the start that Pearson was there to learn about leadership and power and how to form relationships with seemingly conservative lawyers and their clients. That was why Ron Castan had urged him to go to ABL, rather than to a law firm with connections to the ALP:

> At ABL, I was exposed to conservative ideas by some of the senior lawyers and I was taken around to meetings with Jewish families and Jewish business leaders. It was an education.
>
> When ABL got involved in the Yorta Yorta case and other Indigenous cases, I saw that once Mark gave his blessings, ABL would go into bat and you then had a big force behind you. I could see that in the dealings with Jewish businesses and Jewish families, ABL was a mighty force and it was a mighty force in its Indigenous pro-bono work.

Pearson said that when he met Leibler for the first time, he noticed Leibler's striking presence. He exuded power. At the beginning, Pearson was overawed, even frightened of him. How long did that last? "Forever, to a certain extent. He was immediately a sort of role model, someone

I knew I could learn a lot from. And I did learn a lot and I still learn a lot from him."

Pearson described Leibler as a father figure. His own father had died when he was 23 and, after that, Pearson felt like he was alone and that everything he did, he did on his own. That was until Castan came into his life and later, Leibler. "Ron was a source of brightness to me and more gentle. Mark, he was harder. He was a gentle man at heart but he spoke hard, very very hard," Pearson said of the two men.

Asked whether Leibler was hard on him, Pearson's reply was:

> Oh, he was. He was unequivocal about his advice in relation to discipline. "Return calls, return calls," he would tell me. "That's the business of being a lawyer and a leader." He sensed a reck-lessness in me and a reticence to seize the opportunity or the moment, to use power, to presume its existence and use it. And I would see the way he operates, you know, careful, but playing on the power. It wasn't just an internship about the law for me. It was really about learning from his role in the Jewish community and his political role, how to exercise power.

Pearson said he had come to understand that Leibler was a special sort of leader, with an orthodox grounding in Judaism, who was able to make a great contribution to the general community.

As Pearson spoke, it became apparent that, like Langton, he saw Leibler's passion for Indigenous justice and constitutional recognition as coming in large part from his understanding of what it meant to be a Jew, and from the exhortation, repeated often in the Torah, that the Jews must never forget that they were once slaves and strangers— outsiders. He spoke of what he had learned:

> I knew virtually nothing about the Jewish community when I first joined ABL. I had friends and mentors who were Jewish,

lawyers like Ron Castan and their families, but that was not the same as getting to know a Jewish leader like Mark, and through him and through working at ABL, getting to know the Jewish community.

It became a model for me for what Indigenous communities could become. How we could transcend being victims, understand our history but not be trapped by it, not be mired in victimhood. Take control of our future.

At ABL I did a lot of thinking about victimhood and about history, and the thing that fascinated me about the Jewish community was how people who have been so victimised nevertheless have not developed a sense of victimhood. I think that's the trap we fell into and that many groups who are victimised fall into, the trap of turning victimisation at the hands of other people into your own sense of victimhood. I thought a lot about this, how we should never allow history to be denied, but at the same time, never stop engaging with the future. I think the Jewish community gets it right.

I also learnt that in the Jewish community people like Mark are central to maintaining the cultural communal heart, that to maintain that heart, you have to have Orthodox defenders, leaders, upholders of faith. They make it possible for the Jewish community to be cosmopolitan and outward looking and engaged in the general community.

After our conversation ended, I thought about Pearson's observations. If he was right that Australia's Jews had refused to be defined by victimhood, why was that so? Herman Wouk had in the mid 1980s observed a community of people who had been through unimaginable suffering and then, almost immediately, had experienced the miracle of resurrection in the birth of Israel. This was something that the American Jewish community, from which he came, had not experienced. That community was mostly third- and even fourth-generation Americans, their grandparents and great grandparents having migrated to America in their hundreds of thousands from Russia and Eastern Europe in the late 1880s and in the first decade of the 20th century. Although thousands of Holocaust survivors did make it to America after World War 2, they were a small minority in the community.

Still, Wouk's explanation for what was special about the Australian Jewish community is only part of the story. Amongst the refugees and survivors who made it to Australia after the war were men and women who had been leaders in the large, now extinguished, Jewish communities of Eastern Europe. Some, like Abraham and Rachel Leibler, had been leaders of Zionist organisations before the war. Others like Bono Weiner had been leaders in Poland of the Bund and its youth organisation, SKIF. There were many others and these people inspired the next generation of leaders, some of whom, like Isi and Mark Leibler, were their children.

Whatever their shortcomings, they were outstanding leaders because they had refused to give in to despair. They had led politically active lives, with belief systems and hopes that they never abandoned, and they set about rebuilding in Australia the organisations that the Nazis had destroyed. They inspired the remnants of Eastern European Jewry who had escaped the Nazis and washed up in faraway Australia to follow them and to help rebuild, as far as possible, what had been lost. They remained believers—in Zionism, Bundism or Judaism—and they transmitted their belief to their fellow survivors and to their children. No doubt, many of the Jews who managed to get to Australia had been traumatised, and that trauma stayed with them for the rest of their lives and affected the lives of their children. But, as a community, because of the things that Wouk saw, because of the quality of the Jewish leadership, and critically, because Australia had none of the anti-Semitic history of Europe, the Jews of Australia were able to move beyond their trauma and their victimhood.

Noel Pearson, a singular Indigenous leader, had sensed all this. From when he was a student, Pearson was engaged in the hard intellectual and practical work of trying to find ways to integrate Indigenous traditions, ideas and beliefs with the ideas and traditions of Australia's European heritage, which he considered his heritage as well. The Jews, he came to believe, showed how this could be done, and how important it was for Indigenous people to become actors in their own destiny, to refuse to be put in the box of victimhood. Indigenous people had to become empowered, control their destiny. Pearson has long been critical of the left's tendency to treat Indigenous people as essentially victims and thus to disempower them. That view helped to explain why Pearson came to believe that Indigenous leaders had to reach out to those on the conservative side of politics and not just to those on the left. Without their support, constitutional change and true reconciliation would be impossible.

Asked about Pearson, Leibler remembers the first time they met. He saw Pearson's brilliance and charisma straightaway. "He was so passionate and so articulate. He was a force of nature." Leibler thought that he could have a great future in the law. He also thought Pearson would make a great politician, even the first Indigenous prime minister, if that was what he wanted. He noted that "he had a chance to get into politics when Keating was prime minister, but Noel didn't want it then, he wanted to be a leader of his community. Now it might be too late."

I asked how quickly Leibler came to know that the relationship between the pair would be so significant, and that Leibler would become a mentor for Pearson, to which he replied: "Well I am not sure whether I was his mentor or he was mine, but I knew quickly that he would be an important person in my life. Particularly when it came to understanding Indigenous affairs. We spent a lot of time talking to each other."

Peter Seidel believes that Pearson's arrival at ABL affected Leibler in a very personal way. Their connection became, and still is, a father–son relationship, according to Seidel. Pearson has a well-earned reputation for being volatile, quick to lose his temper, but "never with Mark as far as I know," Seidel said:

> You know, from the start, Mark spoke his mind. He was blunt. He calls it as it is. Some of us are guilty of being over-sensitive with Indigenous people. Not Mark. And I think Noel loved that about Mark. I think there was—and still is—love between them. I know there is.

When I told Leibler that Seidel thought there was love between him and Pearson, he reddened. He was embarrassed. I had never seen him like that. Then he said: "I have and always have had, great respect for Noel, for his intellect for instance and how he has grown as a leader. We are close, that's true." Leibler found it hard to talk about himself. Seidel's comment about the love between Leibler and Pearson made him uncomfortable, as if it opened up something about him that he did not want opened. Glimpses of his inner life emerged only occasionally. Yet one came in another story that Seidel told about the role of William Cooper in Leibler's commitment to Indigenous causes relatively late in his life:

> After we lost the High Court appeal, Rob Hulls, the Victorian Attorney-General, said he wanted to meet with Monica Morgan and Uncle Henry Atkinson, who had been the leaders of the

Yorta Yorta claimants. Well, Monica and I and Mark and Uncle Henry went up to see Hulls in a taxi from ABL. It was a really packed car.

Mark mentioned that he had just read in the *Jewish News* a little article about William Cooper and what Cooper had done in 1938. Mark was very excited about this. And Monica just said, "He was my grandfather." Mark said, "You helped us in our time of need, and we're here for you for as long as it takes." It was palpable, the feeling that Mark was deeply moved by what William Cooper had done.

CHAPTER 18

Portland House is how you'd imagine the headquarters of one of Melbourne's old establishment businesses might look. It is at the top end of Collins Street, not far from the Melbourne Club, long the club of choice for Melbourne's old money. This end of Collins Street—the so-called Paris end—five tram stops away from ABL's office at 333 Collins Street, still has a good number of the old Victorian and Edwardian buildings built when Melbourne was flush with money in the aftermath of the Victoria's gold rush of the 1850s and 1860s. The three-storey Victorian building has a thick, highly polished, wooden front door. No plaque or sign indicates what is inside. The high-ceilinged interior is painted in pastel colours. A spiral staircase goes all the way to the third floor; there are no lifts. After reporting to the receptionist on the first floor, you go up the carpeted stairs to be met by a young woman who leads you through a reception area with antique chairs, an old but immaculate armchair and a small polished wooden coffee table. Past an office with a large antique wooden desk and what looks like an antique sideboard, is a room with book-lined walls and soft furnishings, and, beyond that, a small alcove with two chairs on either side of a polished wooden table. It was there that I met David Hains.

Hains, now in his late 80s, has owned Portland House since 1964, about two decades before he established the Portland Group and built it into one of Australia's largest funds management empires. The Hains family is number 21 on the *Australian Financial Review*'s 2018 Rich List, its wealth estimated—some people believe underestimated—at $2.69 billion. Hains gives few, if any, interviews; none come up in a

Google search. On the day we met he was wearing a dark-blue sweat-shirt and blue trousers with an elastic waist. He offered tea, which the young woman went to fetch, bringing back a teapot, bone china cups and saucers and a small jug of milk. Hains made sure that everything sat on a coaster. He was careful and considered in what he had to say and softly spoken, as if he wanted the conversation to be private. There were no plaques or photographs in the room of any of Hains' horses winning major races. The walls had no displays of his life and achievements.

Hains is best known as one of Australia's most successful breeders of racehorses, the champion Kingston Town among them. Kingston Stud at Merricks, an hour and a quarter drive from Melbourne in Western Port, is one of his great passions and he spends as much time there as possible. Now that he has handed control of much of the Portland Group to three of his sons, he has more time to devote to his other great passion, golf.

He has known Mark Leibler for close to 25 years, ever since he went to see him when Hains was in a battle with the Australian Taxation Office over demands that he furnish financial information about his companies and investments over a seven-year period. He had sought a declaration in the Federal Court that the notices were not authorised by the tax laws and therefore invalid. But one way or another, Hains knew that he faced being audited by the ATO. Someone had suggested that he see Leibler, a lawyer he knew by reputation only. He'd had some dealings with one or two of ABL's clients. He tells a story of how he was about to buy a block of flats on Queens Road in Albert Park in inner Melbourne when he discovered that the seller was one of ABL's well-known Jewish clients. Hains withdrew from the sale. He figured that if this guy was selling, he must have a good reason. This man was too smart to be handing him a bargain.

Hains had first consulted other lawyers and accountants about how his tax issue should be handled, but he found the advice hedged and unclear. That's when he decided to see Leibler. From the moment they met, he found Leibler to be a man who did not waste time on niceties but gave advice as succinctly and clearly as possible. Hains said that Leibler was sensible about how to deal with the ATO, and remained so for the nine years it took for the dispute to be settled, when "everybody went home sort of happy."

As a result of that case, ABL, and Leibler in particular, became the Portland Group's lawyers, not just on tax but on a range of corporate issues. At the start, Leibler dealt with Hains almost exclusively. Other ABL lawyers would eventually do work for the Portland Group, but always with Leibler overseeing it. Leibler became Hains' personal lawyer as well and, over time, the two became friends.

For more than 20 years, Leibler has been a member of the board of the Portland Group, which consists of several private companies. The other members of the board are Hains and his five children. Leibler attends every quarterly board meeting, which reviews the Portland Group's property holdings, equities, fixed interest investments and managed funds, in Australia and internationally. Leibler still handles all the group's tax issues, but his role has expanded to include all its corporate issues as well.

Hains described Leibler as being like a member of his family:

> He knows all my children. We have lunch together once a month or so. We occasionally socialise together but not so much at big functions. He and Rosanna have visited the stud several times. At our lunches, we talk about politics and sometimes we talk about family issues. We talk about the world in general but our interest in each other is not just business. Family is very important, too.

CHAPTER 18

One reason Leibler knew the Hains children so well was because he had been a key adviser to Hains on what Leibler called estate planning—the best way for Hains to transfer the running and ownership of the Portland Group to his children. Leibler did not decide how much of the Portland Group should be transferred to the children and in what proportions; those were decisions for Hains to make, yet even on these intensely personal and often fraught family issues, Hains had sought Leibler's advice:

> We have this arrangement where my children have as much say in these things as I do, and Mark has a say, too, and we get the benefit of his wide experience in these things. He's good to talk to. He has helped in the sense that sometimes I am too personally involved with my children and sometimes when I am angry about a particular issue I'll talk to Mark and he'll bring a balance to what's happening. And sometimes he'll talk to the kids if he thinks it could help. He brings that sort of external influence on all of us, to some degree.

I asked whether passing on his business to the next generation was one of the biggest challenges Hains had had to face:

> Oh, absolutely. And I think I have handled that well. We don't expect the grandchildren to come into the business. They will go their own way. They will get some help but they won't inherit huge amounts. My children are well off but they won't inherit the business. Three of them will run the business, they run it now, but no single child will control it. Mark has been important in this arrangement.

Over the past 20 years, and particularly over the past decade, an unprecedented generational transfer of wealth has taken place among Australia's wealthiest people. It has gone largely unreported. Fortunes worth billions of dollars, in some cases, have been passed on from the pre-baby-boomer generation to the baby boomers and from the baby boomers to their children.

Given the nature of his clients, especially the long-term Jewish clients who came to ABL as recently arrived migrants or refugees and had built business empires of great wealth, and had then grown old and were thinking about how to pass on their fortunes to their children, it was inevitable that Leibler would become one of Australia's foremost estate planning lawyers. Apart from anything else, estate planning has big tax implications.

Not all generational transfer of wealth has been done in secret. In some cases, there have been major legal disputes, not only between siblings, but also between parents and their children. Bob Jane's bitter dispute with his son is just one example; Gina Rinehart's with some of her children another. Shakespeare's *King Lear* should be required reading for the wealthy elderly who are thinking of giving away their fortunes to their children, although it seems that there can be terrible consequences both in giving it away to the children and in hanging on to it.

John Gandel, the shopping centre magnate, said that Leibler, his lawyer and long-time friend, had given him advice at his request on how to plan for the time when he was no longer around. Gandel is Australia's seventh richest person with a fortune estimated at $6.45 billion, according to the *Australian Financial Review*'s 2018 Rich List. Gandel said that Leibler was not shy about jumping up and saying, "John, do you realise what you're doing to your family?" Once, Gandel was trying to decide an issue involving his children. Leibler had said, "Don't do this John, it's bad for the family." Gandel said that looking back, Leibler had been 100 per cent right.

CHAPTER 18

Marc Besen and his family rank 25 on the *Australian Financial Review*'s 2018 Rich List with a fortune estimated at $2.4 billion. Eva Besen, in her 90s, is Gandel's sister. At one time, Gandel and Eva's husband, Marc Besen, jointly owned the Sussan Group. It is now owned by the Besens' daughter, Naomi Milgrom, who, like her parents, has a reputation for her business acumen and generous philanthropy, especially in the arts. The Besen family owns TarraWarra Estate, a well-known winery in the Yarra Valley, an hour or so northeast of Melbourne. In 2003, they built the TarraWarra Museum of Art on the estate, opening it as a not-for-profit public art museum whose operations and acquisitions the family continue to fund generously. The 500 works in the collection are all funded by the Besens.

Marc Besen, at 95, still goes at least three times a week to the headquarters of the Sussan Group in inner-city Richmond. His office is in a building that assembles three remodelled warehouses and feels as if it would sit well in the increasingly gentrified Lower East Side of Manhattan. Besen was in good spirits when he talked about his association with Leibler, which goes back more than 40 years, to when Arnold Bloch was senior partner at ABL and Leibler was starting to make a name for himself.

Besen agreed that Leibler was an expert on trusts, which "was important back in those days. We had quite a lot of meetings because of succession planning. You had taxation issues to deal with and that was Mark's area. But he gave general advice as well. He had a lot of experience." Of the outcome of Leibler's advice, he said: "I'm very happy. These things can be very difficult, making the transition to the next generation."

David Hains had had little to do with the Jewish community or with Jewish business when he became a client of ABL. He said that, despite the fact that he had now known Leibler for a long time, they had never discussed Leibler's role in the Jewish community. They never discussed Leibler's faith, never discussed Israel and the Palestinians. Perhaps, Hains said, his position on the Middle East was to the left of Leibler's. He had come to Leibler because of his reputation as a tax adviser, not because ABL was regarded as a Jewish firm. But, over time, he had got to know some of the old Jewish entrepreneurs, billionaires like the Besens. John Gandel is Hains' neighbour in Toorak. His children and the Besen children know each other socially. But he said he never had any business dealings with the Jewish businessmen, who were "generally too smart for me."

Hains said that, as the Jewish community had changed, so had Jewish business people. He had always been aware that they had been subjected to prejudice and, in his view, that explained why they were clannish, stuck together, cooperated and competed with each other all at the same time. They pursued their business interests with an intensity that he thought a bit foreign in Australia. They were very competitive with each other and still are:

> Oh, they still compete alright. There's a strong competition, with the size of their planes and their yachts and their houses and their vineyards and everything you like to name. If one does something, you'll usually find one of them will do it a bit better.

> But the community in general and, the business people in particular, have become more urbane, much less clannish. I mean lots of their children have married non-Jews. They have gone into public companies, almost always ones that they can control.

Asked about Leibler's strengths, Hains did not hesitate; Leibler had an extraordinary knowledge of tax law and was a brilliant negotiator, but, more importantly, he was respected by people at the ATO for his knowledge of the law. Leibler knew people "up and down the scale" at the ATO, including the Tax Commissioner and very senior officials:

> He's a terrific networker but that wouldn't matter if he didn't have skill and ability. He is a formidable opponent for the Tax Office. And he can talk to anyone there. They answer his calls. Often problems with the Tax Office are the result of some idiot lawyer extending a dispute between a client and the office. Mark does not extend disputes. He is about resolving disputes.

Leibler would not answer questions about Hains, his client. He said many times that he would not talk about individual clients and their tax issues, or about the way they had handled the transfer of some or all of their wealth and business empires to their children, and sometimes grandchildren. He did agree, however, that there had been a major transfer of wealth from one generation of the wealthy to the next, and he was proud of the work he had done.

Over the years, many of his clients had become friends, not necessarily close friends, but more than clients, and it was here that the different parts of his life, the lawyer and the Jewish community leader, always intersected. Many of his clients were major contributors to the United Israel Appeal, of which Leibler had become president in 1995. Some were also major funders of the lobby group, Australia/Israel & Jewish Affairs Council. Their Jewish connections and their business connections informed their relationship with Leibler.

It was complicated, the business of estate planning, Leibler said. Yes, it was about tax and the tax implications of any transition, but it was about much more than that. He had to get to know the family, the children, their relationship with their parents, so that he could properly advise his clients, understand where they were coming from, and what they wanted to achieve. It was about how the older generation wanted to manage the transfer of assets and whether it would be during their lifetime. He said that it could be done in ways that "do not trigger tax events"—in other words, in ways that minimise tax liabilities.

Asked whether he had been involved in succession planning that involved the passing on of billions of dollars, he replied: "Yes, absolutely. We've been doing this for many years. You know, during the lifetime of this practice we have separated out at least three generations. We started acting for the parents, then the siblings and then the children of the siblings. It is a highly specialised area."

I asked whether these fortunes should be able to be passed on without the need for the beneficiaries to pay tax. His reply when I asked him whether he was in favour of death or estate taxes was not surprising. It would have been extraordinary, to say the least, if Leibler had come out in favour of death taxes. He is a leading tax lawyer for some of the wealthiest people in Australia. He knows that many Australians believe the rich get away with avoiding paying any more than a minimal amount of tax and that they do so based on the advice of people like him. Nevertheless, he answered my question with characteristic vehemence:

> I have been fundamentally against death taxes as a matter of ideology, and every single principle I can conceive of. My view is that if you make money then you should pay your tax dues to the government during your lifetime and once you've paid your taxes, the wealth you have accumulated belongs to you to do with as you wish.

CHAPTER 19

By the time Michael D'Ascenzo retired in 2012, he had been at the Australian Taxation Office (ATO) for almost 40 years, and had been Commissioner of Taxation for the last seven. His first contact with Mark Leibler was in the late 1970s, not long after he had joined the ATO, when D'Ascenzo was part of a team that examined the way trusts were being used to potentially avoid significant amounts of tax. He wanted to understand how trusts worked and his supervisor had told him to read several articles that Leibler had written on the subject.

A few months later, D'Ascenzo instigated a project that would investigate what he described as trust-stripping schemes that he thought were costing the ATO hundreds of millions of dollars in tax collections every year. These schemes involved trust income being diverted from the intended beneficiaries, often family members of the trust, to an entity that was tax exempt or had losses. These entities then paid back the income—as a loan, for instance—which was then distributed to the intended beneficiaries, tax-free. D'Ascenzo identified 16 variations of trust-stripping schemes and he put together ways of issuing assessments involving these schemes that he believed would give the ATO a good chance of challenging the schemes in the courts.

The next question was whether he could create guidelines that would encourage those involved in the schemes to negotiate settlements with the ATO. He needed a settlement that would be a win for the ATO and a win for the trust-strippers. In the end, the settlement that was offered would impose no penalties for the tax avoided to that time. If no settlement were negotiated, however, those who failed to settle would face legal action.

Leibler contacted D'Ascenzo almost immediately to say he wanted to recommend that his clients take up the settlement offer spelt out in the guidelines. Because Leibler was so influential in the trust area, D'Ascenzo knew that his advice to his clients would enable the ATO to pretty much clean up the trust-stripping schemes. Once people heard that someone as influential as Leibler was advising his clients to settle, others would settle, D'Ascenzo told me. "Remember, these were pretty much blatant, artificial and contrived schemes. I think Mark understood that." In fact, the ATO ended up collecting well over $0.75 billion dollars, D'Ascenzo said. It was big.

A few years later, in the early 1980s, D'Ascenzo had been promoted to Assistant Commissioner and was in charge of dealing with the bottom-of-the-harbour schemes and a raft of others that were essentially big tax avoidance operations. Leibler came to see him in Canberra to settle claims against a number of his clients. By then the legislation that John Howard, as Treasurer, introduced to outlaw the schemes and to retrospectively collect tax that had been avoided had been passed. Many of Leibler's clients would receive fresh assessments from the ATO, some for avoided tax possibly going back many years. Again, D'Ascenzo provided a range of settlement offers that enabled Leibler's clients, if they came forward early, to get some remission of interest and a few other benefits. D'Ascenzo said that Leibler negotiated settlements that "worked for the ATO" and for Leibler. He was always interested in getting a win-win outcome.

D'Ascenzo dealt with a few other issues that involved Leibler. He said Leibler had provided valuable advice on the introduction of self-assessment in the mid-1990s, which was a major change in the way the ATO operated. Individuals and companies would be required to self-assess their tax liability and lodge their returns with the ATO.

The ATO would randomly audit assessments, but the change did involve a level of trust that made it a controversial move. According to D'Ascenzo, however, the evidence suggests that it has worked well. As D'Ascenzo became more senior at the ATO, he found that Leibler came to him from time to time over assessments done by more junior auditors that Leibler found objectionable in some way. Some of the contacts between them involved tax avoidance schemes used by some of Leibler's clients. He described the lawyer as a formidable presence.

I asked D'Ascenzo about Leibler's reputation at the ATO, to which he replied: "There were people who thought he was deeply involved in blatant, artificial and contrived schemes. I was happy to take Mark at his word and move forward." As to whether there was any evidence for that belief, D'Ascenzo said he couldn't "comment about that. I questioned him about whether he was involved in a particular scheme. He said he was not and I moved on."

I said that it was on the public record that some auditors thought that Leibler often went over their heads to more senior people, or threatened to do so, if he was dissatisfied with them over a particular audit. Some thought he had undue influence. D'Ascenzo's response was:

> Well, that's true. He had that reputation at the ATO. You always get that in any organisation, claims that people are being bypassed, that some outsider has undue influence. We were very careful in the organisation not to do anything improper, not to be seen to be allowing people to go over the heads of auditors. If there was a call, the consideration of the case was always done with the auditing team present, if possible. You would never negotiate on your own.

The former Commissioner, who went on to join the Foreign Investment Review Board, wanted to be clear that he had always accepted that Leibler was a lawyer who acted in the best interests of his clients and had never treated D'Ascenzo with anything but respect, even when they disagreed, sometimes robustly. The two men still exchange Christmas cards.

Kevin Fitzpatrick also remains on friendly terms with Leibler. From time to time, Fitzpatrick, who spent 47 years at the ATO, and the veteran lawyer have talked about their shared involvement in major tax issues, from the mid-1990s until Fitzpatrick retired in 2011. They have discussed tax policy in general, or Leibler has asked Fitzpatrick for his view of a speech or paper Leibler was planning to deliver. Leibler has made submissions in the past decade to a dozen or more parliamentary committees that examined Australia's tax legislation or the operations of the ATO. He has been the keynote speaker at a number of conferences on tax attended by senior ATO officials, many of whom Leibler has known and dealt with for a long time.

Since he retired, Fitzpatrick has done some private tax consulting, and he lectures in tax administration at Melbourne University. A plain-spoken man who came by tram to our interview location, he brought with him several articles published in the 1990s to jog his memory about his work as head of the High Wealth Individuals Taskforce. The taskforce had been set up in 1995 by the Keating government to address a widespread community perception that the wealthy, once again, were engaged in schemes to avoid paying their fair share of tax. Individuals and families with net worth of more than $30 million came under the taskforce's scrutiny. Many were Leibler's clients. What's more, one of the first areas the taskforce was going to examine was the taxation of trusts, another area in which Leibler's profile was prominent. Federal Treasurer Ralph Willis had told Parliament that Treasury had advised him that more than $800 million in tax was being avoided through various trust schemes. Leibler told journalists at the time that the claim by Willis was "without foundation" and that Willis was playing populist politics, attacking the wealthy who could not defend themselves and would be unable to muster any community sympathy.

Fitzpatrick, in charge of the taskforce, which had been set up partly because of pressure from Willis, recalled that the ATO was troubled by Willis's claim. The $800 million figure for tax avoidance had not come from the ATO and was probably inaccurate. The issues were not black and white; there was a grey line between tax avoidance and legitimate minimisation.

The introduction of self-assessment was a significant reason for establishing the taskforce. It examined three or four years of the *Business Review Weekly* Rich List to identify individuals who could be the subject of audits. As a result of its work, the ATO had about 50 groups or individuals under audit at any one time, Fitzpatrick said. The audits were meant, in part, to deter people from aggressively doing the wrong thing. Fitzpatrick said there was no doubt that Leibler got involved with the taskforce's work because many of his clients would come under scrutiny: "People were using trusts to avoid tax in simple terms. And Mark Leibler was probably regarded as the leading adviser around the use of trusts. I think that's fair to say."

Tax avoidance by high-net-worth individuals became an issue in the 1996 election campaign. Willis had promised to introduce legislation to address tax avoidance associated with the use of trusts. Shadow Treasurer Peter Costello said that a Coalition government would look at whether legislation was needed and, if it was, it would act. The ATO, and Fitzpatrick in particular, had formed the view that legislation was needed to make the taxation of trusts clearer and more certain, and to stop tax minimisation or avoidance. "Australia has more trusts in its tax system than any other country, proportionately, in the world," Fitzpatrick said. "Over a million people have trusts. It's not only the wealthy. But the taxation law on trusts was, and remains, unclear."

However, after the Liberal/National Coalition parties won the election in a landslide, Treasurer Costello, after a period of consultation, decided to make only minor, and largely inconsequential, changes to the tax laws affecting trusts. Fitzpatrick said that he was sure that Leibler had made representations to the government, as he had a right to. He would not comment on why Costello decided not to go ahead with legislation that the ATO had recommended.

By the time he was dealing with Leibler regularly, Fitzpatrick had become the ATO's Chief Tax Counsel. At times, he was acting Second Commissioner, the second most senior official in the ATO. Apart from trusts, Fitzpatrick said that Leibler's clients used what he described as a variety of schemes designed to avoid tax. One was a scheme that took advantage of general tax write-off provisions for research and development. As far as Fitzpatrick was aware, Leibler had not promoted any of these schemes, although some of his clients may have participated in them. When the High Wealth Individuals Taskforce was disbanded shortly before Fitzpatrick retired in 2011, the Commissioner of Taxation established a High Wealth Private Groups Unit to continue its work. Fitzpatrick said that the unit would undoubtedly continue to scrutinise Leibler's clients.

The ATO has changed the way it connects with taxpayers, including those of high net wealth. It is more open to contact with them, and their lawyers, to discuss issues and explain rulings. As a result, Fitzpatrick believes that the behaviour of tax lawyers and advisers has changed:

> It is a more readily accepted notion that those who advise others on tax have a responsibility. There are less and less of what I

would call rogues, in the sense of people who go out and find tax avoidance loopholes. In my view, Mark has probably changed the way he advises clients in that broad sense.

Asked how officials in the ATO regarded Leibler, Fitzpatrick said that many saw him as a person who had influence and as someone who used this perception to bully more junior auditors by threatening to go over their heads to the Commissioner or some other senior official in order to get his way. He said Leibler marketed himself as a person of influence, and "of course on some things, he was right. Over the years, we spoke about ways to improve the administration of the tax laws and I took some of those suggestions he made on board."

Asked whether Leibler had ever bullied him personally, Fitzpatrick said he had not. Leibler had always been calm and measured and rational with him when dealing with individual cases. As to whether staff had complained to Fitzpatrick about bullying by Leibler, he said that they had:

> He threatened to go above their heads, to the Commissioner in some cases. There was a feeling in the Tax Office, some parts of the Tax Office, that he had undue influence among senior officers on tax matters. It was not improper, this marketing of himself as a person of influence at the ATO. He marketed himself as a person who could have the ear of the Commissioner.

Did Fitzpatrick talk to Leibler about the bullying allegations? He replied:

> In general terms I did. I told him he needed to be careful about how he dealt with some of these auditors. I am not sure it changed his attitude. I always found him to be fair and reasonable and open. I must say, one of the issues for me at the time was that I had to be careful that I wasn't seen by my staff as being overly influenced by him.

Fitzpatrick thought for a while about my question about how Leibler had used his influence before saying that, in his view, Leibler had never influenced senior people, and certainly not Commissioners, as much as others outside the ATO, including Leibler himself, thought he did.

When I asked Leibler about what D'Ascenzo and Fitzpatrick had said, Leibler said that he was not surprised. Yet he seemed disturbed and frustrated, perhaps even angry, about what these two former officials, people he had known for decades, had said. I told him that both D'Ascenzo and Fitzpatrick had said that there was perception at the ATO that he bullied auditors by suggesting he had influence and threatening to go to the Commissioner or another senior official. "How is that bullying?" Leibler demanded. Could he understand that they may have felt bullied? "I can understand that they might have been unhappy."

Leibler said that one challenge in dealing with the ATO was how to escalate matters on a particular case when there was huge resentment about him going above the heads of auditors and speaking to senior people who could get the issue moving when it seemed not to be going anywhere. He said that he did it sparingly and only when he thought that it would help settle an audit that had been going for a long time, in some cases for years:

> You know, there were auditors who became emotionally involved, who acted for ideological reasons or who I felt were not properly applying the law. In some of those cases, I did go to senior officials and, you know what, mostly these cases were quickly resolved. Yes, I often made it clear that I was going above their heads. Or threatened to do so. I don't regard that as bullying.

Did he, as Fitzpatrick claimed, market himself as a lawyer with influence at the Tax Office? "That is not true, just not true," Leibler replied. Where do I market myself like this?" To his clients? "How would he know? If he is saying that if I had a client sitting around the table here who had a particular problem that was going nowhere, and I said to him 'Well, I can contact the Commissioner or the Second Commissioner', is that marketing? I don't think so."

Allegations that Leibler has undue influence inside the ATO go back a long way, In 1992, John Thorburn, a mid-level auditor in the ATO's Melbourne office, told a parliamentary Joint Standing Committee on Public Accounts hearing into the use of discretionary trusts that Leibler was applying "severe pressure" to auditors by making them aware that he had "fairly high" connections and would use them to make the auditors change their views on certain audits. Thorburn had earlier told the hearing that "hundreds of millions of dollars" could be involved in the use of discretionary trusts to avoid tax. He referred specifically to the distribution of income from discretionary trusts to overseas beneficiaries, most of them living in Israel.

At the time, Leibler angrily denied the allegations. In the last two decades, there have been no such complaints. One reason, according to Leibler, is that he no longer serves on any of the various committees that advise the ATO. Yet there are some undeniable facts; as a lawyer, Leibler has immaculate, perhaps unmatched, political connections, in part because of his reputation and experience in tax issues, in part because of his standing as a Jewish community leader, perhaps even in part because of his standing as an advocate and leader on Indigenous issues. And he does, indeed, have fairly easy access to senior officials in the ATO. He has had a relationship with every Commissioner of Taxation since the 1980s. He has hosted some of them, as well as other senior ATO officials, at lunches at ABL. He has been able to pick up the phone and call whoever the Commissioner of the time might be

—including the current Commissioner, Chris Jordan—and expect that his call will be taken.

Leibler said that in his dealings with the ATO, he had mainly been concerned with specific issues involving one or other of his clients. Given the nature of his clients, these issues were often complicated, with a lot at stake for both the clients and the ATO. Over several decades, he had come to know senior officials well and had sometimes talked to them about the way the ATO was operating. Senior ATO officials had come to conferences at which Leibler was speaking, such as the 2018 conference on taxation in Cairns at which he gave a paper on the wide-ranging powers of the Commissioner of Taxation; Chris Jordan was there to hear his paper.

At the age of 75, but in full flight, rubbishing claims that he considered unsubstantiated or unfair, Leibler seemed to be as fierce and blunt and engaged as he was reputed to be when he was a younger man. In response to any question about whether he and other tax lawyers worked according to ethical principles, his answers were almost invariably brief and direct, as if they were black and white.

Yes, he had views about the tax system—it was too complicated, for a start. More importantly, he believed that much of the unfairness in it could easily be resolved if the company tax rate and the top marginal personal tax rate were the same. This would mean bringing the top personal tax rate (45 cents in the dollar in 2019) down to the company rate of 30 cents in the dollar. What Leibler recommends would be a major change to the tax arrangements, which would hugely benefit the well off and the rich. No government is likely to implement such a change in the foreseeable future. Nevertheless, Leibler maintains that, as long as company tax rates are substantially lower than income tax rates, people, especially the wealthy, will find ways to divert personal income to companies. He said that he had made the case for fixing this with every Treasurer he had dealt with, and he had dealt with all of them since John Howard in the early 1980s.

Leibler was proud of the fact that, overwhelmingly, he had managed to settle disputes with the ATO without the need for expensive court action. He said he had always negotiated on the basis that a settlement involved a win for both sides, for his client and the taxman.

Perhaps his greatest win for his clients, at least since the bottom-of-the-harbour schemes, was his involvement in Project Do It, an amnesty scheme announced by Commissioner Chris Jordan in March 2014. The scheme sought to encourage those who had large amounts of money put away in overseas banks to bring the money back to Australia. If they did, they would be assessed for tax going back just four years. The penalty would be minimal and, crucially, unless they had committed crimes unrelated to taxation, they would not be prosecuted for breaching tax laws. The scheme's critics argued that the ATO had agreed to forgo hundreds of millions of dollars of potential tax revenue over fortunes that in many cases had accumulated over decades. They argued that the decision by the Swiss banks, following pressure from the United States, to open their accounts to scrutiny would have meant that most people holding accounts in overseas banks would, in time, be identified. There was no need for such a generous amnesty.

D'Ascenzo, when asked, said he would not have agreed to such a scheme. He knew that Leibler had worked to get the scheme up, that he had produced drafts of the scheme, that he had been in touch regularly with the Commissioner of Taxation. He knew because such a scheme had been proposed to him, and that he and Leibler had talked about it. According to D'Ascenzo, Project Do It was a minor project compared to Project Wickenby, which D'Ascenzo had overseen.

Wickenby, which was set up several years before Project Do It, had a cross-agency task force that included the Australian Federal Police. It went after major tax avoiders, many of them with links to organised crime. According to D'Ascenzo, it recovered many billions of dollars more of tax that had been avoided than Project Do It and it resulted in a number of successful criminal prosecutions. D'Ascenzo said that Leibler had tried to negotiate a similar amnesty with him, but there had been a major sticking point—Leibler wanted a guarantee of no prosecutions and D'Ascenzo was adamant that he could not agree to this, that it was beyond his power to do so. He said that during Project Wickenby he had developed guidelines with the Director of Public Prosecutions (DPP) that meant he could not make any deal that involved non-prosecution guarantees.

I pointed out that the current Commissioner clearly thought Project Do It was a major achievement. D'Ascenzo replied, "I can only assume that the current Commissioner did not understand that he had the protocol that had been agreed with the DPP." Clearly, D'Ascenzo did not believe that there was a need for an amnesty and that it was not for the ATO to offer one. If crimes had been committed, only the investigative authorities, such as the Australian Federal Police, and the DPP could decide whether prosecutions should be initiated.

In an article published in the *Australian Financial Review* in September 2014, journalist Fleur Anderson quoted Leibler as saying that Project Do It had "relieved years of guilt and worry about potential bankruptcy or even prosecution for the families of Holocaust victims and their survivors arising from relatives' financial decisions during World War Two." They had felt guilty at having survived when many of their relatives had been murdered, and they had felt increasingly guilty about holding assets overseas in secret, Anderson wrote. The old Swiss bank accounts of these Holocaust survivors contained the remnants of their pre-World War 2 fortunes that had grown large over the decades. They were worried about the cost of declaring these assets, and the tax penalties, even prosecutions, that might be imposed on them.

The consequence of Project Do It for Leibler and ABL was that, in 2015, there was a surge in fees, from old clients who wanted to take advantage of the amnesty, and new ones who came to Leibler because they knew he had been involved in devising the amnesty and probably understood it better than anyone. Leibler would not say how much in fees he brought in that year, but it was in the tens of millions of dollars, more than any other partner. He was not at all abashed about this. He maintained that the critics were wrong, that, without this amnesty, the ATO might have spent years and significant resources tracking down the owners and beneficiaries of these overseas accounts. Other amnesties had been tried, but they had not been generous enough to get the account holders to come forward.

Many of his clients came forward as a result of Project Do it. They had not done so under previous amnesties. He had advised his clients to give their names to the ATO, or to allow him to do so. It was a good deal. Perhaps they would not be caught if they refused to come forward, but, if they were caught, they would be hit with significant penalties, and with the possibility of prosecution for breaches of the law.

What role, I asked, did he play in the development of Project Do It? He replied:

> Well, I think I played some role. In the end of course, the decision to go with Project Do It was wholly a decision made by the Tax Commissioner who I am sure, sounded out the Government, unofficially, to see whether there would be a political fallout. But I did speak to the Commissioner about an amnesty. I advised him

about what I thought would be the response of my clients to various proposed schemes—whether, essentially, they were generous enough to work, to get people to declare their overseas accounts.

As for removing the threat of prosecutions, Leibler said that any agreement on prosecutions would not cover criminal offences unrelated to taxation law. The agreement not to launch prosecutions was not official. The Commissioner of Taxation could not direct the Director of Public Prosecutions how to act. But the Commissioner could agree that apart from criminal breaches of the law, there would be no referrals by him to the DPP. "What's more," said Leibler, "the prosecuting agencies, the DPP and the Federal Police among others, had indicated their support for Project Do It."

He indicated that "at least $5 billion dollars" was brought back to Australia as a result of Project Do It, but was not prepared to give an exact figure for the amount brought back by his clients, although he agreed it was billions of dollars.

The release of the Panama Papers by a team of investigative journalists based in the United States in 2015 revealed how some of the world's richest people used offshore companies to hide their wealth. Leibler was quoted in *The Weekend Australian* as saying that people who had come forward under Project Do It and whose names appeared in the Panama Papers would be covered by the amnesty and would have "significant legal protection."

At the time the ATO was investigating more than 800 Australian residents, including about 80 for allegedly serious organised crime offences, in connection with the Panama Papers. These people would not be covered by the amnesty under Project Do It. Two years later, following further revelations by the investigative journalists, Leibler said that he supported the ATO's investigations of people who may have been involved in serious non-tax crimes and that Project Do It had never been about protecting criminals. Those clients who had listened to him and come forward under the amnesty, some of whom were named in the Panama Papers, had nothing to fear. They had settled their tax issues.

Fair or not, Project Do It meant that many of ABL's clients, and in many cases, their heirs, were able to repatriate to Australia hundreds of millions of dollars on which they would pay what can only be described as minimal tax and minimal penalties. Leibler agreed that there had been something personal for him in Project Do It, not in the sense that he had profited from it, but that he had managed to come up with a solution to an issue confronting many of his clients who had been through the Holocaust. But he said that it was not just Holocaust survivors and their descendants who came forward as a result of Project Do It. There were also Italians, Greeks, Chinese and other migrants and refugees who came to Australia leaving behind assets overseas because they were not sure what would happen to them in their new country. Now they had the opportunity to clean up their tax affairs.

Project Do It had, once again, involved Leibler the lawyer, Leibler the Jewish leader, and ABL clients who were Holocaust survivors and their descendants. Leibler's maternal grandparents had been murdered in Auschwitz. In the 1950s, his parents had gone back to Belgium to retrieve diamonds his grandparents had hidden in their home in Antwerp before they were rounded up in a cattle truck. This personal dimension must have added to Leibler's satisfaction in what was one of his greatest triumphs as a tax lawyer.

CHAPTER 20

Most people who have had public disagreements with the Australia/ Israel & Jewish Affairs Council over their views about some aspect of the conflict between Israel and the Palestinians will know that the experience can be bracing, to say the least. There are journalists, editors, academics, politicians and public servants—some of them Jewish— who have felt the wrath of AIJAC, including former Prime Minister and Foreign Minister, Kevin Rudd, and former Foreign Minister Bob Carr. It is undeniably AIJAC, and not the Zionist Federation of Australia or any of the representative Jewish bodies such as the Executive Council of Australian Jewry, that is the most formidable lobbying outfit for Israel and for what AIJAC perceives to be Jewish community interests in Australia.

Privately funded—many of its biggest funders are clients of ABL— and not answerable to any Jewish community body, AIJAC is widely regarded by the Australian political class and by journalists who cover the Middle East or have been on one of AIJAC's study trips to represent the views and interests of the Australian Jewish community when it comes to Israel and Australia's position on its conflict with the Palestinians.

From its birth, there were Jews, some of them community leaders and committed Zionists, who were, at best, uneasy about AIJAC. Sam Lipski was one of these people. In the late 1970s, Lipksi, by then a well-known journalist, quit journalism to set up Australia/Israel Publications (AIP), funded by the businessmen Isador Magid and Robert Zablud. It was a modest operation that produced a monthly publication of news and commentary on Israel and on Australia–Israel relations. Asked about it, Lipski said that he wanted to produce something with journalistic integrity that put Israel's case in a way that the general media was not doing. It never pretended, he said, to represent the views of the Jewish community or of any community organisation. Lipski had always believed that only the Executive Council of Australian Jewry should speak for the Jewish community's interests in Canberra.

The ECAJ leadership was not exactly democratically elected, but the organisation was made up of representatives from a wide range of community bodies, from schools to welfare organisations. In the dispute between Isi and Mark Leibler over who should speak for the Jewish community, Lipski sided with Isi Leibler, then president of the ECAJ. The Zionist Federation of Australia, Lipski argued, even with a leader as good and as well-connected as Mark Leibler, could not speak for the Jewish community. Mark Leibler has never accepted this.

Lipski was Editor-in-Chief of the *Australian Jewish News* when AIJAC was born through the merger of Australia/Israel Publications, which he had established, and the Australian Institute of Jewish Affairs that Isi Leibler had created in 1984 to fund research into a broad range of Jewish issues. The Institute was on its last legs in 1996, when the merger was proposed; Isi Leibler was on the verge of moving to Israel and his interest in leading Australian Jewish organisations had waned. In that year Mark Leibler had finished his 10-year stint as President of the ZFA and was about to take up the presidency of the United Israel Appeal, Australia's biggest fundraising body for Israel. Solomon Lew convinced Leibler to become chairman of AIJAC. Colin Rubenstein, a Monash University lecturer in Middle East Studies, after working unpaid for the new body and had just taken over as its Executive Director. With Lew contributing significant funding and persuading some of his fellow Jewish billionaires to help fund AIJAC, it was clear that the new body would not follow in the modest footsteps of Lipski's AIP. Leibler and Rubenstein built AIJAC into one of Australia's most formidable lobbying outfits, with a budget of more than $4 million—a figure that neither Rubenstein nor Leibler would confirm, but Rubenstein did not dispute when I put it to him.

Not included in that budget is the cost of AIJAC's Rambam Israel Fellowship. Named after the 12th-century Jewish philosopher Moses Maimonides—Rambam is an acronym of his full name and title—the program sends Australian politicians and senior public servants to Israel to be briefed by senior Israeli and Palestinian politicians, journalists, commentators and military and security officials. AIJAC has funded Rambam fellowships for scores of Australian politicians, including Scott Morrison and Bill Shorten when they were backbenchers, and Julia Gillard when she was Shadow Minister of Health. About 500 journalists, commentators, senior public servants and academics have also participated in the program, which is funded by donations, mostly from some of Australia's wealthiest Jewish families.

In 2014, AIJAC was heavily involved in the campaign against the Abbott government's move to change or eliminate Section 18C of the Racial Discrimination Act. AIJAC also initiated the Australia–Israel military dialogues that bring together top counter-terrorism experts and others from Israel and Australia.

It also brings guest speakers to Australia, mainly from Israel but also from the United States. The high-profile lawyer, Alan Dershowitz, famously a member of O.J Simpson's defence team and, more recently, of Donald Trump's defence team during the impeachment hearings in the US Senate, spoke at an AIJAC function held at ABL in 2018. Once a Democrat, Dershowitz is now a regular on Fox News where he often supports Donald Trump on specific issues. He is a zealous supporter of Israel and always a scathing critic of what he has described as the anti-Semitism of anti-Zionists. The visits of some of the speakers AIJAC brings to Australia are timed to coincide with sittings of the federal parliament. It also brings politicians and officials from India, China and Southeast Asia to Australia, some of whom are unable to take up Rambam Fellowships because most Muslim majority countries, such as Malaysia, forbid travel to Israel; AIJAC also organises programs for these people in their home countries.

No Jewish representative body in Australia has such resources, contacts and clout. In fact, some of the state community bodies, such as the Jewish Community Council of Victoria—until 1989 the Victorian Jewish Board of Deputies—are struggling to survive financially. AIJAC's headquarters is an impressive suite of offices in inner-city South Melbourne. It has a staff of 17, eight of them full-time policy analysts and journalists. Its Sydney office is run by long-time Jewish community activist Jeremy Jones. Jones has been a force in Jewish–Christian relations for decades and has more recently concentrated on developing relationships with Australia's Muslim community, a process still very much in its infancy.

For Leibler, AIJAC is a perfect fit. He does not have to get involved in the day-to-day running of the place; Rubenstein does that. While Rubenstein and Leibler are constantly in touch over issues that affect Australia's relationship with Israel, Rubenstein is AIJAC's main spokesman. Nevertheless, when AIJAC puts out a statement on a big issue, it is often in Leibler's name. When there's lobbying to do in Canberra, Leibler is invariably part of the AIJAC delegation. Because it is not a community organisation, but rather a lobbying outfit with no Jewish community oversight, there are none of the frequent and interminable meetings that Leibler had to put up with as leader the ZFA and of the United Israel Appeal. The AIJAC board, appointed by Leibler and senior AIJAC staff, meets every three months in one of the ABL boardrooms.

Rubenstein has known Leibler since they were students at Mount Scopus College. When I met him in his office at AIJAC's headquarters, Rubenstein answered questions as if they had all been asked before— as indeed they had, by journalists and by Jewish critics of AIJAC. At 75, Rubenstein, like Leibler, showed no sign of slowing down.

Rubenstein's family goes back four generations in Australia. They were not Orthodox Jews, going to synagogue only on the high holidays —Jewish New Year and Yom Kippur, the Day of Atonement—and occasionally on the Sabbath. Because they were also sports-mad, on Saturdays sport came before God and his mandated day of rest. Rubenstein played basketball for the Maccabi which was part of the Jewish sports club, Ajax, and went on to become the basketball team's long-term coach. Unlike most post-war Jewish leaders, who were either Holocaust survivors or the children of survivors, Rubenstein's family was, in his words, "heavily involved in Australia and they had fought for Australia in two wars."

While lecturing at Monash University, Rubenstein got involved with Lipski's Australia/Israel Publications. In 1977, he set up the group, Australian Academics for Peace in the Middle East, providing venues at Monash for Israeli politicians and commentators Lipski brought to Australia, which he continued to do after Melbourne Ports federal Labor MP, Michael Danby, took over from Lipski. By the early 1990s, Rubenstein was telling people, Leibler included, that AIP was not viable and needed to be professionalised along the lines of the American Israel Public Affairs Committee (AIPAC), one of the most powerful lobbying bodies in Washington. A dogged networker, Rubenstein went to see a number of wealthy Jewish families in Melbourne and Sydney. Rubenstein says they quickly agreed to support his vision of a professionally run and well-resourced replacement for the AIP.

The Jewish community, Rubenstein believed, needed a body that would put Israel's case in Canberra and in the wider community. It needed to be "independent" and nimble, quick to respond to any issue. It could not be answerable to any of the community organisations. Like Leibler, the new AIJAC major donor, Solomon Lew, had been Rubenstein's schoolmate at Mount Scopus, and they had stayed friends. "Solly, he's very street sharp and is a can-do guy," Rubenstein said. "He took it by the scruff of the neck and he persuaded others to come on board."

It was Lew, a client of ABL by the 1990s, who persuaded Leibler to chair the new body. With many of ABL's clients on board, AIJAC was born. Lew remains a major figure at AIJAC, although his name does not appear on the masthead of its monthly publication, *Australia/ Israel Review*. When I asked about his involvement, Lew feigned a sort of cheeky reticence, as if to say, "I know where these questions are going." Did he remain a major donor of AIJAC? "I have been a donor for decades." A major donor? "A donor."

I asked whether he could go to Leibler and say, "I want you to be the chairman of this new AIJAC." "Yes, I could do that," he replied. "I had been instrumental in bringing Colin in and making sure he was properly paid. At the same time, I had to marry Mark and Colin, no easy task, but I underwrote the relationship and they never looked back." Lew agreed that AIJAC was well funded and resourced. "It's privately funded. It's not a community body. You couldn't operate AIJAC as a community body."

Asked who AIJAC represented, Lew's reply was. "Australian Jewry." How did he know that? "That's its mantra. It represents Australian Jewry and it represents Israel. We are recognised by more politicians in Australia from all sides. They never make a speech without checking with us."

Rubenstein, by contrast, said AIJAC had never claimed to represent Australian Jewry. AIJAC did, however, claim to represent the "mainstream views" of the Australian Jewish community. Proof of that was "the wide range of people who are involved with it as donors and people who come to AIJAC events." By "representing the views of the Australian Jewish community," Rubenstein said he meant support for Israel—but not for any political party in Israel.

AIJAC has rarely, if ever, criticised any Israeli government, including the Netanyahu government, over the way it has handled the peace process with the Palestinians. AIJAC supports a two-state solution, but has consistently argued that the peace process is stalled indefinitely. It blames the Palestinian leadership, both in Gaza, where Hamas is in power and is openly committed to Israel's destruction, and on the West Bank, where the Palestinian Authority, according to AIJAC, has rejected every attempt to resume the stalled peace process.

On the face of it, AIJAC's position is shared by the moderate right in Israel and by the centrist parties that came close to defeating the Netanyahu-led coalition government in the April 2019 elections. With neither side able to form a government, new elections were held in September 2019, which resulted in deadlock again; a new poll was called for March 2020. There is little evidence, however, that Prime Minister Netanyahu supports a two-state solution; on the contrary, no matter what Netanyahu may say, he is a captive of his more extreme coalition partners, who have publicly disowned any prospect of a two-state solution to the conflict between Israel and the Palestinians.

In Australia, AIJAC lobbies on issues that affect Australian Jews, such as anti-Semitism and the health of multiculturalism. Rubenstein believes that multiculturalism has served the Jewish community well and that Australian Jewry is a great multicultural success story. I asked why this lobbying should be done by AIJAC rather than long-established community organisations like the Executive Council of Australian Jewry. Smiling, Rubenstein answered, "The more voices the better. We do not believe that only the communal organisations can raise these issues. But we do try and coordinate our work with them."

Nevertheless, for some, AIJAC presents a troubling reality. To its critics it is essentially a private lobbying body that acts as if it speaks for the entire Australian Jewish community on a wide range of issues—not just on the Middle East. Both Leibler and Rubenstein are adamant that they have never said that AIJAC speaks for the whole community, but they do not deny that the political class in particular sees AIJAC as the community's main voice, certainly on the Middle East.

There are, however, Australian Jews, perhaps a good number of them, who reject any suggestion that AIJAC reflects the views of the Jewish community. Most of these Jews are left-leaning, and some of them long-time critics of Israel. A few consider themselves to be anti-Zionist, although it is never entirely clear what they mean by that. Growing numbers of Jews who are active in the community, who went to Zionist youth organisations, who are involved in their local congregations, and who still regard themselves as Zionists, are, nevertheless, fierce critics of AIJAC.

Mark Baker is a writer and academic and former director of Monash University's Australian Centre for Jewish Civilisation, where he still plays a part in its international visitors' program. He is deeply involved in Jewish life in Australia. As a university student in the early 1980s, he worked for the State Zionist Council of Victoria when Mark Leibler was its president. It would be fair to say that since then, Baker's views on Israel, and even on what it means to be a Zionist, have diverged significantly from Leibler's views. Baker acknowledges that Leibler has been a significant leader who has helped create institutions that have made the Jewish community strong and committed to Jewish life and to Israel. Baker is a Zionist and says that it is, in part, as a Zionist that he is a critic of what he describes as the right-wing politics of AIJAC, or Leibler, for that matter, and most of the Jewish community leadership. "For too long," he said, "AIJAC in particular has taken onto itself to define Zionism, so that anyone who criticised Israel or the Netanyahu Government or supported the Palestinians in any way could not be a Zionist. I am a Zionist and I am 'guilty' of all those things."

Baker said that AIJAC tried to silence people, that their criticism of people who held views they didn't like was almost always extreme and sometimes personal. He said that AIJAC wounded people. Baker sounded wounded, and angry, as he spoke: "They never think, 'What's going to be the consequence of what we are saying about these people?' They make enemies of people. Some of the people they treat as enemies are committed Jews, committed Zionists, who are critics of the Netanyahu Government in its dealings with the Palestinians."

Did AIJAC represent the mainstream views of Australian Jews, I asked; Baker replied:

> They have created an organisation that represents the far right in Israel. Every word that comes out of AIJAC is of the far right. I don't think the Australian Jewish community is monolithic. Some would support the AIJAC position. But many people would not.

I think the attempt to silence people radiates out in many ways, and we have a community as a result where many people feel that the official institutions that claim to represent them don't represent them at all. So there is this attempt to marginalise people like me and what I represent.

Baker said that he refused to be silenced. He was not intimidated because he was "still one of them," a committed Jew and Zionist. "I come from Holocaust stock," he added.

Asked about Baker, Leibler said that he had never questioned Baker's sincerity or his commitment to Jewish life and Israel. He just vehemently disagreed with him. Yes, AIJAC had at times been critical of Baker's views, but never, Leibler said, had he attacked him personally. Nor had anyone at AIJAC:

> As for AIJAC being of the far right, I reject that totally. We are careful how we address security issues in Israel, that's true, but we have been critical at times of the Netanyahu Government: on the way it has treated the Eritrean and South Sudanese refugees, for instance, on the Jewish Nation State Law (that formally proclaimed Israel as the state of the Jewish people without referring to the equal rights and treatment of all its citizens), which we said was unnecessary and counter-productive.

It is true that, when Israel's Jewish Home Party (formerly the Religious Zionists party) agreed to Netanyahu's plea and merged with the far-right and racist party, Jewish Power, in order to contest the first of the two national elections in 2019, AIJAC released a statement that condemned the merger and said there was no place in Israel's politics for a racist party like Jewish Power. In effect, they were condemning Netanyahu because the merged party would be part of any Netanyahu coalition government.

Nevertheless, I understand why some people feel that AIJAC can be bullying and extreme in its response to what it sees as bias and animus against Israel. As Editor of *The Age*, I would receive, at times almost daily, AIJAC's criticism of the newspaper's coverage of the Middle East, especially of the work of its Middle East correspondent, either by email, phone or in meetings at newspaper's offices. The AIJAC spokespeople were smart, relentless, knew their stuff, and were blunt, sometimes to the point of rudeness, in their criticism of the paper and some of its journalists and commentators.

I also received emails and phone calls, some of them abusive and hostile, from people whose views on Israel were to the far right of AIJAC, about some aspect of our coverage of the Middle East. Invariably, I was accused of being an anti-Semite or a self-hating Jew. The representatives of AIJAC were never abusive, but they were always confronting and often outraged and never took a backward step. I did not find the approach intimidating, but often wondered what effect all the calls and emails had on my fellow non-Jewish editors and on the politicians AIJAC criticised, who had no doubt been subjected to the sorts of phone calls and emails that I had received. I wondered whether AIJAC's approach sometimes made enemies of people who had not been enemies before.

These issues burst into the public domain in 2003, when Sydney University's Peace Foundation awarded its annual Sydney Peace Prize to the veteran Palestinian activist and politician, Hanan Ashrawi. The citation praised Ashrawi's commitment to human rights and to the peace process in the Middle East, but it was a controversial decision. Asked about Ashrawi on the ABC Radio National's *PM* program in October 2003, a month before the prize ceremony, Rubenstein said the suggestion that she was a force for moderation was "laughable."

In his view, she had "a track record and a very distinct and clear track record really, as an apologist for violence and terrorism." Rubenstein called on Bob Carr, then Premier of New South Wales, to refuse to present the Prize to Ashrawi. Carr, a long-time supporter of Israel and a founding member of Labor Friends of Israel, said that he would not withdraw from the ceremony and would present the prize to Ashrawi, "for the simple reason that the security of Israel will only be achieved by a peace settlement with the Palestinians and we've got to seize every opportunity to engage with both sides and urge peace on both sides."

The City of Sydney, one of the main sponsors of the Prize, announced that it would boycott the ceremony. The Lord Mayor, Lucy Turnbull, told the *PM* program that she had spent time researching Ashrawi's writing and speeches and that "it became clear to me that more often than not, she did not do what peace makers should do and speak the language of peace and reach out across a chasm of extraordinary conflict and hostility." Turnbull rejected claims made by Professor Stuart Rees, head of the Sydney Peace Foundation, that she, like him, had been subjected to "severe pressure", including abusive phone calls, over the Ashrawi decision. Rees talked in vague but dark terms about what he said were threats made to "our supporters to the effect that their interests might be affected if they pursue their association with this peace prize."

There is little doubt that AIJAC and other Jewish organisations lobbied Carr, in particular, and others to boycott the Peace Prize ceremony. Given my experience, I have no doubt that Rees and Carr were subjected to abusive phone calls from individuals who see anti-Semitism and hatred of Israel everywhere, but these would not have been from AIJAC, and certainly not from Rubenstein or Leibler. I have not found any evidence that AIJAC threatened to get Jewish donors to withdraw their donations from Sydney University programs, for instance, if the Peace Prize were given to Ashrawi, and the University denied that such threats had been made. The threat that Rees referred to would have been foolish and counter-productive, and neither Rubenstein nor Leibler are fools. The talk of threats, unsupported by any real evidence, says more about Rees than about Leibler and Rubenstein.

But I also believe that their criticism of Ashrawi was over the top. In Palestinian politics, she was a moderate. It is true that she said different things for an Arab audience than for a Western one, and it is true that at times she seemed to accept Palestinian terrorist attacks on Israeli civilians, but she did not, at least in her public statements, support such attacks. Whether or not she should have received the Peace Prize is another matter, but AIJAC's criticism of her and of Carr's decision to present the award was counter-productive.

Carr came to believe that AIJAC—the Israel Lobby, as he called it—had succeeded in distorting Australia's position on the Middle East in Israel's favour. Had AIJAC turned a friend into an enemy? When I asked Leibler whether AIJAC tried to intimidate critics, whether it was outraged in its criticism to the extent that outrage becomes bullying and counter-productive, he said that, if AIJAC had its time again, it would not have been so concerned about Ashrawi's Peace Prize. "It was not that important. Sometimes, we have to know when silence is best. Let things go. I think I have certainly learnt not to react to everything. And I think I have learnt to say things in a more measured way."

But did AIJAC sometimes turn friends—or people who hold no strong views one way or the other on the Middle East—into enemies? Leibler's response was forthright: "Making us responsible for our enemies is to blame Jews for anti-Semitism. I utterly reject that."

CHAPTER 21

The close relationship that Mark Leibler enjoyed with Paul Keating and John Howard during their time as prime minister did not extend to Howard's successor, Kevin Rudd. Having reported on Rudd's campaign in 2007, and with the benefit of hindsight, it seems inevitable to me that Leibler and Rudd would, at best, irritate each other and, at worst, dislike and distrust each other. That they seriously fell out, however, is attributable in large part to a major crisis in relations between Israel and Australia. Two events soured the relationship between Rudd and the leadership of the Jewish community, especially the relationship between Rudd and Leibler. The first was the so-called passports affair, and the second a dinner at The Lodge, the Prime Minister's residence in Canberra, both of which occurred in the two months before Rudd was deposed as Prime Minister in June 2010.

On 16 May 2010, Australia expelled an Israeli diplomat, who was also a senior agent of Israeli security service Mossad, after Mossad agents had used fake Australian passports to enter Dubai. There they had assassinated one of the top arms dealers of Hamas, the Palestinian Islamist organisation that since 2007 has been the de facto governing authority in the Gaza Strip. The dealer, Mahmoud al-Mabhouh, was found dead in his hotel room on 20 January 2010. Prime Minister Rudd declared that the relationship with Israel had been affected by this "outrageous" use of fake Australian passports. He said this was especially so, given that Mossad had used Australian passports for another operation in 2003, the details of which neither Israeli nor Australian security officials have ever disclosed. After the 2003 incident, according to Rudd, Mossad had given the Australian Security

Intelligence Organisation (ASIO) a secret undertaking never to use Australian passports for any Israeli security exercise again.

The passports affair came just before an operation by the Israeli military involving one of the six ships of the Gaza Freedom Flotilla, launched by a coalition of pro-Palestinian and human rights groups to break the Israeli-Egyptian blockade of the Gaza Strip. There is little doubt that some of those on board some of the ships were armed with knives and clubs; there were also unconfirmed reports that some were armed with handguns. Nine people on board the ship were killed and 10 Israeli soldiers wounded after the soldiers landed on the ship from helicopters on 31 May 2010. All six ships were escorted to an Israeli port and everyone on board detained for several days before they were expelled from Israel. There was international outrage at what the Israelis had done.

Rudd reacted immediately, condemning "any use of violence under the circumstances that we have seen." While he didn't spell it out, it was clear that he was referring to the use of violence by the Israeli military. He called for the blockade of Gaza to be lifted, and for the Israeli government to set up an independent inquiry into the incident: "If the Israeli authorities, the Israeli government does not do that, then consideration should be given to what other form of inquiry occurs."

Leibler's notes about the passports fiasco and the Gaza blockade show the extent to which these two crises challenged and consumed him. They also show that he could reach out to Cabinet ministers and senior public servants, who invariably took his calls or agreed to see him. The passports incident was especially difficult, time-consuming and troubling for him, because it was specifically about the relationship between Australia and Israel, and because it was hard to defend what the Israelis had done.

CHAPTER 21

During the crisis, Leibler spoke almost every day with the Israeli Ambassador in Canberra, Yuval Rotem. When I called Rotem in Israel, he remembered that time well. Since 2009 he had risen through the ranks to become Director General of the Foreign Ministry, making him one of the most senior civil servants in the country and a close adviser to Prime Minister Benjamin Netanyahu. The passports affair was "a major crisis, the most serious in the history of Australia–Israel relations," Rotem said.

> During this time of 2010, our relationship was tested in the most meaningful and deep way. And so, when at the end of the day, under Kevin Rudd and later Julia Gillard, our relationship returned to normalcy and to some kind of cooperation that had strategic meaning, it showed that we were able to overcome even major obstacles when they presented themselves.

What Rotem hinted at, but would not spell out, was that, for a while, the strong cooperation between the Australian and Israeli security organisations was threatened after Australia expelled the Israeli diplomat and Mossad operative from the country. Working feverishly to prevent a rupture in this cooperation, Rotem lobbied senior members of the Rudd and Gillard governments, and worked closely with Leibler to get the relationship repaired as quickly as possible. Rotem described Leibler as "an amazingly discreet person" who served the interests of Australia and at the same time worked across the Israeli political spectrum to help repair the relationship between the countries. Leibler "was a great facilitator of negotiations."

Asked what he had thought of Rudd during the crisis, Rotem said that his view was unimportant. He had to deal with the prime minister of the time and, anyway, he said, it would be wrong to characterise Rudd as hostile to Israel or not supportive of the relationship between the two countries. Of Julia Gillard, however, Rotem added that she "had an emotional intelligence that was special. I found her relatively easy to deal with. We had arguments, too, but I think they were conducted in a civilised manner. She was an outstanding person and politician."

Leibler has notes of conversations with Foreign Minister Stephen Smith and with other members of the Rudd government and of the Coalition in Opposition, as well as with senior Foreign Affairs officials, including Dennis Richardson, then head of the Department of Foreign Affairs and Trade. His notes record a meeting with Richardson, who had been head of ASIO when Israeli agents had used fake Australian passports in 2003, on 27 May 2010. At the meeting, Leibler noted, Richardson said that a Memorandum of Understanding had been drawn up after the 2003 incident which spelt out that Mossad would not use Australian passports again. Leibler told Richardson that on his next visit to Israel he would arrange a meeting with the head of Mossad to convey his concerns, and Richardson's, about the further use of Australian passports. Leibler's notes also reveal that he believed Rudd had overreacted by expelling the Israeli diplomat, but Leibler knew that Israel did not have a strong case to argue over the expulsion. He wanted to settle this issue and for things to "move on."

Leibler would not go into the details of his conversation with Richardson but must have known that it was Richardson who had urged Rudd to expel the diplomat. Rotem, to whom Leibler was speaking every day, had reached that conclusion, which is why the meeting with Richardson was, as Leibler's notes state, "critically important." He wanted to make it clear to Richardson that he, Leibler, could convey to Israeli leaders, including the head of Mossad, Richardson's concerns. Leibler did not defend the use of the passports.

Rudd gave his version of these events in the second volume of his memoirs, *The PM Years*, published in late 2018. In a report on the book in *The Age* on 19 October of that year, Rudd was quoted as saying that Israel's use of fake Australian passports in 2010 was the second time this had happened and that, after the Israelis were caught the first time, they had agreed not to do it again. This was true and it is reflected in the notes Leibler wrote at the time. Rudd also writes in his book that what he called the "Israel Lobby" had tried to "menace" him for his strong response to the passports affair. He goes on to write about how Mossad had been found out forging passports in 2003 and that Richardson, as head of ASIO, had "hauled them over the coals" and extracted from the Israelis a promise not to do it again. Rudd's account more or less coincides with the substance of what Richardson told Leibler, but with an added degree of grandiosity; Richardson, according to Rudd, had disciplined Mossad and forced it to promise to be good in future.

In his memoirs, Rudd then goes on to describe a meeting of the National Security Committee of Cabinet after the second passports incident. Richardson, as head of the Department of Foreign Affairs and Trade, had urged them to "act firmly and decisively." Everyone apparently nodded in agreement except, Rudd wrote, for Julia Gillard. "I asked her explicitly whether she supported the recommendations. She grunted her assent. I knew for a fact that Julia had been cultivating the Israeli Lobby in Australia."

On 1 June 2010, Mark Dreyfus, later Gillard's Attorney-General, called Leibler, whom he had known for many years. Dreyfus told Leibler that Rudd wanted to have a dinner with Leibler and a few other Jewish community leaders at the Prime Minister's Canberra residence on 3 June to discuss the passports issue and the Gaza flotilla. The dinner was intended to begin the process of repairing the strained relationship between Rudd and the Jewish community, at least with its leaders like Leibler. Jewish MP, Michael Danby, was present, as was Dreyfus. The presidents of the ZFA and the ECAJ attended, as did Leibler's former adviser, Helene Teichmann, who knew Rudd and had maintained her extensive contacts in the Australian Labor Party.

What happened at that dinner is contested. Rudd writes in his book that he agreed to host the dinner out of respect for Labor's Jewish MPs from Melbourne, Danby and Dreyfus, who had lobbied him to put on a dinner for the Jewish leaders. According to Rudd, he sat politely at the table while Leibler berated him for committing the "hostile act" of expelling the Israeli diplomat. Rudd writes that he told Leibler that it had been the second time that Israel had used fake passports and that Leibler had responded, "I don't believe you." When he offered Leibler a briefing with Richardson, Leibler turned angry and made a "menacing threat." Rudd records Leibler as saying, "Julia is looking very good in the public eye these days, Prime Minister. She's performing very strongly. She's a great friend of Israel. But you shouldn't be anxious about her, should you, Prime Minister."

None of these incidents that Rudd recalls so vividly are in the nine pages of notes, dated 7 June, that Leibler typed after the dinner. Leibler had made handwritten notes in his hotel room immediately after the dinner, before he flew back to Melbourne the next morning. According to his notes, Leibler, at Rudd's invitation, had raised a range of issues, and the Prime Minister had responded to each. Leibler acknowledges he had been blunt with Rudd, telling him that the Jewish community was "pissed off" by the expulsion of the Israeli diplomat. He had labelled the expulsion an "overreaction", but he had not, according to the notes,

contradicted Rudd's suggestion that this had been the second time
that the Israelis had used fake Australian passports.

Others at the dinner, including Teichmann, had taken part in the
discussions that followed Leibler's presentation. At the end of the dinner,
Rudd had pointed out that he had spent more time on Australia's
relationship with Israel than on its relationship with any other countries
except the United States and China. He had not extended to any other
group representing a particular community "an invitation of the kind
that he had extended to us, to have dinner with him and engage in a
frank exchange of views."

"Everyone regarded the meeting as positive, constructive and
friendly," Leibler wrote. "The PM made it clear that he valued and
was very supportive of a close and warm relationship with Israel and
the Australian Jewish Community." Leibler's notes only mention
Gillard once. At one point, Leibler praised her for her statement she
made while she was acting Prime Minister during the Israel–Gaza
war of December 2008 and early January 2009. In a statement, she had
called for a ceasefire in the war, but had said that Israel was justified in
responding to missile attacks by Hamas, which had threatened Israeli
civilians. As his notes record:

> Rudd responded by saying that he discussed and approved the
> statement with Julia Gillard. I said, "Don't be so sensitive—this
> is something we assumed." For about 30 seconds there was dead
> silence and I thought Rudd's eyes were going to pop out of his
> head, and then we reverted back to normal conversation.

Leibler writes that when he was leaving, he took Rudd aside and
assured him that he was going to raise Rudd's concerns over the passports issue with both the head of Mossad and with Prime Minister
Netanyahu. Less than two weeks after the dinner at The Lodge, Leibler

flew to Israel. He met Netanyahu on 20 June and raised his concerns about the use of fake Australian passports, before meeting the head of Mossad, Meir Dagan, on 23 June, and expressing similar concerns.

When I asked how the meeting with Dagan had been arranged, Leibler would not comment. It was surely interesting that an Australian could organise a meeting with Israel's spy chief? Leibler remained silent. When I checked with Rotem, he also would not comment. He indicated that Leibler had deep contacts in the Israeli Foreign Ministry and in the Prime Minister's Office. Benjamin Netanyahu's office had probably organised the meeting. Leibler was clearly sensitive about this meeting with the Mossad chief. He told me that he had made it clear to everyone that the discussions took place on the basis that he would brief the Australian authorities fully on what had transpired at this meeting with Dagan.

Three days after Leibler met Dagan, and just over three weeks after the dinner at The Lodge, Julia Gillard defeated Rudd in a leadership ballot and became Australia's first female prime minister. This event would change Rudd's view of the "Israel Lobby" for good. On 18 August, Leibler had a two-hour meeting with Richardson and David Irvine, Director-General of ASIO. On 26 November, he met with Rudd, by then Foreign Minister. In his notes, Leibler writes that Richardson and Irvine indicated that they were both determined to ensure that the tensions caused by the passports affair would be a "temporary blip" and that the warm relations between Australia and Israel at all levels, but particularly on security issues, would be restored as soon as possible.

There is little doubt that part of the reason why the Australian security services were keen to quickly restore the relationship with their Israeli counterparts was that the Australians were the major beneficiaries of the relationship. When it came to identifying the terrorism threat from any region of the world, the Israelis were considered the masters. There is also little doubt that Leibler played a significant role in repairing the relationship through what Rotem described as his "outstanding diplomacy." Leibler had ready access to the Israeli Prime Minister and, more importantly in this case, to the head of Mossad.

The conflicting versions of what happened at that dinner on 3 June are revealing. Rudd's version looks back, after everything that had happened to him. It seems that Gillard's "betrayal" of him and the way she became close to Leibler when she was Prime Minister came together for Rudd, in retrospect. He had decided that the Israel Lobby, Leibler in particular, had supported Gillard's challenge to him and was in some way responsible for his subsequent defeat.

Rudd's conclusion has echoes of Bill Hayden's suspicion, when he was Opposition Leader in the early 1980s, that Bob Hawke, hero of the Jews, was mustering the support of Jewish community leaders in his bid to replace Hayden as leader. Hawke had apparently said as much to many of his caucus colleagues, but there is no evidence that Jewish leaders were lobbying caucus members on Hawke's behalf, and no reason to believe they could do so even if they wanted to. Similarly, there is no evidence to support Rudd's claim that the Israel Lobby was working against him for Gillard. There is evidence, though, that Rudd was obsessed with the Israel–Palestine issue. Why did he say that he spent more time on it as PM than on any other foreign policy issue bar the United States and China? More time than he spent on Indonesia? Or the other Southeast Asian countries, or Europe?

Is it significant that both Hayden and Rudd are from Queensland and therefore had had very little to do with Jews or the Jewish community, which was concentrated in Sydney and Melbourne? Both men had somehow absorbed the notion that Jews were so powerful they could play a role in deciding the fate of an Australian prime minister. But, unlike Hayden, who changed his mind and developed a long friendship with Leibler, Rudd's language about Gillard and the Israel Lobby has remained extreme, verging on a conspiratorial darkness. In *The PM Years*, he describes how Gillard became a "wholly owned subsidiary of the far-right Australian Israel Lobby." Together, Gillard and "the Lobby" plotted to undermine him for at least a year before she challenged him for the leadership. "The meticulous work of moving Gillard from left to right on foreign policy had already begun in earnest a year before the coup."

Leibler's account of the dinner, unlike Rudd's, was written immediately afterwards, in the notes he began to make in his hotel. Others who were present at the dinner have publicly disputed Rudd's version. In a joint statement released after an article about the dinner was published in *The Age* in October 2018, Danby and Australian Jewish business-man and philanthropist, Albert Dadon, said that the incidents Rudd described "had not happened, at least not in our presence." They added that Rudd had been a friend of Israel when he was Prime Minister and remained one after he left politics.

Dadon's intervention was significant. He was at the dinner because at the time he was close to Rudd, the Prime Minister's go-to leader in the Jewish community. Rudd reportedly found Dadon far more congenial than some other Jewish community leaders, especially those at AIJAC, including Leibler. Yet in his book, Rudd neither mentions his relationship with Dadon nor includes the businessman in the Israel Lobby that he said captured Gillard in the year leading up to his overthrow in 2010.

Of Leibler, one former senior Labor politician said that Rudd found his forthright style "extremely challenging and disliked it, as he had disliked it from public servants and cabinet colleagues as well." He disliked it from staff, and they knew how to protect him from that sort of confrontational person. But to deal with the Jewish community, "he had to deal with Mark Leibler. There was no way around it."

Leibler responded with fury to the 2018 report in *The Age*. In a press release, he labelled Rudd's accusations as "far-fetched conspiracy theories". Rudd's account of the dinner was "completely false, virtually from top to bottom…Nothing even approximating the threat… was said by me or anyone else. I am shocked and disappointed that completely false accounts of the meeting are now being used to prop up far-fetched conspiracy theories by a former prime minister."

Gillard did not attend the dinner, but had clearly been briefed on what happened. She would not comment on the incident, beyond saying that the fact that she had grown close to some people in the Jewish community, including Dadon and Leibler, was never an issue between her and Rudd before the leadership challenge. Nor would she respond to Rudd's charge that she had been grudging, at best, in her support of Richardson's recommendations at the National Security Committee meeting because she had been "cultivating the Israel Lobby."

It is known, however, that by 2009 Gillard was fielding complaints from a range of community groups to intervene on their behalf with Rudd, whom they found erratic, temperamental, disorganised and often contradictory in his dealings with them. Gillard confirmed to me that there had been

a set of challenges relating to the Jewish community…By then, Kevin's leadership style meant that his manner of working, and some of the ways in which he dealt with people, were very difficult. I think the Jewish community was not the only community to feel that it was being treated in an off-hand kind of fashion.

Soon after she became Prime Minister in June 2010, Gillard was accused by Ross Burns, who had been Australia's Ambassador to Israel from 2001 to 2003, of having been "remarkably taciturn on the excesses of Israeli actions in the past two years." In a letter to the *Sydney Morning Herald*, Burns was responding to the disclosure that Gillard's partner, Tim Mathieson, had been employed since 2009 as a property sales consultant by the Ubertas Group, a fund management and property development company jointly owned by Albert and Deborah Dadon. Gillard had declared this on her register of interests, but it only became controversial after she became Prime Minister. Mathieson probably met the Dadons after he and Gillard, together with a group of Australian Liberals, including politicians Christopher Pyne and Peter Costello, attended the first Australia–Israel Leadership Forum in Jerusalem. Albert Dadon had set up the forum. Eventually Mathieson resigned from the Ubertas Group, but Gillard had defended her partner's right to a career and dismissed the suggestion that her views on Israel were somehow influenced by the fact that Mathieson was employed by Dadon. She told me that any suggestion that Dadon had influenced her views on Israel in any way was ridiculous.

Burns, a long-time critic of Israel, went on to write that Gillard should be condemned for refusing to criticise Israel during Operation Cast Lead in the statement on the war in Gaza that she made as acting Prime Minister in January 2009. It was this statement that Leibler had raised approvingly at the Rudd dinner with Jewish leaders on 3 June. Rudd's response, according to Leibler's notes about the dinner, was that he had vetted and approved that statement.

Three months after she became Prime Minister, Gillard appointed the defeated Rudd as Foreign Minister. She did so with great reluctance, knowing that Rudd's undermining of her would not cease once he was in Cabinet, but she felt she had no choice. As Foreign Minister, Rudd's anxiety about the Israel Lobby did not abate. In his book, he alleges that Gillard's "ever-loyal American factotum, Bruce Wolpe, her lifeline to the Australian and American Jewish communities," had exercised a Svengali-like influence on her, even before she had taken over from Rudd as Prime Minister. Rudd wrote that Wolpe had moved her to a position of uncritical support for the American Alliance and for the Israel Lobby's position on Israel and Palestine.

Wolpe is an American Jew, a New Yorker who married an Australian and eventually settled in Australia more than a decade ago. He had been a senior adviser to the prominent Democratic congressman, Henry Waxman. Journalists whom Wolpe had helped when they reported from Washington knew that he had, and still has, seriously impressive contacts in the United States Congress and in the Democratic Party. (Wolpe was communications director at Fairfax from 1998 to 2009, and for six of those years I was Editor of *The Age*. I knew him well and he helped with contacts among the Democrats when I was Washington correspondent for the paper from 2004 until 2007.) Wolpe joined Gillard's staff as a senior adviser in 2010, soon after she became Prime Minister. His role was twofold: to develop contacts and interaction with the Australian business community, and to be the contact person between the Prime Minister and the Jewish community. Rudd was right about one thing; he was dedicated and loyal to Gillard. Wolpe remained on Gillard's staff, based in Adelaide, after she left parliament, until he resigned in late 2018 when he became a fellow at the United States Studies Centre at the University of Sydney.

Was Wolpe Gillard's Svengali on Israel, or was it Leibler, the power behind AIJAC? When asked about this, Gillard said these questions would only be asked of a female politician and prime minister. Of course, she said, to some people a female prime minister could not have a mind of her own on an issue as complex as Israel and Palestine. She said that she gave Wolpe the liaison role with the Jewish community because there was increasing dissatisfaction within that community about the way Rudd was behaving. She wanted her own sources in the community, so that she could assess what Rudd was saying to community meetings and leaders. On the face of it, it seems extraordinary that an Australian prime minister so distrusted her Foreign Minister that she could not believe what he was telling her and felt she needed an alternative source of information about his relationship with Jewish community leaders. But they were extraordinary times.

Wolpe continued to play that role after Bob Carr became Foreign Minister. "It remained an important role as far as I was concerned," Gillard said. "As for the accusation that I was somehow a puppet of the so-called Israel Lobby and that Bruce Wolpe was its agent, well that's laughable, worse than laughable."

As Gillard had feared, Rudd turned out to be a problem for her on many fronts, including the Middle East. He embarked on a campaign to get Australia a seat on the United Nations Security Council, and probably to improve his chances of getting a senior post at the United Nations, perhaps even the Secretary's position, when he left politics. Several times, Gillard vetoed press releases that Rudd intended to send to the media on Israel and Palestine that she said did not reflect her government's position.

By this time, Leibler had come to seriously distrust Rudd, whom he found frustrating to deal with, slippery, unclear, distracted a lot of the time by self-pity, and not always truthful. He felt that Rudd said different things to different people, depending on what he wanted them to hear. In a note Leibler wrote after a meeting with a senior Foreign Affairs official while Rudd was Foreign Minister, he said that the official had told him that Rudd was not telling the truth when he said that he was not actively pursuing a senior role at the United Nations. According to the note, the official said that Rudd was "courting the Arab bloc" at the United Nations by signalling that Australia might vote for a resolution in the General Assembly declaring Palestine a state, though with non-voting status. Gillard had privately rebuffed Rudd and instructed Australia's Ambassador to the United Nations to vote against any resolution on statehood for Palestine.

Leibler had become close to Gillard, whom he had first met after she visited Israel on a Rambam Fellowship in 2001. In 2010 she had appointed him as co-chair of her Expert Panel on Constitutional Recognition of Indigenous Australians. He said publicly that she was performing admirably in the difficult circumstances of having to lead a minority government. Gillard struck Leibler as brave and honest—a far better prime minister than Rudd had ever been.

CHAPTER 22

In February 2012, Kevin Rudd resigned as Foreign Minister in order to challenge Prime Minister Gillard for the Labor leadership. He lost his challenge comprehensively, with only 31 of 102 caucus members voting for him. With Rudd finally out of Cabinet, Julia Gillard turned her attention to choosing his replacement as Foreign Minister. She considered it something of a political coup when Bob Carr, former New South Wales Premier and a senior figure in the New South Wales Labor Party, agreed to fill the Senate vacancy left by the resignation of the prominent New South Wales Right faction member, Mark Arbib, and to take over as Foreign Minister.

Asked why she had appointed Carr, Gillard said that it made sense politically. She was running a minority government that was under constant challenge, and Carr was considered to have been successful in his 10 years as leader of the New South Wales government; he was someone with gravitas. She did not know that his position on Israel and the Palestinians had changed over the years.

When Mark Leibler heard the news, he felt apprehensive. Nevertheless, his relationship with Gillard was strong. He trusted her and believed that as Prime Minister she would have the final say on her government's policy on Israel and the Palestinians. He did not know Carr beyond a nodding acquaintance, although he had been vaguely aware of Carr's role in Labor Friends of Israel—a minor role, he had thought, given that Carr was a New South Wales state politician when it had been set up and given that Bob Hawke was considered the driving force behind Labor's closeness to Israel after the difficult Whitlam years. Leibler did know that, long before he became Foreign

Minister, Carr had travelled a long road in his views on Israel, from passionate supporter to scathing critic.

In his memoir, *Run for Your Life*, published by Melbourne University Publishing in 2018, Carr sketched his journey of disillusionment with Israel and with its supporters in Australia in particular. In a chapter entitled "Me and 'The Lobby'", Carr writes like a spurned lover—as someone who over many years did much to promote the cause of Israel and the Australian Jewish community, only to be rejected, betrayed, cast out of the Jewish family. The point when the love affair went sour, at least publicly, was in 2003 when, as New South Wales Premier, he accepted the invitation to present the Sydney Peace Prize to the Palestinian activist, Hanan Ashrawi, of which he writes:

> The storm of criticism that then occurred was a shock…and an insight…Soon after my participation was announced, Jewish leaders launched an international campaign to force me to withdraw from the award…There were threats of funding being withdrawn from the University…Letters of protest were dispatched about the awards going to a Palestinian, switchboards were set aflame with indignation.

Carr goes on to set out his long history of support for Israel, how he had always been on hand to "greet delegations and troop along to the Independence Day celebrations." But he also describes how, over the years, his views on Israel and the Palestinians changed, though he continued to make himself available to meet "Israeli delegations and visitors, mostly gloomy and dogmatic diplomats." One of these visitors to Australia was Yitzhak Rabin's widow, Leah. Her "haughty brows arched in contempt as she shrugged off questions about a two-state solution and the welfare of the Palestinians," Carr wrote. Given that Leah Rabin had been a fierce critic of Benjamin Netanyahu and had opposed the expansion of Israeli settlements in the West Bank—a position held by her husband before he was assassinated by a right-wing extremist while he was Prime Minister in 1995—Leah Rabin's "contempt" for a two-state solution seems questionable. She died in 2000, so she can neither confirm nor deny Carr's description of his meeting with her.

Carr writes that it was not until the Israel Lobby publicly spurned him, pressured him to change his mind over Ashrawi, sent him scores of messages and called him all sorts of names, that he realised how powerful it was, how it distorted and controlled Australian policy on the Middle East, and how seemingly ungrateful these Jews were for what he, Bob Carr, had done for the Jews and for Israel. The most prominent and influential members of this Israel Lobby, according to Carr, were the people who ran AIJAC—Leibler and Colin Rubenstein in particular. Of the Lobby, Carr wrote:

> The hold of the Israel Lobby over Australian politicians is based on two facts. First, donations to the political parties from the Jewish community leadership; second, paid trips to Israel extended to every member of parliament and journalists. From the Australia/Israel and Jewish Affairs Council (AIJAC) over 700 trips alone…No other community, in my experience, treats politicians as their poodles.

One of those treated as a poodle, Carr implies, was Prime Minister Gillard, in whose Cabinet he had served as Foreign Minister.

Leibler did not have much to do with AIJAC's response to the Ashrawi issue. He said that AIJAC had vigorously opposed the decision to grant the Peace Prize to Ashrawi because she spoke as a moderate to foreign journalists, and as a supporter of terrorism to her Palestinian and Arab constituencies. And yes, AIJAC had urged Carr not to present the prize to her. According to Leibler,

The rest [of Carr's claims] are just lies. We did not threaten the
university with a withdrawal of Jewish donations, we did not
organise an international campaign—whatever that means—and
we did not organise any boycott of the Peace Prize event. Look,
as Carr himself writes, the event went ahead and was a sell-out.
He was stopped on the street and called a hero for resisting Jewish
pressure, wasn't he? So much for sinister Jewish power. And the
suggestion that Australian politicians are poodles of AIJAC is
outrageous and disgusting.

Eight months after Carr's appointment as Foreign Minister, his relationship with Gillard had become troubled, at best. In late November
2012, the government had to decide what position to take on a
looming United Nations vote on a resolution granting "non-member"
status to Palestine. Carr was determined that Australia should vote in
favour of the resolution; Gillard was adamant that Australia should
vote against it. She was convinced that a vote in favour of recognising
Palestine as a state would do nothing for the Palestinians, and would
at the same time extinguish what she accepted was the faint hope of
a negotiated two-state settlement between Israel and the Palestinians
in the foreseeable future. Given how strongly she felt about this, she
thought that it was ultimately her call as Prime Minister. She was sure
that Cabinet would back her.

Carr lobbied his fellow Cabinet Ministers and members of the New
South Wales Labor Party Right to back his position on the United
Nations resolution. Some of the more prominent Cabinet ministers,
such as Chris Bowen and Tony Burke, held seats in Sydney's western
suburbs with large Muslim populations. Carr was now committed to
rolling Gillard on this issue in Cabinet and Caucus, no matter what the
consequences for her. This would be a rare occurrence, were it to happen,
for any prime minister, but particularly troubling for one leading a

minority government, with Rudd a constant and malevolent presence, determined on revenge and winning back the prime ministership of which he had been robbed. Gillard accepted a compromise. Australia would abstain from voting; in reality, she had been defeated.

Carr, however, was not pacified. Like Rudd before him, he was convinced that Bruce Wolpe, Gillard's liaison person with the Jewish community, was Leibler's spy in the Prime Minister's Office. According to Leibler, nothing he could say to Carr would convince him otherwise. The relationship between Carr and Leibler deteriorated in April 2013, when Carr agreed to attend a breakfast with Jewish community leaders organised by AIJAC and held at ABL. On the afternoon before the breakfast, Leibler and Carr met in Leibler's office. According to an email Leibler sent his brother, Isi, Carr spent an hour "ranting and raving and yelling to the point that it could be heard all over the office." Wolpe's name got several mentions. The email continued: "The breakfast the next morning turned out to be very positive and Carr kept repeating to me, 'You are very smart', a sentiment which he repeated to others at the breakfast." As a consequence of the less positive meeting the day before the breakfast, the two men hardly spoke again and avoided each other as much as possible, such was the level of distrust between them.

In his *Diary of a Foreign Minister*, published in 2014, Carr describes how the Israel Lobby made his life hell whenever he wanted to issue a statement as Foreign Minister on any issue involving Israel and the Palestinians. He found it frustrating that he couldn't even issue a "routine expression of concern about the spread of settlements" without getting pushback from the Lobby. In an interview after the publication of *Diary of a Foreign Minister*, Carr said that what he had tried to do in the book was "spell out how the extremely conservative instincts of the pro-Israel Lobby in Melbourne was exercised through the then-prime minister's office."

Although he did not say so directly, it was clear Carr believed that Gillard had vetted—and sometimes vetoed—his statements on Israel and the Palestinians, just as, he believed, she had done to Rudd when he was Foreign Minister. No doubt, Carr's remarks about the Israel Lobby's power in the Prime Minister's Office were about Wolpe, the man who had so offended Kevin Rudd. No-one was prepared to confirm this on the record, but more than one person I spoke to described an incident outside the Prime Minister's Office in Canberra, where Carr ran after Wolpe shouting that he was an "agent of the Israel Lobby" and of the Jewish leaders in Melbourne, in particular.

Bob Carr did not respond to requests for an interview. I had hoped to ask him how, if AIJAC and the Israel Lobby were so powerful, he had been able to roll Gillard in Cabinet and in Caucus over Australia's vote on a United Nations resolution granting Palestine observer status, and about how both the 2016 New South Wales Labor Party conference and the 2018 Australian Labor Party National Conference could pass resolutions supporting the official recognition of Palestinian as a state, when AIJAC and Leibler opposed the resolutions.

More than a year after I had made the requests for an interview, Carr called. He said he had not responded to the requests because he had no interest or reason to say anything about Mark Leibler. He would answer questions now he said, because that time when he had dealt with Leibler and the Israel Lobby was over. But before I asked any questions Carr wanted to say that he had received great public support during the Ashrawi Peace Prize controversy. People had come up to him in the street to congratulate him for the stand he had taken. He said that he had always had overwhelming support from "my side of politics" on the position he had taken on Israel–Palestine.

I asked him how he squared his belief that the Israel Lobby was so powerful that it could distort Australian foreign policy with the fact that he had such overwhelming support on Ashrawi and in general, on Israel and the Palestinians. If the Lobby was so powerful, how was it that it failed to stop the 2018 resolution at the ALP federal conference, a resolution he had campaigned for? He answered:

> The December 2018 resolution was passed unanimously. It was the same resolution that I had put to the New South Wales state conference and that had been passed at other state ALP conferences. The passing of the resolution in 2018 at the federal conference was the biggest defeat the Israel Lobby had ever suffered.

So, the Lobby was not as powerful as he had painted it in his books? Carr said that, as far as the ALP was concerned, the Lobby was no longer "as powerful, no longer able to influence Australian foreign policy on the Middle East." He did not, he said, "resile from anything I said about the Israel Lobby's influence and power in the past."

All this may indeed be history now, but as Carr spoke it did not sound like it was history for him. He could not disguise the fact that he had contempt for AIJAC and for its leaders, including Leibler, a passionate contempt that to me seemed to suggest that he had been wounded by these leaders, that they had rewarded his long history of support for Israel with vicious criticism. There is a syndrome I have observed; some people who have a long history of support for the Jewish community and for Israel feel betrayed when Jewish leaders do not support their position on a particular issue, and indeed publicly reject their position. Andrew Bolt expressed his sense of betrayal explicitly;

after all the support he had given the Jewish community, after his unwavering support for Israel, the Jewish leaders had failed to support his campaign to get rid of Section 18C of the Racial Discrimination Act. Carr certainly sounded wounded and angry with the Jewish leaders who had failed to recognise and honour his long commitment to the Jewish community and to Israel.

And then there was Julia Gillard. I asked Carr whether Julia Gillard had vetoed statements he had wanted to make on the Israeli–Palestinian conflict when he was foreign minister. He answered: "She did so on more than one occasion. Some of the statements merely repeated government policy, for instance that the settlements were obstacles to peace." Was he angry at these interventions? "What do you think?", he replied. So, was Gillard a captive of the Israel Lobby? He said he was "not going to speculate about that. There is no point in doing so now."

When I went to interview her, Gillard readily agreed to talk about her relationship with Leibler. She was more reluctant when it came to talking about Rudd and Carr. She was in Melbourne to speak at a Labor Party fundraising event and was talking to a group of young Labor women in the boardroom of a technology company when we met. In the presence of these young women she had a sort of energy and optimism, as if they had grasped the opportunities that she had created for them. That embattled, sometimes wooden, person who carried the burden of battling Kevin Rudd throughout her time as Prime Minister had long been discarded.

Gillard also spoke a little about Carr, although she was careful in what she said. He had been an important politician and Labor premier, and no, she did not regret appointing him Foreign Minister, though yes, she was surprised how emotional Carr became about Israel and Palestine. She said that he must have known of the issues she had with

Rudd about Middle East policy and that she was on good terms with Leibler. She had made no secret of any of this:

> There had been an emerging drumbeat about our position on UN resolutions but I never thought it was a major issue until Bob Carr got Caucus and Cabinet all het up about it. I don't personally feel like I understand the degree of emotional attachment that Bob ended up having on this issue. I didn't understand it then and I don't understand it now.

Unlike Carr and Hawke and others in the ALP who had always been passionately involved in the subject, Gillard had never had much interest in the Middle East conflict. During her student days, when she was on its executive, she had opposed the Australian Union of Students taking any position on Israel and the Palestinians. In her view, this was not an issue that the student body should be concerned with, not officially anyway.

When she won the seat of Lalor in the 1998 federal election, Gillard had never spoken publicly about Israel and the Palestinians, nor had she had much to do with the Jewish community. She had grown up and gone to university in Adelaide, which had a very small Jewish community. She did get to know the Smorgon family, which had deep business roots in Melbourne's western suburbs going back almost a century. From 1996 to 2010 David Smorgon was president of Australian Football League club, the Western Bulldogs, and Gillard, a committed Bulldogs' supporter, became number one ticket holder in February 2012.

It was not until 2001, when she was Shadow Minister of Health, that Gillard first went to Israel in a group of Labor and Liberal politicians chosen for AIJAC's Rambam Israel Fellowship. For some people, including Rudd and Carr and others who believe that AIJAC has too much influence, if not power, over politicians, journalists and even academics when it comes to the Middle East, Rambam is a contentious program. Carr maintains that the program has produced scores of politicians and journalists who are poodles of AIJAC; by inference, Gillard was one of these poodles.

When Gillard spoke about her visit to Israel, she did not sound like someone who had been brainwashed. She remembered that she had met medical researchers who had expertise in mass casualty trauma. Because of her special interest in health issues she spent time talking to Israeli officials about the health system and how it was funded and run. But what about Israel and Palestine? How had that visit affected her? She replied: "Look, the idea spread by some that I was totally ignorant and uninterested in international affairs and Israel and Palestine in particular is nonsense, designed to harm me politically. I did not go an ignorant naif."

Rambam Fellowship participants are asked to write a report of their experience. Some are invited to a function to talk about what they saw, whom they spoke to, and the impact the visit had on them. Gillard remembered meeting Leibler at the function where she spoke. She found him intelligent and forthright. For the next few years, they had little contact because her portfolio interests remained in areas of domestic policy—health, education, industrial relations:

> You know in opposition, you are occupied with areas that are contested, and on Israel there was a deep bipartisanship about how we should conduct ourselves—at the UN, for instance, how we should vote on those resolutions that came up every year. And as you get higher up in the scheme of things, you're a shadow minister, I had more than enough to do in my areas, in population and immigration at first and then in health.

Gillard said that one of the things she liked about Leibler, from the start, was that "you were never going to die wondering in conversation with Mark about what he really thinks." She also found that she could say to him, "I agree on the first thing and not on the second thing you've said, so let's talk about it."

Leibler's relationship with Gillard continued to grow. After Australia's abstention in the vote in the United Nations, the two met. Gillard had come to appreciate Leibler's keen sense of what was happening in politics and she appreciated his encouragement and concern for her. He, in turn, thought Gillard was an outstanding prime minister operating in uniquely difficult circumstances. Both of them must have known by the middle of 2013 that, even if Gillard survived a challenge by Rudd, she would not win the next election. On 26 June 2013, Rudd successfully challenged her and became Prime Minister again.

From what both Gillard and Leibler say, there is no doubt that the relationship between Leibler and Gillard was much more than one based on the fact that Leibler was a veteran leader of the Jewish community who had a history of close relationships with a number of prime ministers.

Asked whether she thought that AIJAC, and Leibler in particular, were powerful, Gillard replied:

> Look, yes in the sense that the Jewish community in Australia—the Melbourne community in particular, because I know it best—is well connected. Put it another way, the community has done a good job over many years of developing deep connections across both sides of Australian politics. They therefore have the networks and the access to put a particular point of view.

What did that mean, I asked. "It doesn't mean that you get to snap your fingers and tell a prime minister or a foreign minister what to do. That's not true, and I think people who hold that view are putting forward a kind of conspiracy theory."

How, then, did she decide her position on Israel and the Palestinians? She replied:

> I think that it would be fair to say that those who would want to put an alternate view, Australians of Palestinian heritage or people with a particular sympathy for the Palestinian cause, have not been as good over time at developing those political networks. I hope they do because it's best if decision makers hear from all sides of the debate.

Asked about the influence AIJAC, and Leibler had on her decision-making as prime minister, she said:

> I was always open to hearing different views, but people make their own choices, and you don't fall from the sky in making those choices. You are an inheritor of a political tradition. I was very conscious of being a Labor prime minister, of being an inheritor of what I think is a very precious political tradition and that political tradition is one of support for Israel and advocacy for a two-state solution. The actions I took as prime minister were in line with that long-term inherited Labor wisdom and tradition.

On further aspects of Leibler's influence on her, she commented:

> There was a friendship, that's true. That remains. He came to have a respect for me in those testing times and I came to feel from him a care and concern about me as a human being, you know not just Mark Leibler to a prime minister, but Mark the person actually coming to have respect for and care and concern about the welfare of Julia the person. I felt that develop over the time, and that's persisted ever since.

Leibler told me on a number of occasions that he had very few close friends. Sometimes he said he had no close friends at all; yet he described his relationships with Hayden and Keating as friendships. The friendships that public figures have with each other are almost always, in some fundamental way, transactional. They are hardly ever intimate. In Leibler's case, perhaps there was one exception—his friendship with Gillard. He and Gillard expressed an affection for each other that seemed to have elements of the intimacy that is part of every true friendship.

CHAPTER 23

Arnold Bloch Leibler is spread across three floors of the grand old Commercial Bank building at 333 Collins Street in central Melbourne. The white walls of the firm's reception area on the 21st floor are hung with large paintings—the sort of business art that some artists specialise in, big bold paintings that are essentially decorative and speak of success and power. To one side of the reception is Mark Leibler's big corner office and three boardrooms. One is named after the firm's founder, Arnold Bloch, one for Ron Castan, the barrister who led the legal team in the Mabo case, and one for the former Governor-General, Sir Zelman Cowen. Sliding walls enable the rooms to be opened into one large area to host lunches for up to 200 people.

Long before you arrive on the 21st floor, walking through the foyer of the building, through the arched entrance with its marble columns on either side, gives you a sense of how ABL has changed in positioning and confidence over the years. The change reflects how its old clients, most of them Jewish and many of them Holocaust survivors, have gradually become more comfortable and recognised in business in the 60 to 70 years since they arrived in Australia.

A short walk up Collins Street is the Melbourne Club, where much of the business establishment and its lawyers gather and where Jews were not welcome until recently. Even now it is not clear whether Jews can join, as any prospective member can be anonymously blackballed, with no reason given.

Is ABL still a Jewish firm? Is there still a convergence of interests between Leibler's leadership of the Jewish community and the wealthy Jews who were ABL's base? Behind these questions are larger ones about the influence of the Jewish community, not only in business and the professions, but in the arts, philanthropy and politics, in virtually every aspect of Australian life.

In 1986, five of ABL's six partners, all of them men, were Jews. In 2018, only 13 of the 33 partners—27 men and six women—were Jewish. Aside from the partners, ABL had 92 senior and junior lawyers. Just 11 were Jewish; more than half of the 92 were women. Some of these women described Leonie Thompson, one of ABL's first female partners, who died in 2017, as an inspirational mentor for many women at the firm. When ABL named two more boardrooms in 2018, one was named after the late Alan Goldberg QC, a Federal Court judge and one of a group of barristers whom ABL lawyers regularly briefed. The other was named after Thompson. Goldberg was Jewish; Thompson, married to former Federal Court Judge Ray Finkelstein, was not.

About half of ABL's clients are Jewish, although Leibler said that no-one has ever researched this because there is no reason to. Thirty-five of Australia's 200 wealthiest individuals and families in the *Australian Financial Review*'s 2018 Rich List are ABL clients; of these, 19 are Jewish. They include long-time clients of ABL, such as the shopping centre developer John Gandel, Sussan chain owner and property developer Marc Besen, the Werdiger family and retail magnate Solomon Lew. Some of their children—the Lews, Besens and Werdigers—have remained clients of ABL. So has the billionaire investor, Alex Waislitz, who was once married to Heloise Pratt, daughter of Dick Pratt, the international cardboard box manufacturer and long-time ABL client. Dick Pratt's son and successor at Visy, Anthony, another ABL client, topped the 2018 Rich List with an estimated fortune of $12.9 billion.

These clients help make ABL one of Australia's most profitable law firms. It is not large compared to Clayton Utz, Freehills and Mallesons, for example. Some lawyers refer to it, snidely and never on the record, as a boutique firm. While the big establishment firms have hundreds of partners and annual revenues of up to $600 million, ABL's fees revenue in 2018 approached $100 million. Although neither Leibler nor Henry Lanzer would divulge the exact profit, people at ABL who should know say it is over $45 million, which is a handsome dividend and would put average earnings of partners at roughly $1.8 million a year. Of course, the earnings of partners vary greatly, depending on their seniority and share in the partnership, so there is no doubt that some earn much more than that average. According to an article in *Business Review Weekly* in 1988, Mark Leibler was earning over a million dollars even then. Asked about this, Leibler did not contradict that figure, but he would not disclose his current income. If his income had only kept up with inflation, it would now be close to $3 million a year.

Another of ABL's advantages is its close connections with several major New York firms, especially those in part established and run by Jews. Firms such as Wachtell Lipton and Skaddan Arps have referred many major cases to ABL. They dwarf ABL in terms of size and revenue, but it is understood that their lawyers feel comfortable dealing with ABL, a firm with origins in the Jewish community that still retains a significant Jewish client base.

Most of the senior partners, including Leibler, managing partner Henry Lanzer and ABL's "celebrity lawyer" Leon Zwier, are Jewish. The sons of Leibler and Lanzer, both called Jeremy, are partners at ABL, as is Jonathan Wenig, who is married to Leibler's daughter, Simone. Zwier's daughter, Rebecca, is an associate in the firm. ABL is a small dynasty, and the connections between families, the law and the Jewish community still run deep. In 2018, Jeremy Leibler was elected president of the ZFA. Colin Rubenstein's son, Paul, is ABL's managing partner in Sydney and is the New South Wales chairman of AIJAC and also a possible successor to Leibler as AIJAC's national chairman. A transition of power from one generation to the next is in train, both at ABL and in two of the Jewish community's most influential organisations.

Some of the senior partners—and rising future leaders such as Wenig and Jeremy Leibler—have connections to the Jewish community through leadership positions in community organisations or on the boards of Jewish schools or philanthropic foundations run by ABL's wealthiest Jewish clients.

Henry Lanzer, for example, has been on the board of governors of his old school, Mount Scopus College, since 1988. He is a board member of the TarraWarra Museum of Art, which was built and funded initially by the Besen family in the undulating hills of the Yarra Valley northeast of Melbourne. He is also honorary solicitor for the Australian Friends of Tel Aviv University, the Caulfield Hebrew congregation and the Jewish Museum of Australia. All of these roles have both a Jewish dimension and a connection to clients of ABL. When asked about this, Lanzer was quick to point out that he had also served as a director for five years of the major medical research body, the Burnet Institute. Nevertheless, he acknowledged that the legal work of some senior ABL partners was enhanced by their Jewish community work, and vice versa. In his view, these seamless connections had benefited both ABL and the Jewish community from the day Arnold Bloch first put out his shingle in 1953. A happy consequence of ABL's work for Jewish community organisations, Lanzer said, was that the firm's lawyers got to know the community and, therefore, some of ABL's major clients—who they were, what made them so successful, and how to meet their needs.

Nevertheless, most partners agree that ABL's staff and client profiles have been changing for a decade or more and that, over time, the proportion of Jewish partners and clients will continue to decline. John Gandel, who was with ABL from the days when Arnold Bloch set himself up as a sole practitioner, has taken most of his legal work away from ABL. The property developer, who built the Chadstone Shopping Centre in Melbourne's southeast into the biggest shopping complex in the southern hemisphere, considers Leibler a close friend and has donated significantly to organisations closely linked with Leibler, such as AIJAC and the United Israel Appeal. In spite of their friendship Gandel moved the major part of his business legal work from ABL to Mallesons in the early 1990s. Gandel is unabashed about his reasons for doing so; in his view, ABL is too small to handle the complex legal issues of his business empire:

> I still have some of my personal legal work done at ABL but the bulk of it, not anymore. Still, I spend perhaps a million and a half a year with ABL. That's not nothing. Mark is very clever. He is a terrific lawyer. He's been very successful in the Jewish community. I think if Mark Leibler had not had his enormously heavy commitment to the community, his firm now might have been one of the top firms in Australia.

Leibler rejected the suggestion that his community work had been responsible for what Gandel described as ABL's modest size. He said that ABL had never pursued growth for growth's sake. It had always focused on profitability and looking after clients.

Indeed, most Jewish billionaires have stayed with ABL, even as the bigger law firms fought for their business. Yet some of their children are not building businesses like their parents and are not generating large legal fees. Others have taken their business elsewhere, not wanting to be represented by the lawyers who acted for their parents.

ABL continues to attract wealthy individuals and families, but now many are not Jewish. An examination of its top 50 clients from 2014 to 2018 shows that the firm has moved beyond its base of high-net-wealth individuals and families. Of ABL's top 10 revenue-earning clients over this period, an average of five were public companies. However, while ABL does represent big listed companies such as Nufarm, Slater and Gordon, BlueScope Steel, Seek, and Carsales, it typically does not act for large institutional clients such as Australia's big four banks.

Asked about this, Lanzer said there had been a time when ABL did represent some big institutional companies, such as Telstra and National Australia Bank, but they turned out to be a wrong fit for the firm. The work often involved ABL joining a panel of lawyers from different firms to work collaboratively. ABL's strength is in representing clients who are entrepreneurial decision-makers looking for advice beyond black letter legal advice. Lanzer said that was why the listed companies that were clients often had a dominant shareholder who was the prime decision-maker.

A classic case is Premier Investments, whose dominant shareholder is billionaire retailer Solomon Lew, one of the first of the old Jewish entrepreneurs to float his private company on the stock exchange. Lew has had a long, often tumultuous, at times litigious, relationship with Coles Myer, Australia's largest retail company and biggest employer. While Lew was in a battle for control of Coles Myer, which he eventually lost, Leibler was on the company's board for nine years from 1995. Today Lanzer and Jeremy Leibler handle Premier Investments' legal work, which means they often deal with Lew, and Lanzer sits on the board of Premier Investments.

Lanzer's corner office is on the 22nd floor, one up from Leibler's, with much the same view across Melbourne. A large framed cartoon of a tiger holding the 2017 Australian Football League premiership cup is perched on an armchair in his office. When the Richmond Tigers won the flag in 2019, the old poster was changed for the 2019 one, but the tiger was unchanged. It's as if the tiger is there to take part in meetings. Leibler hired Lanzer in 1982, when he was in his mid-20s, during the crisis following Arnold Bloch's departure. Hiring Lanzer, Leibler said, was one of the best decisions he has ever made.

Lanzer can't sit still as he talks and, when he looks at you, it is slightly disconcerting because his left eye seems to stay fixed in one place even as his right eye darts around the room. He is in his early 60s but looks younger as he talks first of the joy of the Tigers finally winning a premiership and then of his love for ABL. Despite his restless energy, Lanzer answered carefully when asked whether ABL was still a "Jewish firm" and about the convergence between the firm and the Jewish community. He pointed out that ABL's business was now roughly a third in mergers, takeovers and other corporate law issues, a third in litigation, including acting for people accused of white-collar crime, and in insolvency and bankruptcy. About 10 per cent was in tax and the same percentage in property; a further 10 per cent was in banking and finance. In other words, close to two thirds of ABL's work now involved companies, some of them large.

ABL is not the only legal firm to have gone through significant change in the past decade or so. Australia's five or six largest firms have more than 200 partners and revenues of hundreds of millions of dollars each. But globalisation has made it meaningless to talk about the largest Australian firms. In 2012 and 2013 five of the most prestigious, including Mallesons, Freehills and Blake Dawson, either merged with or were taken over by overseas firms, including firms from the United Kingdom and China. They are now international legal firms representing clients from all over the world. In the 1960s and 1970s, some of these firms had an unspoken bar on hiring Jews. Nowadays, Leibler said, some of the big law firms are keen to hire Jewish lawyers, partly to attract Jewish clients.

In 2002 ABL opened a Sydney office on the 36th floor of the Chifley Tower Building in Chifley Square. The view of the harbour and the Sydney Opera House from most offices and the large win-dowed foyer is spectacular. The fact that ABL opened its Sydney offices so late in its history reveals how much the firm was rooted in Melbourne, and especially in its Jewish community. The Sydney opening was surprisingly modest, given that Sydney had become Australia's financial headquarters, with the head offices of most of the large banks and companies located there. Only seven of ABL's 33 partners are in Sydney.

Sydney does not have as many Jewish billionaires as Melbourne. Although businessman Sir Frank Lowy and apartment king Harry Triguboff ranked in the top 10 of the *Australian Financial Review*'s 2018 Rich List, the wealth in Sydney was more widely spread in its Jewish community. It is also growing perhaps more rapidly than in Melbourne, in large part through the business success of South African Jewish migrants, most of whom settled in Sydney and Perth from the 1970s to the 1990s. Increasingly, the new generation of Jewish entrepreneurs is based in Sydney.

Susanna Ford is a partner in ABL's Sydney office. She first moved to the firm in 2006 from Freehills, one of Australia's big establishment law firms, after a stint as a senior adviser to Daryl Williams, then Attorney-General in the Howard government. In 2007, she left ABL to take up a position in the Attorney-General's department as assistant secretary in charge of the International Crime Cooperation Central Authority, but rejoined ABL in 2010 as a senior associate, becoming a partner in 2014. Ford speaks with great enthusiasm. She is articulate as you would expect from a senior litigator, but there is no sense, as she speaks, that she is censoring herself, as if she is being cross-examined. At one stage, she wonders whether she is revealing too much.

She first met Leibler when he was acting for the Grollo Group and she was working for Attorney-General Williams. A prosecution involving the Grollo Group had been abandoned mid-trial because, Ford said, it had been misconceived and Leibler had submitted that the Grollos should be compensated for their costs. Ford said that Williams was very nervous about Leibler coming to see him and that they had done "a whole heap of prep" beforehand. Leibler had an extraordinary reputation and Williams wanted to be as ready as possible for what was bound to be a challenging meeting.

Born in Melbourne but raised in Canberra, Ford had known few Jews when she was growing up and as a student at the Australian National University. Freehills had Jewish lawyers and clients, but she did not work with any. From the day she joined ABL, she found the culture totally different to what she had experienced at Freehills. ABL immediately gave her cases that would never have gone to such a junior lawyer at Freehills. I asked Ford whether it meant anything that ABL was known as a Jewish firm. "Absolutely, I mean that's its heritage—the fact that the firm was started in those particular post-war circumstances," she replied.

Mark couldn't get a job back then in one of the bigger firms. Here we are 60 years later, with an extraordinary clientele and there's a little bit of "up yours" about it. And as a woman having been through more conservative experiences, I like that about ABL. Not that these clients are underdogs anymore. They run significant family companies that have grown into huge corporations with international connections. They are an extraordinary group of people.

Ford said that she felt lucky to have clients who had been through World War 2 and the Holocaust and who had then created an "entirely new experience" by being incredibly determined and savvy. She said these clients were very different from those establishment figures who had gotten onto a board because their father had been on it, or they went to the right school. She continued:

> The other thing is that focus on giving something back, which I think is a very Jewish thing. An element of that really comes through in the pro-bono work. Yes, we make a lot of money and we're a very successful firm but there's a huge emphasis on also contributing something, particularly to the Jewish community but also to other communities.

Ford thought that the Jewish identity of the firm would continue, but that it didn't "mean we non-Jewish lawyers are not given a fair go. That's not the case. ABL hires and promotes the best lawyers. I think we need to work on having more female partners, Jewish or non-Jewish."

The shifts at ABL reflect changes in, and perhaps attitudes to, the Jewish community. It is no longer characterised by refugees and Holocaust survivors, by people whose lives and families had been destroyed. The time when Jews felt they had to huddle together, live and do business with each other, a time when they felt alien and were still overcoming the trauma of their beginnings in Australia, is over.

Those migrants and refugees, who were excluded from the Australian business establishment and so built their fortunes with private companies and brought their business to ABL, no longer feel like newcomers. Their children and grandchildren certainly do not see themselves that way. Daphne Stamkos, ABL's long-serving receptionist, said that the descendants of the Eastern European Jews she first encountered in the 1970s were different from their fathers and grandfathers. They were less driven and more at home in Australia. They had not gone through what the earlier generation had gone through.

In a speech he gave at a 2012 ABL retreat, Lanzer captures some of the firm's transformation. The firm, he said, maintained "unrivalled" strengths in acting for private clients "in their deeply personal and important strategic transactions." Among them were "some of our largest clients, our traditional clients—such as Pratt, Lew, Besen and Alter—for whom we have acted over many years, including as control has passed to successive generations." Some of these clients —Solomon Lew at Premier Investments and Max Beck at Becton—had grown to be controlling shareholders of listed companies. In his speech, Lanzer celebrated the work of Leon Zwier in the "insolvency and restructuring and distressed debt space." As a result, ABL had been central to some of Australia's biggest insolvency and restructuring cases, with the dissolution of the airline group, Ansett Australia an early example.

Zwier has built the litigation practice of ABL into a major part of its business. Apart from Bloch and Leibler, few lawyers have had as much impact on the firm as has Zwier. Media-savvy, flamboyant, determined to take on paid or pro-bono cases that are guaranteed to get big coverage, Zwier looks as if he would be at home in any of the big New York law firms or in a TV series like *The Good Fight*. He certainly seems to have made it his goal to be one of the most reported on lawyers in Australia. As he sat in his office and talked, there was a restlessness about Zwier, a breathiness in the way he spoke, and a sort of designed casualness that belied the fact that he was watchful, intent on saying neither too much nor too little. He knew from experience that saying too little would irritate the writer and he would never want to irritate anyone who was going to write about him. He is gregarious and fast-talking, but so quietly spoken that you have to concentrate rather hard to hear what he is saying.

Recruited to the firm by former senior partner Joe Gersh in 1991, when he was 34, Zwier was Bill Shorten's legal adviser during the Royal Commission into Trade Union Governance and Corruption in 2014–15 and Tony Abbott's lawyer when he was sued for libel. He is a friend of Shorten and of former federal Labor minister and Australian Council of Trade Unions Secretary Greg Combet, but he has also acted for a number of politicians in the Coalition government when questions were raised in 2017–18 about their eligibility for election to parliament, because of dual citizenship issues. He has acted both for trade unions and for businesses in disputes with unions.

Zwier gave legal advice to the former Australian cricket captain, Steve Smith, when, in 2018, Smith was banned for a year from test cricket. In 2019 he acted for actor Eryn-Jean Norvill, the key witness for Sydney's *Daily Telegraph* when Geoffrey Rush sued it for defamation after it published allegations that Rush had sexually harassed a young actress, later revealed as Norvill, during a Sydney Theatre Company production of *King Lear*. He also advised Yael Stone, star of *Orange Is the New Black*, who, in interviews with the *Washington Post* and the ABC Television's *7.30* program, also accused Rush of inappropriate sexual behaviour. Zwier took all these cases pro bono, a sideline to his lucrative work as a litigator and solvency adviser in major business cases. But the pro-bono cases pay him well in terms of media attention. Several lawyers said, off the record, that Zwier was obsessed with the media. Zwier takes that as a compliment, saying that his job was to find the best way of representing his client.

When Zwier turned 60 in July 2017, his friends organised a roast at the fashionably shabby Newmarket Hotel in Melbourne's inner-city suburb of St Kilda. The *Australian Financial Review*'s business gossip columnist, Joe Aston, reported that a bunch of lawyers from some of Melbourne's big law firms were there, along with Bill Shorten, Victorian Appeals Court judge Simon Whelan, who acted as master of ceremonies, and former Federal Court judge Ray Finkelstein.

On Zwier's walls hang framed newspaper stories and photographs of Zwier with some of his clients—Richard Pratt, the builders Bruno and Rino Grollo, and Ray Williams of HIH Insurance, which collapsed in ignominious circumstances in 2001, earning Williams three years in jail. Near a couch in his 21st-floor corner office overlooking Melbourne's western suburbs is a small replica plane carrying the Ansett logo; Zwier represented the Ansett administrators after the company's collapse in 2001. More recently, he was involved in the rescue of the steelmaker, Arrium, and the legal giant Slater and Gordon, when it got into serious trouble following its disastrous expansion into the United Kingdom.

When Zwier joined ABL, he was, by his own admission, a lawyer with a "chequered past," having been through an acrimonious partnership dispute that had cost him a lot of money. He had worked at a number of small law firms when Gersh and Lanzer decided that he had enormous potential and, if properly managed, would be a great asset. His practice grew rapidly, enhanced by his reputation as a litigator and by his media-savviness. By 2018, revenue from

Zwier's clients represented around a third of ABL's fee revenue. Of ABL, Zwier said:

> I loved the place from the start. We worked really well together and we had fun and it was a very, very smart operation full of very smart people. Even the jokes at the partners' table were very sophisticated, sharp. If you weren't on your game, people could tear apart a proposition you might make.

What, I asked, was his experience of the old client base, the Jewish entrepreneurs and business people? He replied:

> I have always believed that one of the reasons we have been successful is that we acted for a group of people who were smart, savvy, sophisticated and strong. They were the strongest people you could ever meet. They were brutally direct, they could yell and scream, but they were smart and so you learnt by osmosis, and you know those older guys could solve a problem quicker and smarter than you could imagine.

Asked to name the case that affected him most, Zwier answers immediately: the criminal charges brought against Richard Pratt in 2008 on the recommendation of the Australian Competition and Consumer Commission (ACCC), then headed by Graeme Samuel. Zwier's breathiness grew more pronounced as he said, "I devoted my life to making sure we took on Graeme Samuel's ACCC and that the charges be withdrawn before Richard died." In 2007, in a case brought by the ACCC, Pratt's giant packaging and recycling firm, Visy, was fined $36 million for price-fixing with its rival, Amcor. At the time it was the largest fine ever levied for price collusion in Australia. This civil penalty case had been settled on the "agreed facts", which Zwier was quick to say were not statements of truth but an "artifice" used to settle complex civil penalty cases. According to Zwier, these Visy statements of "agreed facts" were expressly prohibited from being used in any criminal case.

In June 2008, the federal Director of Public Prosecutions announced criminal charges against Pratt for allegedly lying under oath about the price collusion and giving false and misleading evidence to the ACCC. There is no doubt these charges were initiated by Samuel. His decision caused terrible divisions both in legal circles and in the Jewish community. Some in the community who had been friends with Samuel severed all contact with him. Mark and Rosanna Leibler had a personal relationship with Samuel and his wife, but since the Pratt case was launched, Leibler and Samuel have not spoken.

Eventually, several months after the prosecution was launched, all charges against Pratt were dropped. By then Pratt was terminally ill. The prosecutor, Mark Dean SC, told the Federal Court that it was not in the public interest to continue the case because of Pratt's condition. Zwier opposed that move, arguing that Pratt had never wanted the charges dropped because of his health but because they represented an abuse of process. That morning, Justice Donald Ryan had ruled that key evidence in the case—the agreed statement that had been used in the civil case—was inadmissible. Zwier said it was the only evidence that the prosecution had against Pratt.

Talking about that time more than 10 years ago, Zwier gave the impression that he was once more outside the courtroom, talking to reporters, adamant that Pratt had been cleared, that the charges should never have been brought, that Pratt would have been "comforted by the outcome in his final hours." As he told me:

> I've always said that Graeme Samuel is the second-best spinner in Australia after Shane Warne. He went out afterwards and said, "We didn't withdraw because we lost the court case, we

withdrew because he was critically ill and public policy suggests you don't prosecute someone who's not going to get to a trial anyway." Well, why did he [Samuel] wait until the judge threw out the key evidence on which his case was based? He'd known for the previous six months that Richard was critically ill.

When I asked Samuel about the case, he said in a brief phone conversation that he had no interest in talking about it or about Leibler, except to say that he believed that Leibler had acted "dishonourably". What did he mean? He had nothing further to say. Zwier said he did not know what had motivated Samuel to initiate criminal proceedings against Pratt after Samuel had "already won big" in the civil proceedings against Pratt and Visy. Pratt had been fined $36 million for price-fixing. I asked Zwier what pursuing Pratt with criminal charges was about and whether Samuel had a personal issue with Leibler. He replied:

> Mark did not run the case. I ran the case, and yes, at times I was brutal in my defence of Richard. I think it was justified and necessary. No doubt some of those on the other side felt I was too brutal, but I thought a great injustice was being perpetrated. Justice had to prevail.

Samuel paid a price for the way he acted in the Pratt case, Zwier said. He became "a pariah to a lot of people in the [Jewish] community." Samuel did not have to initiate the criminal case, as he had already won big in the civil case. Zwier said that Pratt had paid a price for the wrong thing he might have done, but he also had done a lot of good things for the community and not just the Jewish community. Samuel had just gone too far.

Jeremy Leibler had told me that Zwier would be one of the hardest of the senior partners to replace when he retired. When this was put to him, Zwier feigned modesty. He looked out the window and then around the room. Without a doubt, he said, the hardest person to replace at ABL would be Mark Leibler. Yet the future of ABL is no longer with the father but with the next generation, with Jeremy Leibler, and the young lawyers around him. Jeremy Leibler is seen in the legal fraternity as a rising star, a savvy lawyer, and a marketer of ABL and of himself. Among his clients are Solomon Lew and billionaire investor Alex Waislitz, who are Jewish, but increasingly, ABL is moving beyond its Jewish client base. Jeremy Leibler and his brother-in-law Jonathan Wenig run a team that focuses on mergers and acquisitions, the fastest-growing part of ABL's business.

The younger Leibler embodies the changes at ABL. He is adamant that it is wrong to describe ABL as a firm of Jewish lawyers and clients, or as a firm mainly for high-net-wealth individuals:

> That old generation of Jewish migrant entrepreneurs was unique. Their children are often less entrepreneurial and at the same time, they don't feel as connected to the Jewish community as their parents and grandparents. We had to move beyond that special generation and we have done so. Yes, in part that's because Jews have felt more and more comfortable with getting involved with public companies. But only in part.

Like his father, Jeremy Leibler grew up having very little to do with non-Jews until he went to university. He went to a Jewish day school and to synagogue on Saturday mornings with his father. When he was eight, he joined Bnei Akiva, where his parents had met. Through his teenage years, he went to its meetings most Saturday afternoons and to its camp during the summer holidays. Also like his father, Jeremy, the youngest of Leibler's four children, won the Supreme Court Prize as the top honours law student, although he had studied at Monash University, not the University of Melbourne. But, unlike his father,

Jeremy could without question have gone to one of the big establishment law firms in Melbourne. The time of Jews not being welcome had passed. Nevertheless, he joined ABL as an articled clerk in 2004 and was made a partner in 2011. He had worried whether he would have to live in his father's shadow, or be seen to be a beneficiary of nepotism. Yet ABL was probably always his destiny. From his childhood, he had known many of the firm's clients, and his father had been his mentor.

At an ABL retreat in 2016, Jeremy Leibler, Jeremy Lanzer and another young ABL lawyer, Jason van Grieken, presented a slide show entitled *Transactions*. It was all about what made ABL unique, and how to build on these qualities. The lawyers outlined three case studies to show how the firm could continue to "differentiate ourselves in a very overcrowded, competitive and dynamic legal market."

The future was about something they called "Nirvana"—yes, after the legendary group—which described the strengths that made ABL so difficult for rival firms to compete against. These strengths were about developing relationships with clients, an emphasis on "creativity and ingenuity" and critically, on influence and power. "The combination of our high level relationships with both sides of government and our well known, consistent record of fierce advocacy [is] a powerful draw-card for existing and potential clients alike." The language of the slide show read like something from a business school manual. These three young lawyers, likely to be the future of ABL, did not mention the immigrant and refugee Jews who for so long were the bedrock clients of the firm that Bloch and Leibler had built. Neither these clients nor even their offspring were ABL's future. ABL had to find the new generation of entrepreneurs now.

CHAPTER 23

Leibler has pulled back from daily legal work, to some degree. He still develops the strategy for big tax cases, but other partners and associates do the detailed work. He remains the first point of contact for long-term clients who have dealt with him directly for decades, but younger lawyers mostly take carriage of individual cases. However, if a major case involves changes to legislation or rulings by the ATO that might adversely affect his clients, Leibler will step in. He still nourishes his contacts at the ATO's senior levels, including with the Commissioner, and his contacts with senior politicians on both sides of politics. The networking and schmoozing never stops; it's part of his DNA and he has helped to instil it in many lawyers at ABL.

Some ABL people said that Leibler could be blunt and gruff and could look right through you. He was not great at small talk. His awkwardness could come across as arrogance. He probably had no idea who many of the people were at ABL. But people also spoke of a quiet, confidential, caring side to Leibler, especially when anyone had a problem. Claire Tedeschi, a former journalist who is ABL's senior communications adviser, said that when she had breast cancer 13 years ago, she felt wonderfully looked after by Leibler and by other people. "He could seem so remote and inaccessible," she said, "yet his door was open to everyone. If you have a problem and wanted to see him, Mark will see you."

Daphne Stamkos has witnessed the way Leibler has changed from the young lawyer she first met in 1976. As a boss, she said Leibler was demanding, both of himself and of his employees. He could be very direct, and some people feared him. Yes, Stamkos said, he could sometimes seem arrogant and aloof, but really, he was shy and sometimes socially awkward. He never had the easy charm of Arnold

Bloch. "He is still the most respected lawyer at ABL," Stamkos said. "I think that irrespective of how old or how wealthy they are, people like John Gandel and Marc Besen, when they come here, they are so respectful with him."

No doubt, Leibler can be blunt. At a lunchtime meeting of ATO officials and representatives in an ABL boardroom in 2018, the atmosphere was friendly and polite, the questions were asked deferentially and the answers from the officials were measured and respectful. During questions, the mood abruptly turned; Leibler got up and said that a tax change being considered by the Morrison government was a disgrace, outrageous, ridiculous and would not stand. These people, he said—referring to the Treasury officials who had put out a discussion paper on the issue—had no bloody idea what they were doing. The smiles and knowing glances that crossed the room suggested that this was Leibler in full flight: always blunt and emphatic—some might say rude—and not open to contradiction.

Leibler also does an increasing amount of pro-bono work. Peter Seidel, who runs the firm's pro-bono practice, has tried to keep a record of this work but Leibler often does not tell him what he is doing. Seidel thought that half of Leibler's pro-bono hours might involve Indigenous issues. Leibler still chairs the monthly partner meetings and, according to some partners, one thing he still focuses on with the same ferocity is the late payment, in some cases long-term non-payment, of fees. According to Lanzer, Leibler is not so much desperate to have the fees paid on time, but worried that late fees can be a symptom of something else: of disrespect, dissatisfaction with the service some clients are getting. That Leibler cannot abide.

Every year, Leibler addresses the new intake of graduate lawyers and interns, and the Indigenous interns and law students that ABL mentors as part of the firm's Reconciliation Action Plan. He gives them essentially the same messages he gave to Noel Pearson when he came to work at ABL in the mid-1990s, the same messages Bloch passed on to Leibler half a century ago: Always be there for clients; Nurture and grow your contacts; Do not be erratic; Understand power and learn how to exercise it; Return calls; Respond to every phone call that same day.

CHAPTER 24

On a hot summer's day in 2019, Leibler was getting ready for his first flight of the year to Israel. For more than 25 years Leibler has flown to Israel for meetings of Keren Hayesod, the Israeli-based institution that governs United Israel Appeal (UIA) organisations that operate worldwide except in the United States, and of the Jewish Agency for Israel. The Jewish Agency is the most financially powerful Jewish organisation in the world. From its birth in 1929, it was a sort of government-in-exile for the Jewish State that the Zionist movement worked and lobbied for and, since 1948 has funded Aliyah programs around the world and projects that support diaspora Jewish communities.

Perhaps half the money raised by the United Israel Appeal in Australia and forwarded to Keren Hayesod is spent by the Jewish Agency. Keren Hayesod distributes the rest to projects that support Aliyah from Jewish communities with relatively meagre financial resources, such as those in Russia and Eastern Europe, and to NGOs in Israel working with immigrant communities and the poor.

The Jewish Agency has a budget of about $US400 million supported by funds raised by American Jewish organisations, from Jewish Agency appeals in America and from Keren Hayesod. Increasingly, it funds projects in the diaspora that are designed to bolster Jewish identity and connection to Israel in communities where assimilation looms large and where there is evidence of weakening ties to Israel. It funds the Birthright programs that send young Jews on organised tours to Israel and around 1800 *shlichim*, the young Israeli emissaries sent to diaspora communities to work in schools, universities and Zionist youth groups in order to promote the migration of young Jews to Israel. The Jewish Agency also funds diaspora Zionist organisations such as the ZFA.

Leibler was the first Australian to chair Keren Hayesod's World Board of Trustees and the second to serve on the Jewish Agency's Executive. These two organisations, with their headquarters in Israel, have been at the heart of the Zionist enterprise for almost a century. Increasingly, they are the main expression of Leibler's Zionism, since he has long given up any formal connection with the Australian Zionist organisations and any other Australian community bodies.

Leibler has never harboured an ambition to follow his brother and put himself forward to lead the Executive Council of Australian Jewry, the community's roof body. Isi Leibler had made the ECAJ his turf and Mark Leibler had always focused more narrowly on the Zionist project and on fostering financial support and love for Israel among the Jews of Australia.

In his six years as President of the United Israel Appeal, from 1995 to 2001, its state affiliates, especially in New South Wales and Victoria, had raised around $200 million. In some years they sent more to Keren Hayesod, in absolute terms, than equivalent organisations in Canada, which has a Jewish community three times the size of Australia's, and more than any Jewish community in Europe, including the French community of more than 350,000. These fundraising results gave Leibler influence and a degree of power in international Zionist organisations well beyond the Australian Jewish community's modest size.

Even though the world's largest Jewish community—that in the United States—is not part of it, Keren Hayesod is one of world Jewry's most influential organisations. It operates in Australia and Canada and across 40 other countries in Europe, Latin America and the former

Soviet Union. In 2018 it raised about $US180 million, of which about $US40 million went directly to the Jewish Agency and the rest to projects either funded by Keren Hayesod or, increasingly, chosen and funded by major donors.

The American community, which makes up two-thirds of all Jews in the diaspora, not only has significant influence on United States policy on Israel and the Palestinians but dwarfs other diaspora communities in terms of fundraising. Consequently, it can in effect decide how money raised for the Jewish Agency will be spent, including some of the money raised by Keren Hayesod's diaspora affiliates, such as Australia's United Israel Appeal.

Several research projects conducted by Monash University's Centre for Jewish Civilisation over two decades have found that over 70 per cent of Australian Jews in all age groups, no matter what their religious affiliations—even secular Jews—describe themselves as Zionists. Donating to the appeals of organisations such as the UIA is an expression of their Zionism and a part of what gives them a sense of close connection with Israel. This perhaps explains the consistent outperformance of the Australian UIA in comparison with countries with much larger Jewish populations.

Israel now relies less and less on money donated by Jews in the diaspora. Since Israel is now a First World economy, should not the Israeli government and taxpayers fund the projects, run by the Jewish Agency and scores of NGOs, that the billions of dollars sent by diaspora Jews support? In the first decades after its founding, perhaps even as late as the 1980s, Israel was a developing country and economy. That is no longer true as Israel now has a per capita GDP on par with most countries in Europe.

It was inevitable, therefore, that the tax deductibility of donations to the UIA would come under scrutiny in Australia. Under legislation, donations to charities that ran programs in developing countries were tax-deductible. Even in 1993, when Leibler, with his expertise in tax law, managed to win an exemption for the UIA, Israel was no longer a developing country. Leibler argued that the funds were going to projects that supported immigrants to Israel, such as the Ethiopian Jews who had waited for decades to be granted the right to make Aliyah, and the poor and mainly elderly Jews in some Eastern European countries. After several meetings with Leibler, Foreign Minister Gareth Evans agreed to grant tax-deductible status to the UIA. By 1998, however, the tax-deductible status of the UIA seemed to be in doubt once again. The legislation that regulated charities and philanthropic foundations did not allow tax deductibility for donations to organisations in First World countries, and it seemed clearer than ever that Israel was a First World country. If donations to the UIA were ruled not to be tax deductible, this would have a significant impact on the amount the organisation would raise.

Leibler went to see Foreign Minister Alexander Downer and told him that despite Israel's First-World status, the funds raised by the UIA were going to refugee resettlement in Israel and to Jews living in difficult circumstances in Eastern Europe, Ethiopia and the Balkans. Downer was convinced and shepherded through amendments to the Income Tax Assessment Act that allowed the UIA to retain its tax deductibility and, therefore, its position as the Jewish world's biggest fundraiser for Israel outside the United States. This achievement helped ensure Leibler's standing as one of the Jewish world's outstanding Zionist leaders.

By 2018, all of Leibler's leadership ambitions in the Australian Jewish community had been fulfilled. What remained, in terms of his leadership roles amongst the Jews, was his work for the two largest international Jewish organisations. Their work was essentially about raising funds in diaspora communities that would be allocated for projects to foster Aliyah and support disadvantaged groups in Israel and the settlement of newly arrived migrants. These projects were often jointly run by the Jewish Agency and the Israeli government.

With no Americans involved, Leibler was as influential a leader of Keren Hayesod as anyone on its World Board of Trustees, including those representing much larger communities, such as Canadian Jewry. Together with his lengthy service, his commitment of time and energy, his networking and his connections with senior Israeli politicians, the immensely generous donations of Jewish Australian families to the UIA gave Leibler great clout.

Greg Masel, who until his retirement in January 2020 was Director-General of Keren Hayesod, was born and raised in Australia. He made Aliyah in the early 1990s, having been active in the Zionist movement in Australia, and joined the head office of Keren Hayesod in Jerusalem in 1994, becoming Director-General in 2004. As Director-General he traveled constantly from one diaspora community to another, checking on the health of the local branches of the organisation, meeting with major donors and philanthropic bodies, delivering fundraising targets set in Jerusalem.

Masel is aware that donors are increasingly moving away from making commitments to the United Israel Appeals in the diaspora and to the appeals in the United States. Instead, donors are funding an increasing number of specific projects in Israel that they identify and, in some cases, oversee. They bypass the Keren Hayesod and Jewish

Agency appeals, preferring to fund specific projects of their choosing. Increasingly, the children of old Jewish families in Australia want to donate to projects they want to oversee, consistent with the growing trend everywhere, but probably most pronounced in the United States. Keren Hayesod had to prepare itself, Masel told me, for what would be its biggest challenge—a drop in the percentage of funds it received for distribution by the Jewish Agency, as donors increasingly sent money to specific projects in Israel. These trends in Jewish philanthropy suggest more funding for general, as opposed to Jewish, community projects in diaspora countries. As Masel put it:

> More and more, that next generation of Jewish philanthropists are interested in giving money to things that aren't specifically Jewish. In Australia, Indigenous projects and projects to alleviate poverty are getting more support. Of course, there is nothing wrong with that, but it does mean we face significant challenges. We want them to do both: support projects in the general community and support the United Israel Appeal.

In 2018, Keren Hayesod had a global target to raise $US180 million. Of that amount, Masel said that Australia's target, which he would not disclose, was "challenging". The target is believed to be around $30 to $35 million, which would make Australia close to Keren Hayesod's biggest donor country.

Past and present members of Keren Hayesod's World Board of Trustees have described Leibler as smart, blunt, impatient, and a brilliant political operator. His influence has been profound, and not just because Australia is a significant donor country. He understood the international Jewish community and its strengths and weaknesses. He understood that donating to Israel was a way to express support and even love for the country. Only Aliyah represented a deeper love and commitment, but it had long been clear that there would never be mass Aliyah from the prosperous and increasingly assimilated Jewish communities of the West, even from the embattled communities of Europe.

Leibler said that he accepted the challenges faced by Jewish communities in Europe, where anti-Semitism was on the rise and where Jews felt increasingly unsafe. He understood that the American Jewish community was going through a sort of identity crisis, and that many thousands of young Jews, in particular, felt increasingly untethered from Israel and from any sense of what it meant to be a Jew. But he has always believed that it was not Keren Hayesod's role to raise funds for projects that addressed the challenges faced by the Jews of Europe or of the United States—or of Australia for that matter. The principal mission of Keren Hayesod, and therefore of the Jewish Agency, was to foster Aliyah and fund projects in Israel. Projects to strengthen Jewish identity and communities in the diaspora were not part of Leibler's understanding of the mission of Keren Hayesod and the Jewish Agency.

Masel said that Leibler had never deviated from his understanding of Keren Hayesod's role and that he was respected for the way he argued his case and had managed over the years to put that case to the Jewish Agency Executive. Masel thought that Leibler had influence as a member of that executive, even though the community he represented was small compared to the communities represented by the American Jews.

The extent of Leibler's influence within the Jewish Agency was explored with Jerry Silverman, one of American Jewry's most influential leaders. Until his recent retirement, Silverman had been President and Chief Executive of the Jewish Federations of North America for many years and was a long-serving member of the Jewish Agency's Board of Governors and its Executive. Silverman admitted there had been, and remained, significant differences between him and Leibler about the direction of the Jewish Agency in terms of the projects it funded. He said that Natan Sharanksy, who chaired the Jewish Agency from 2009 until 2018, had changed the agency's strategic direction, moving it some distance from projects in Israel to projects that strengthened Jewish identity, particularly in the United States.

Sharansky was considered a hero of the Jewish people. A former minister in several Likud-led Israeli governments, Sharansky had spent seven years in a Soviet prison camp for his leadership role in the movement of Soviet Jews who demanded the right to emigrate to Israel. Partly as a result of his efforts and those of others, more than one and a half million Soviet Jews were allowed to leave the Soviet Union between the 1970s and its fall in 1991. Almost a million settled in Israel. Isi Leibler had played a significant role in the Free Soviet Jewry movement, as did Australian Prime Minister Bob Hawke.

Silverman said that, as a consequence of Sharansky's strategic changes, Aliyah and projects designed to work with the most vulnerable people in Israel became secondary priorities. The Americans on the Jewish Agency Executive had also pushed for these changes, which were designed to fund programs in America that could help address the crisis of identity in the world's biggest and most powerful Jewish community. Leibler had fought ferociously against them. According to Silverman, Leibler had insisted that Keren Hayesod's constituency was in diaspora communities like Australia's, which wanted to support Aliyah programs and projects in Israel, not projects to address crises in American Jewish life.

In a phone interview, Sharansky told me that the relationship between world Jewry and Israel was very complicated and was in crisis in some ways. Israel had grown much stronger, its economy was booming and, at the same time, ties to Israel in the diaspora were weakening. Sharansky had taken the position that Jewish identity projects, especially in America, were a first-order priority for the Agency, rather than projects in Israel. Of the Leibler family, he said:

> I have great respect for Mark Leibler and his brother, the Leibler family. They are committed Zionists and they have done much for Israel and in my case, for the former Soviet Jews—especially Isi. Did I have disagreements with Mark? Yes, but I don't want to talk about those things. He always argued that, for the Jewish community in Australia, the programs supporting Israel's institutions and Aliyah were more important than the programs strengthening the Jewish identity in the diaspora.

In October 2018, Israeli Opposition Leader Isaac Herzog resigned from the Knesset and replaced Sharansky as Chairman of the Jewish Agency. The former leader of the Israeli Labor Party was not the Netanyahu government's choice, but he had the support of the Jewish Agency's Board of Governors, including Leibler, who had lobbied for Herzog to get the post. Herzog is from a distinguished Israeli family with close ties to Australia, where some of his extended family have settled. Herzog's father, Chaim Herzog, was a former Israeli armed forces chief and served two terms as President of Israel from 1983 to 1993. Isaac's uncle, legendary Israeli diplomat Abba Eban, was close to Herbert ("Doc") Evatt, the Australian Foreign Minister who went on to become President of the United Nations General Assembly in 1948.

Isaac Herzog had known Leibler since 1986, when his father had been Israel's President and had visited Australia. By then, Leibler was an influential figure in Australian Jewish life. Over the years, it was in part through Leibler that Isaac Herzog had developed relationships with senior Australian Labor Party figures, including Kevin Rudd and Julia Gillard. He told me that he had always seen Leibler as an "exemplification of a wise man." Asked what he meant by a "wise man", Herzog replied:

> It means way beyond that he is intelligent. He gives the right advice. You know the ancient Jewish parliament—the Sanhedrin—consisted of 70 wise men. King Solomon spoke about how they acted only through experience. You look at Mark and you listen to him and you see and hear only experience. He is always clear. There is no grey language. And he is known by all the leaders in Israel. So he can walk into Prime Minister Netanyahu's office quietly and speak of very sensitive matters involving even our most "delicate" agencies. Like he did on the passports affair.

Nevertheless, the direction that Herzog would take for the Jewish Agency was not necessarily one that Leibler would wholeheartedly support. Herzog said that as incoming Chairman of the Jewish Agency, one of his greatest challenges was to "mend fences and go to these [diaspora] communities and bring them back on board, tell them that Jerusalem and Babylon have to work together. In these communities there are Jews who keep on arguing and asking questions and undermining the centrality of Israel in the hearts of Jews." Asked if he meant America, he said:

> Yes, of course Australia is totally different. I remember when my father came back from the state visit to Australia, he said that there was no other community like it in the world. So united, so strongly Zionist. I have been to Australia many times and that has been my experience, too.

All this may be true, but Herzog made it clear that, whatever Leibler's opposition might be, the Jewish Agency's major focus for the foreseeable future would be on the American Jewish community, so large and powerful, but so vulnerable, at least in terms of Jewish continuity. This is one battle that Leibler cannot win. In terms of Israel's security, the strength of the American Jewish community and its commitment to Israel is far more important than anything that Keren Hayesod's fundraising for Israeli projects, even those that promote Aliyah, can achieve.

What's more, perhaps those challenges confronting the American Jewish community might be coming to Australia some time. There is some evidence, especially in the rate of "marrying out", which is up to 70 per cent among secular Jews, that points to serious challenges to Jewish continuity in Australia. If Australia does follow the United States down the path of loosening ties to Israel and weakening Jewish identity among the young, it would surely not make sense for Israel to remain as the main focus of Jewish community fundraising.

That focus has in a sense been Leibler's great achievement as a Jewish and Zionist leader. But there are now people in the Jewish community, even committed Zionists like his brother, Isi, who have long believed that there has been too much focus on fundraising for Israel when many of the needs of Australian Jews were not being met. The Jewish day schools were under pressure because parents increasingly were not able to pay the rising fees. Organisations like the Victorian Jewish Community Council were almost broke and unable to pay for the professional staff these bodies needed to meet their challenges.

Asked about this, Mark Leibler said that his brother had always wanted some of the funds raised by the UIA to go to struggling community organisations, but he had never countenanced such a change. That was not the mission of the UIA or the Zionist Federation of Australia. The measures of the success of these organisations, and of his success as a Zionist leader, were the strong attachment to Israel among Australian Jews, the relatively high rate of Aliyah from Australia, and the large number of young Australians visiting Israel on a variety of programs. "The future, well, the future could be challenging," he said, "but it could not be known." He had had his time as a leader in the Australian Jewish community. Whatever challenges existed in future, he said, they would not be his to meet.

CHAPTER 25

Yuval Rotem is the head of Israel's Foreign Ministry and probably the country's most powerful civil servant. During his six years as Israel's Ambassador to Australia during the 2000s, Rotem got to know the Australian Jewish community and what he described as its cultural richness, its "unshakeable love" for Israel, and its leaders like Mark Leibler. Of Leibler's links with Israel, Rotem said:

> What you have to understand is that Mark Leibler's leadership, his connection with Israel, is personal. His brothers live there. His mother lived and died there. His son lives there and, most importantly, his grandchildren, two of them, are serving in the Israeli army. You think he does not worry about them? I have seen the look in his eyes when he talks about them. You know, few, if any, American Jewish leaders have that sort of connection with Israel. Few Jewish leaders anywhere.

This sort of family connection with Israel, if not always as close as Leibler's, is common in the Australian Jewish community. It is, in part, a consequence of the fact that many Jews in the displaced persons' camps of Europe after World War 2 had to decide whether to make the hazardous journey to Palestine, as the young men and women sent to the camps by the Jewish Agency were urging them to do. The British government, which controlled Palestine, refused to allow any of the Jewish refugees and Holocaust survivors into the country, but eventually gave in when tens of thousands boarded the boats organised by the Jewish Agency and other Zionist groups and went to Palestine anyway. Having been refused visas to countries like Australia, Canada and the United States, they had nowhere else to go. Others, like my immediate family, were lucky enough to be sponsored by relatives in Australia, but my mother's two sisters, her brother and their families had no sponsors and went to Israel. Because many families were split up in this way, many Australian Jews have family connections in Israel.

Many family connections also stem from the fact that 70 per cent of Australian Jews describe themselves as Zionists, as established by Gen17, a major survey of the Australian Jewish population conducted in 2017 by Monash University's Australian Centre for Jewish Civilisation and funded by the charitable foundations of some of Australia's wealthiest Jewish families, including the Gandels and Besens. The figure is about the same among Canadian Jews, but is much lower in the United States.

The Gen17 study surveyed just over 8000 of Australia's estimated 120,000 Jews, most of them in Sydney and Melbourne, where more than 90 per cent of Australia's Jews live. They were asked questions designed to paint a detailed portrait of the community in 2017: Where was it headed? What were its constituent parts? How did it compare with the community that had been surveyed 10 years earlier, in the Gen08 report?

The study found that more than 90 per cent of Australian Jews over the age of 18 have visited Israel, many more than once. Two in three have close family living there. These figures are higher than in any other diaspora Jewish community. Between 7000 and 10,000 Australian Jews have made Aliyah, proportionately more than from any other Western country. Gen17 researchers, Andrew Markus, head of the Australian Centre for Jewish Civilisation, and David Graham, demographic consultant to the Sydney-based Jewish fundraising organisation NSW Joint Communal Appeal, found no significant change in the Jewish community's commitment to Israel between 2007 and 2017. The fact that 80 per cent had called themselves Zionists in 2007, compared with 69 per cent in 2017, was due to a change in the way the question was asked in the 2017 survey. In 2007, it was framed in terms of a connection with Jewish history and the Jewish people as well as a connection to Israel; in 2017, the question simply asked whether the respondent was a Zionist. According to Markus, Australian Jews overwhelmingly describe themselves as Zionists. Despite the young Jews who express their disillusionment with Israel and the mainstream leadership of the Jewish community on social media and digital Jewish news websites, the Gen17 survey shows that the percentage of Jews who say they are Zionists is highest among 18- to 29-year-olds.

For Leibler and the leadership of AIJAC, these figures are proof that they do represent what they call the "mainstream" views of the Jewish community. The Gen17 report states that a unifying issue within the community "is a sense of personal connection with Israel. The security of Israel is the immediate issue of concern that unifies Australian Jews more than any other." Markus told me to

> Look at the figures for young people going to Israel for their gap year, or on organised programs like Birthright, funded by major donors, which has sent hundreds if not thousands of young Jews to Israel for a 10-day study tour. The figures are astoundingly high, well over 70 per cent. This is a reflection of the community's connection with Israel. It's more than just ideology. They have been there. They know the place. Many have family there.

Markus said that the trauma and lessons of the Holocaust had been transmitted from the survivors—who made up a large proportion of the post-war Jewish community—to their grandchildren. The so-called Second Generation baby boomers—the children of Holocaust survivors—had come to see themselves also as survivors, because the trauma and suffering of their parents had been passed on to them. Now there was a Third Generation, the grandchildren of the survivors. The Australian Jewish community remained one in which remembering the Holocaust was overwhelmingly a defining factor of Jewish identity. Israel had saved the Jews from total despair and helplessness.

Veteran Jewish journalist Sam Lipski had a slightly different view from Markus. He thought that the Jewish community was in a sense frozen in time and, therefore, somehow immune from the threatening trends to Jewish continuity in communities in America and in Europe. The richness and vitality of Jewish life that had been the work of the post-war migrants and their connection to Israel as the saviour of the Jewish people had been passed to their children and grandchildren. Lipski agreed that credit was due in part to the quality of Jewish leadership—the Leiblers, amongst others—who, unlike their American counterparts, were religious Jews steeped in Judaism and Jewish history and Zionism. As for the non-Zionist leaders of the Bund, they, too, were steeped in Jewish history and culture, in their Jewishness.

As a result, Australia's Zionist youth movements, which cater for children aged eight to 18 and are funded and supported by the ZFA, are thriving and their membership is growing. This achievement is unparalleled anywhere in the world. The youth movements, especially the religious Zionist movement, Bnei Akiva, are Jewish leadership laboratories. Mark Leibler emerged from Bnei Akiva to become president of the ZFA eventually; Jeremy Leibler followed in his father's footsteps, from Bnei Akiva to leadership of the ZFA.

One of the things that put the Australian Jewish community into a "time bubble", as Lipski called it, was the fact that more than half of its children went to Jewish schools. Without generous federal government funding of private schools, which is unconstitutional in the United

States and not available in Britain, there would be far fewer Jewish schools with far fewer students, even though the Jewish community is probably the wealthiest ethnic community in Australia. Even with government funding, the two largest Jewish schools in Melbourne, Mount Scopus College and Bialik College, ranked second and fourth in the 2019 list of Melbourne's most expensive private schools, with annual fees for Year 12 (final year) students at $37,880 and $35,950 respectively. Sydney's Moriah College, Australia's largest Jewish school, is not ranked in the 10 most expensive private schools in Sydney, with fees for Year 12 students amounting to $31,540.

The community's wealth goes beyond the tycoons revealed in the *Australian Financial Review*'s Rich 200 list. In the Gen17 survey, 78 per cent of Jews said they were "comfortable or better." Jews are more likely to be in the upper brackets of income, with 18 per cent of those surveyed having an annual personal income of $104,000 or more, compared with 7 per cent of the general population. Australian Jews live, in the main, in the middle-class or upper-middle-class suburbs of Sydney and Melbourne. A significant number live on Sydney's North Shore and in Toorak and South Yarra in Melbourne. Markus considers the way a community of refugees and migrants went from poverty to great wealth to be a remarkable story, and an outcome of all that had made the Jewish community so vibrant in the post-war years.

The picture is very different in America, where the Jewish community is three or four generations older than the community in Australia and, inevitably, more assimilated. Unlike Australia, it is mostly a pre-Holocaust community. For a decade or more, Jewish leaders in the United States have felt challenged by the rate at which Jews marry non-Jews who do not covert to Judaism, which is now well over 70 per cent. This has led to a weakening of the connection with Israel among young Jews and a community identity crisis over what it means to be Jewish and what it means to have a special connection to Israel. These trends threaten Jewish continuity in the world's largest Jewish community. In the medium term they also threaten the American Jewish community's support for Israel, which could, in turn, change the dynamics of United States policy on Israel and the Palestinians.

This particular issue has come to a head with the mainstream American Jewish response to the Boycott, Divestment, Sanctions (BDS) movement. The BDS movement is a worldwide campaign to boycott Israel and Israelis, including academics and companies, although what it aims to get Israel to do is not clear. For some—a minority in the movement—it is about getting Israel to end the occupation of the West Bank and Gaza and to enter peace talks with the Palestinians, with goal of achieving a two-state solution. In the main, the BDS goal has become to replace Israel with one secular state "from the Jordan to the sea." There is little doubt that some BDS supporters are not just virulently anti-Israel but are anti-Semitic, or at least they couch their arguments in anti-Semitic tropes about Jewish power, money and malign influence. BDS organisations are still supported by a minority of American Jews, but they are growing, especially on university campuses. In Australia, no Jewish organisation supports the BDS movement, but there are individual Jews who do. Some of them, like Larry Stillman, long-time member of the left-wing Jewish Democratic Society, and journalist Anthony Lowenstein, write as Jews, which gives their opinions a particular legitimacy in some quarters. Such people are but a small group of Jews whose influence in the Jewish community is negligible.

When it comes to Jewish continuity, it seems that the American Jewish community is facing the challenge that Melbourne academic and writer Mark Baker has identified, involving a generation of young Jews who are moving away from being Jews in any meaningful sense of the word. That challenge, according to Baker, will confront Australian Jewry in the not too distant future. Baker remains a committed Jew, who attends a Modern Orthodox synagogue, and a Zionist, even as he abhors the Netanyahu government and its oppressive occupation of the West Bank and its Palestinian population. He is not a supporter of the BDS movement.

But even if few of the trends apparent in the United States are replicated in Australia, for Jewish leaders like Leibler, whose life's work has been about ensuring a Jewish future in Australia, all is not rosy in the Gen17 report. Since the early 1990s, the rate at which Australian Jews "marry out" has doubled; about 35 per cent of Jews in Sydney and 26 per cent in Melbourne now "marry out". Breaking down these figures is even more revealing. Among the Orthodox, very few marry non-Jews. The rate among the ultra-Orthodox is 5 per cent and among Modern Orthodox, 7 per cent. Among self-described secular Jews—about a third of the community—62 per cent "married out" between 2010 and 2017. Since the Gen17 research shows that "by almost all attitudinal measures, intermarried Jews exhibit weaker levels of Jewish identification and Jewish behaviour than their in-married counterparts," these figures suggest that a large number of secular Jews will eventually "disappear" into the general community.

Markus, asked how different he thought the community might be when the planned Gen27 research project is conducted seven years from now, said he believed that not much would change, apart from the intermarriage rate, which would continue to rise, and that would have all sorts of ramifications. The community may cease to grow, given that a major migration of Jews to Australia is unlikely. The proportion of Jews who are ultra-Orthodox or Modern Orthodox will increase, and the community might become even more conservative.

Markus believes that the Jewish community is already much more conservative than it was 20 or 30 years ago: "Once there were left-wing groups and voices in the community like the Bund that were quite powerful. These groups no longer have a significant communal voice." His view is supported by the voting patterns of Australian Jews over the past half century. In a 1966 survey of Victorian Jews which asked what party they had supported in the 1963 general election, 39 per cent of respondents said the Australian Labor Party and 40 per cent the Liberal Party. (No equivalent surveys of the New South Wales community at that time were located.) Forty years later, the Gen08 survey asked participants how they would vote in a general election in 2007, and the results showed that just 23 per cent of respondents across Australia said they would vote for the ALP, while 50 per cent supported the Liberal Party and 4 per cent the Australian Greens. Support for the ALP had fallen to 19 per cent by the time of the Gen17 Survey, while support for the Greens had risen to 9 per cent, and Liberal Party support had remained constant. This increasing support for conservative politicians over the long term has not been evident in the United States where Jewish community support for the Democratic Party remains above 70 per cent.

There are trends dividing Jewish communities around the world. Some of them concern a fundamental question: who is a Jew? According to Halacha (Jewish religious law), a Jew is a person born to a Jewish mother, or to a woman who has converted to Judaism through an arduous and lengthy process overseen by Orthodox rabbis. Women whose conversion is supervised by Reform or Progressive rabbis—the liberal streams of Judaism—are not considered to be Jewish by the vast majority of Orthodox rabbis and their congregations, nor by Israel's Rabbinates, which determine who in Israel is a Jew and, therefore, can be married under Jewish law.

It is one of the great ironies of Israeli history and politics that a country founded largely by left-wing secularists has no civil marriage or divorce. After the state was created in 1948, its founders, feeling they needed the support of the religious parties in order to form government, gave the rabbinical establishment control over marriage and divorce. Since then the religious parties, which represent a minority of Israelis, have almost always held enough votes in the Knesset to make and unmake governments. As a result, they have been able to decide who in Israel is and is not a Jew.

Reform Judaism, as it is known in America, or Progressive Judaism, as it is known in Australia, does not follow a literal reading of the Torah or Halacha. The most obvious manifestation of this "modernisation" of Torah and Halacha teachings is the acceptance, indeed celebration, of the ordination and promotion of female rabbis. Even in Modern Orthodox congregations, such as the Mizrachi, of which the Leiblers are prominent members, men and women are separated during services and rabbis can only be male. Neither Modern Orthodox nor ultra-Orthodox Jews recognise Reform or Progressive Judaism as authentic forms of Judaism. Most Orthodox rabbis, and most of their congregants, have never been to a Reform or Progressive synagogue. Marriages performed by Reform or Progressive rabbis are not recognised by the rabbinates in Israel. Given that a large majority of America's six million Jews are members of Reform or Liberal branches of Judaism, the question of who is a Jew is highly contested, all the more so because over 70 per cent of non-Orthodox Jews in American "marry out" and most of the non-Jewish partners who do convert do so with Progressive rabbis.

The Leibler family has not needed to wrestle directly with the question of who is a Jew. They were religious Zionists, Modern Orthodox, going back three generations. There had been no intermarriage or slippage into Reform or Progressive Judaism. Unlike in America, Reform Jews represent a small minority of Australia's Jewish population. The question of who is a Jew has, nevertheless, troubled Leibler. As a veteran Zionist leader, he fervently believes in the Law of Return's central position in Zionism. He is an Orthodox Jew who attends Synagogue on Shabbat and at every Jewish festival. His home is strictly kosher, and only kosher food is served at ABL for Jewish functions. He has, however, changed his attitude to Reform Judaism over the years. He attends weddings and bar mitzvahs at Reform synagogues and always addresses Reform rabbis, including female ones, with the proper honorific. He has changed his understanding of who is a Jew, even though he is unsure about how far to go— for instance, whether to accept as part of the Jewish community the children of "mixed" marriages where the mother is not Jewish, as is increasingly the case in America and even in Australia.

For Leibler personally and his family, the question of who is a Jew does not arise. As a Zionist and a long-time Zionist leader, however, Leibler accepts that it is a fundamental question, as he explained:

> There are many difficult questions...who is defined as a Jew, who does the defining and on what basis...who you can marry, who you can't marry. Our Jewish organisations, including the Zionist Federation that I led for more than a decade, don't talk about these issues. These issues engage younger people and, if you don't talk about them, many younger people are less likely to get involved.

The issues are not just about who is a Jew. ABL was one of the first law firms to support the Yes case in the same-sex marriage postal survey. When the Australian rabbinical authorities put out statements urging people to vote against the legalization of same-sex marriage, Leibler was furious. In his view, they should not have got involved. The rabbis could decide what was a marriage under Halacha, but they could have no say about what constituted a marriage under civil law. He had some pretty tough discussions with a couple of rabbis about their behaviour over this issue.

As there is no civil law when it comes to marriage in Israel, does that mean, I asked him, that marriage equality is not possible in Israel? He replied, "Yes, that's true I'd say, unfortunately. It is unlikely to change in the foreseeable future, basically because the Israeli system of proportional representation means that the religious parties will often be in a position to make or break governments."

What about the issue of who is a Jew? Should the Orthodox rabbis decide this question? And what will it mean for American Jewry and sections of Australian Jewry if they do hold on to that power?

> The Law of Return makes it necessary to have a definition of who is a Jew and it has never been the one enforced by the Orthodox Rabbinate in Israel. It is a much looser definition. You only need one Jewish grandparent. The Law of Return is about having a country where Jews as a matter of course are accepted as citizens if they make Aliyah.

Did he accept the Halachic or Orthodox definition of a Jew—someone born to a Jewish mother whose parents were married by an Orthodox rabbi in an Orthodox marriage ceremony and have a Ketubah—an Orthodox marriage certificate—to prove it? In his reply he invited debate:

This is not simple. I am an Orthodox Jew and a Zionist. But I think Zionist organisations should be advocating for civil marriage and divorce in Israel for instance. That might complicate things, but the world is changing, the Jewish world is changing. It won't be easy to get all Zionist organisations to advocate for civil marriage and divorce because there will be opposition. There has been a shift to the right, no doubt about that. Mizrachi for instance, might be opposed to civil marriage in Israel. Well, let's have the debate. I think the powers of the Chief Rabbinate in Israel are too great and the way these powers are exercised is often appalling.

So, what about defining who is a Jew?

I am an Orthodox Jew but I have changed over the years, changed my mind about many things. Yes, I accept that there is a need to define who is a Jew. But that definition needs to be as broad as possible without rendering it meaningless. It needs to be defined within the Orthodox framework.

Talking about all this with Leibler and about the Gen17 Report, it struck me that we two elderly Jews, both children of the post-war Australian Jewish community, had landed in very different places. I was part of that section of the Jewish community, the secular Jews who according to the Gen 17 study are marrying out at an increasing rate. I came to the conclusion long ago that secular Jewishness, which in reality is only a few generations old, has no long-term future, that assimilation and intermarriage for the children and grandchildren of secular Jews is inevitable. My own family and the families of many of the people who were my friends at SKIF provide some evidence that my sort of Jewishness has, at best, a precarious future.

Leibler, by contrast, is part of the Orthodox and ultra-Orthodox section of Australian Jewry that has negligible rates of intermarriage.

Leibler knows what sort of Jew he is, and how important it was for him that his children, and now his grandchildren, married Jews. He can be pretty sure that his family, his children and grandchildren will be committed Jews, committed to their Judaism and to the sort of religious Zionism in which three generations of the Leibler family have played such a prominent role.

But even for the mainstream leadership of the Jewish community, there are challenges ahead. Is there a new generation of leaders that can emulate the achievements of the Leiblers and the Rubensteins and the business people who funded and continue to fund organisations like AIJAC? Both Leibler and Rubenstein are in their mid-70s; so too is Solomon Lew. The community that formed them and that they, in turn, helped shape is changing—profoundly in some ways. The wealthy Jewish donors who funded AIJAC are elderly and are passing on their wealth to their children. Some of these children have no interest in continuing to fund AIJAC.

Colin Rubenstein's son Paul, the New South Wales chairman of AIJAC, is considered a possible replacement when Leibler eventually steps down as AIJAC chairman. Paul, however, said in an interview that AIJAC's future once his father and Leibler retired was not at all clear. He said he was pessimistic in some ways about the future of the Australian Jewish community. People still gave money to the United Israel Appeal and some still supported AIJAC, but they did not want to be involved beyond their donations. They were too busy.

Rubenstein said he accepted the fact that some people's ties to Israel were weaker than those of their parents and certainly their grand-parents. He agreed that this was the trend in the United States and starting to be a trend in Australia. "There's a whole group of Jews who genuinely think Israel is a rogue state. They are a small group but they

CHAPTER 25

didn't exist before. They are active. Many are young. Some have been members of the Zionist youth organisations. Their numbers will grow."

Mark Leibler knows that the time is approaching when he will have to seriously seek out younger people who will be willing and able to replace him and Rubenstein when the time comes for them to step down. Asked about this, he repeated the cliché that no-one is irreplaceable, but is that true in the case of AIJAC? The next generation of leaders will face daunting challenges: the rise in anti-Semitism around the world, including in Australia; a weakening of Jewish identity; and a Jewish community that is in some ways more diverse than its predecessor in its views about Jewishness and about Israel, and whose members are more sure of themselves as Australians than their parents and certainly their grandparents were.

It is possible that AIJAC will never be as powerful and influential again as it is now, and that Leibler was wrong; as times change, some leaders will be found to be irreplaceable. That a meeting between Prime Minister Scott Morrison and AIJAC's three most senior leaders could be arranged not long after Morrison replaced Malcolm Turnbull as leader of the Australian government is evidence of an organisation at the height of its influence.

CHAPTER 26

In October 2018, Prime Minister Morrison, less than two months after he had replaced Malcolm Turnbull, hosted an AIJAC delegation at the federal parliamentary offices in Treasury Place in Melbourne. In the room with Morrison were Leibler, Chairman of AIJAC, Colin Rubenstein, its Executive Director, and Solomon Lew, the billionaire retailer and long-time funder of AIJAC. It was 10 days before a by-election in the federal seat of Wentworth triggered by Turnbull's resignation from parliament. Dave Sharma, Australian Ambassador to Israel from 2013 to 2017, was the Liberal Party's candidate in the by-election. Sharma was known for his pro-Israel views when he was selected as the candidate for the seat that has the largest Jewish presence of any seat in Australia—12.5 per cent of the population of the Wentworth electorate are Jewish.

Leibler said that Rubenstein had proposed the meeting and that Morrison's office had responded in a couple of days. The AIJAC leaders had been surprised at how quickly the meeting was organised, but it surely was not really surprising. Although Leibler did not know Morrison well, he had met him several times when Morrison was Treasurer, and Leibler was close to Josh Frydenberg, the Liberal Party's Deputy Leader and newly elevated to federal Treasurer, whom he had known for 20 years or more, since Frydenberg had worked as an adviser to John Howard. By the time Leibler and the delegation met with Morrison, Frydenberg had become the most senior Jewish politician in Australian history. There is little doubt that Frydenberg had briefed Morrison about the possible meeting with the AIJAC people. What's more, Morrison would have been aware of Leibler's connections in Canberra, probably remembering that his predecessor as Prime Minister had chosen Leibler to MC at the official lunch for Benjamin Netanyahu in Sydney in February 2017.

For the meeting with Morrison, the AIJAC delegation had a list of issues they wanted to discuss with the Prime Minister, the most important of which was to urge Morrison to abandon Australia's support for the Iran nuclear deal. This could only be a symbolic gesture, because Australia was not a party to the agreement negotiated by Barak Obama between Iran and the United States, Germany, Britain, France and Russia, but in Leibler's view, if a respected middle power like Australia changed its position on the deal, it would have an impact internationally. Also on the AIJAC group's list of issues was the question of the Australian Embassy in Israel, which they were going to argue should be in Jerusalem and not in Tel Aviv. But, for them, the Iran nuclear deal was the major issue.

Morrison had been well briefed for the meeting. He seemed to understand the points the AIJAC group was making on Iran. Their main points were that Iran had to be stopped from becoming a nuclear power, that the agreement Obama had negotiated was seriously flawed, and that Iran funded terrorist organisations such as Hezbollah and Hamas and supplied them with the weapons, including thousands of rockets, that threatened Israel. And the Iranian leadership has repeatedly called for the elimination of Israel. The nuclear deal had to be opposed because, ultimately, it would not prevent Iran from acquiring nuclear weapons and it did not deal with Iran's support for terrorism. Indeed, according to Leibler and his AIJAC team, it facilitated it by lifting sanctions on the regime.

It was Morrison who raised the matter of the location of the Australian Embassy in Israel, right at the end of the meeting, when

Leibler thought they had run out of time. As they were leaving, Morrison asked them their view on moving the embassy. They told him that they were, of course, in favour of such a move but did not seriously push for it. Three days after that meeting, Morrison announced that the government was examining the possibility of moving the Australian embassy from Tel Aviv to Jerusalem. Penny Wong, Labor's shadow Foreign Affairs Minister, described Morrison's announcement as a cynical and desperate attempt to attract Jewish votes in Wentworth, vowing that, if the ALP became the government, it would overturn any decision by Morrison to move the Australian embassy from Tel Aviv to Jerusalem.

At a media conference, Morrison refused to say whether he had been briefed by Foreign Affairs or by his own department on the consequences of the embassy move. It was unclear who had advised him on the embassy issue, other than Dave Sharma, former ambassador to Israel and the Liberal candidate in the imminent Wentworth by-election. But was Sharma his only adviser? When I spoke to Frydenberg, he would not say whether he had talked to Morrison about the Embassy, though he made it clear that he favoured its move from Tel Aviv to Jerusalem. Frydenberg said he would not comment on any meeting he might have had with the Prime Minister.

Leibler would not have been surprised when he learnt that Sharma had briefed Morrison on the embassy move and that Sharma was in favour of it. Leibler and Sharma knew each other well. A few weeks before Sharma took up his post in Tel Aviv in July 2013, a month after Gillard had been replaced as Prime Minister by Kevin Rudd and six months before the federal election that would bring Tony Abbott to power, he came to see Leibler. His goal was to establish a relationship with the man he had been told was the most influential leader in the Jewish community, with unmatched contacts in Canberra.

Sharma had worked in the international division of the Prime Minister's Department before he was appointed Ambassador to Israel—at 37, the youngest Australian Ambassador ever appointed. He knew Julia Gillard. He knew Kevin Rudd and he knew the head of Foreign Affairs, Dennis Richardson, former head of ASIO and former Australian Ambassador to the United States. Richardson was his mentor and supporter. Gillard, Rudd and Richardson all had a relationship with Leibler. In all probability, by the time he was appointed ambassador, Sharma knew that AIJAC was the most powerful and successful Jewish voice in Canberra.

Several months before he was chosen as the Liberal Party candidate for Wentworth, Sharma talked to me about how his relationship with Leibler had developed. When he got the job as Ambassador to Israel, a few people told him to go and see Leibler:

> I was surprised at how many people said he was important and how much influence he wielded behind the scenes because he's not a self-aggrandising individual. He's quite subtle about how he does it. People think, "Oh, it's Colin [Rubenstein] who is the powerhouse, and yes he runs AIJAC, but Mark is the power behind the throne. So my objective was to understand him, to charm him a little.

Why, I asked, was that important? He replied:

> You know Dennis [Richardson] told me there was one constituency "you need to keep happy in Australia—there are others—but not very important ones—and that's the Jewish community because if they are not happy with what you are doing, it's not you that's going to hear about it, it's the Foreign Minister back in

Australia." He told me to spend time with them and be responsive and that was very much the approach I took to the job.

During his four years as Ambassador to Israel, Sharma often bypassed Foreign Affairs and sent his reports on Israel and the Palestinians directly to Foreign Minister Julie Bishop's office rather than to the officers running their sections in the Foreign Affairs Department, which was unusual, to say the least. Sharma, however, did not trust his superiors to pass on his reports in full to the Foreign Minister. "I wanted the Foreign Minister to get my take on what was happening unfiltered by Foreign Affairs," he told me. "FA had a particular bias towards the Palestinians and the Arab countries when it came to the Middle East."

Sharma lost the Wentworth by-election in November 2018, but six months later won the seat in the May 2019 general election, in which Morrison led the Liberal and National party coalition to a comfortable victory. Sharma was a politician with prospects; many observers considered him to be a future Foreign Affairs Minister. Before the May 2019 election, Morrison announced that his government was committed to moving the Australian Embassy from Tel Aviv to West Jerusalem when the time was right. As for the Iran nuclear deal, the government would continue to support it, with some reservations. But there is little doubt that Leibler and AIJAC push on open doors when it comes to having access to the Prime Minister and senior ministers in his government.

Past prime ministers have shown the same sort of respect for AIJAC. Regular attendees at AIJAC functions who have told me an anecdote swear that it happened. At an AIJAC function held at ABL in 2013, Prime Minister Tony Abbott was asked what his position was on some aspect or other of the conflict between Israel and the Palestinians. "Oh, my position is whatever Mark and Colin's position is," he answered. Mark Leibler, when asked about it, said that yes, he had heard about that remark but really it was just a joke. Then he laughed; clearly it was a joke that he found quite congenial.

CHAPTER 27

On a hot summer's morning in 2019, Mark Leibler's corner office at ABL was bathed in light. On a small table in front of two cushioned wooden chairs was a framed photograph of Leibler and his wife, Rosanna, taken in June 2005, with Governor-General Michael Jeffery. Leibler had just been made a Companion in the General Division of the Order of Australia (AC), the country's highest award. The citation recognised Leibler's service to business, to the law, to the Jewish community in Australia and internationally, and to reconciliation and the promotion of understanding between Indigenous and non-Indigenous Australians. This citation summed up Leibler's contributions to public life. He had been awarded an AO (Officer of the Order of Australia) in 1987, but this AC was special, and the day when he and Rosanna flew to Canberra to receive the award from Jeffery was one of the good days of his life. It was the first and only time that an AC had been awarded in part for service to the Jewish community. It is likely that Prime Minister John Howard nominated Leibler for the award.

Scattered around the office was voluminous evidence of his many achievements: photos with Noel Pearson and the other members of the Expert Panel on Indigenous Constitutional Recognition; photos with members of the University of Melbourne Council, to which he was appointed in 2017; photos of him with Paul Keating and John Howard whom he regarded as friends. Then there were photos of his children and grandchildren, those living in Israel and those living in the almost cloistered streets of North Caulfield, where they had grown up. It was all evidence of a life lived in different but connected worlds:

the law; Australia's Jewish community; Israel; and the struggles of Indigenous Australians.

Mark Leibler has lived most of his 75 years within half a dozen streets in the middle-class Melbourne suburb of North Caulfield. Caulfield was once full of California bungalows set on quarter-acre blocks, with mown front lawns, immaculate garden beds and fruit trees out the back. That's how it was when the Jews first moved to Caulfield in the 1950s, 1960s and 1970s from the crowded and small Victorian terraces of Carlton. The large and often fortress-like double-storey houses that have now replaced the California bungalows are of an architectural style that has been described as Jewish baroque.

The Leiblers' house is more subdued in style, though it is large and grand in its own way, with its water features in the front garden and well-tended garden bed. Leibler, unlike many of his Jewish clients, has not made the journey of success from Caulfield to Toorak, but not because he could not afford to, even if he is not in the same league as those of his billionaire clients and others worth hundreds of millions. Within walking distance are the places where he has lived his religious Jewish life: the Mizrachi synagogue where three generations of his family have worshiped and the Modern Orthodox school, Leibler Yavneh College, to which the Leibler family donated a million dollars in 1988 and where his children and grandchildren have studied. Also within walking distance are the kosher grocery and butcher shops where Rosanna shops for the family and for the Shabbat lunches with her children and grandchildren. Sometimes, unless they are to be catered, she shops there for the dinner parties where she welcomes the scores of politicians, among them Australian and Israeli Prime Ministers, and diplomats who have visited over the years. She has found these dinners and events sometimes enjoyable, sometimes stressful, but she has hosted them all with a grace and charm not always apparent in her husband.

Over the many months that Leibler talked to me about his life, the many hours spent going backwards and forwards from when he was a boy to his having passed his biblical three score years and ten, one question, more than any other, caused him for a moment or two to drop the mask of lawyerly calm and get impatient. "Why do you keep asking me why I didn't move to Israel? Haven't I answered that question?" he asked at one point. The truth was, he hadn't. He had provided justifications, but no satisfying explanation for what was perhaps the deepest paradox of his life.

As a leader of the international Zionist movement, Leibler is the inheritor of an idea that has helped to shape the course of the modern world. From its beginnings in the 1890s, Zionism was a nationalist enterprise, in many ways energised and influenced by the nationalist movements in Europe that led to the independence of Italy, Germany, Greece and other countries. Some of its main founders, such as Austrian journalist Theodor Herzl, were thoroughly assimilated secular Jews, who had nevertheless concluded that the Jews, however loyal they were to the nation in which they lived, would never be accepted as Europeans—as French or German or Dutch. The history of the Jews showed that they would always be subjected to discrimination and even hatred.

This idea began to gather momentum in the late 19th century, taking on immense, even unstoppable force after the murder by the Nazis of six million mainly European Jews. The Zionists had been right and to most Jews, and to many other people as well, it was now clear that only with a state of their own could Jews be "normal", a nation among other

nations, in control of their own destiny. In
forces they would live their lives as "new"
and at the mercy of the *goyim*.

To committed Zionists, Aliyah is mor
ponsibility. The Leibler family story is in p
consequences for Australian Jewish families
to their sense of what it means to be Jewish

In 1984, when Leibler became the presider
of Australia, he was 40. The *Australian Jew*
"an angry young man" who was "drawing t
around himself to present a platform of co
One of the consensus policies that he insiste
Aliyah to the Zionist enterprise. In his first
he said that a Zionist leader must have a fun
Aliyah; he did not believe that "an individu
if he negates the option of Aliyah for himse

In those days, nearly all the Leiblers lived
each other. They shared Shabbat meals, sho
went to synagogue, celebrated bar mitzvahs
whenever a boy was born, and they brought
the high holidays and at events for their ch
College. Then, one by one, family members
Allan, the youngest of the three brothers, w
Israel with his second wife in 1996. Isi and N
in 1998 and now live in Jerusalem with their

In 2000, at the age of 88, the family matriar
and moved into the building in which Isi and
in West Jerusalem. She had always wanted
her son, Mark that she adored her new life.

Rosa
his A
Yehu
Aliya

M
and A
moth
nor th
Mark
from
assoc
the s
squee

N
o
to
ye
in

F
b
fo
li
m

I c
back
had n
saw th
for w
answe

. Leibler's eldest son, Anthony, left Melbourne for Israel with
rican-born wife Elisheva and their two infant sons, Yair and
In 2017, one of Mark Leibler's grandsons, Ari, also made
But Mark and Rosanna have not.

joined Isi and Naomi and their children and grandchildren,
n and his family, and Anthony and his family to celebrate his
90th birthday party in Jerusalem in 2002. Neither Rosanna
:hildren and grandchildren who lived in Australia were there.
ave a speech in which he said that he had always suffered
iddle-child syndrome". Isi had been given all the privileges
:d with being the *bechor* (eldest son), while Allan had received
ial treatment reserved for the youngest child. He had been
l between the two brothers—neglected, he joked. Then he said:

m, did you ever think about the potentially traumatic impact
ny psyche of your decision to finally settle here...and live
ther with my two brothers in Jerusalem. Of course I miss
a great deal but, really, this is one decision I had no difficulty
nderstanding and in coming to terms with.

the truth is that almost from birth, I, together with my
hers, was nurtured by you and dad in a household where the
s was always on Israel and its centrality in our lives and in the
s of the Jewish people. It is therefore not surprising that the
ority of your family has made Aliyah and today live in Israel.

ed Isi Leibler in Jerusalem. At 84, he is unlikely to ever come
a visit to Australia, where, apart from family, he has never
ny friends, and those he once had have died. Asked how he
future of diaspora Jewish communities, he thought about it
t seemed a long while—at least for him, because he usually
:d questions before the asking was finished. Then he said, in

the language of opinion journalism—in his 70s, Isi had become one of the *Jerusalem Post*'s best-known columnists—that the American Jewish community had been "destroyed by progressiveness." In Europe, the Jews had no future because of a rising anti-Semitism that was often cloaked in anti-Zionism, most of it from the hard left. European Jews, French Jews and, soon, English Jews would be leaving, he said. They were already leaving, he said.

In a column in 2016, Isi Leibler described a diaspora world of growing anti-Semitism and virulent anti-Zionism, in which Jews increasingly felt unsafe, where they were physically attacked and, in some cases, murdered because they were Jews. Aliyah, wrote Leibler, was the only long-term solution, both to acculturation and to anti-Semitism:

> We cannot expect hundreds of thousands of Jews from the Western world to make Aliyah but those concerned that their grandchildren retain their Jewish identity should be contemplating whether to remain in the diaspora, with all that entails, or become a vibrant and active component of the Jewish Nation. The storm clouds are gathering and the time for decision making is now.

Australia's Jewish community, which Isi Leibler described as the best in the world, was a "cocoon that's behind the times and still much better than most communities," but it was rapidly emerging from the cocoon that had kept it safe from being like all the other diaspora communities. God forbid, he said, that it should move towards being like an American or European community. "I see acculturation taking place in Australia," Isi Leibler told me. "A new generation has not inherited the values and commitments of previous generations. I see a lack of commitment to Israel, at least a weakening of it."

Did he feel, I asked, that the trends he described were evidence of the failure of Australian Jewish leaders like him and his brother? Isi replied:

> I think what is happening, the acculturation, was inevitable, an inevitable sociological development. A consequence in a sense of the way Jews have been accepted in Australia. Perhaps had I stayed in Australia and if there were more people like me and Mark still fighting on the front lines, maybe we could have slowed things. I don't know.

Asked what he thought of his nephew Jeremy as a leader having become the president of the Zionist Federation of Australia, following in his father Mark's footsteps, Isi Leibler said he had great hopes for Jeremy, for the quality of leadership he has already brought to the ZFA. "Jeremy comes from good stock", he said and laughed. "He is young, enthusiastic and steeped in Judaism and Zionism. He will do his best to hold back the tide of acculturation."

What struck me listening to Isi was how much the brothers shared as leaders, the forthrightness, the tough language, the lack of grey in their views, at least in the way they express them. They are difficult to contradict, to take on politically. They have made and vanquished many enemies. But they have changed ideologically over the past decade or so. Isi, now an Israeli, feels free to write about any aspect of Israeli politics and about the Jewish diaspora. His columns in the *Jerusalem Post* are often apocalyptic: diaspora Jews have no future; the American Jewish leadership is worse than hopeless when it comes to support for Israel; the left in Israel is deservedly politically fading away; Netanyahu, for all his personal faults, is a great prime minister; there is no prospect in the foreseeable future for peace between Israel and the Palestinians.

In all our time together, Mark Leibler has never been prepared to say on the record whether or not his views coincide with his brother's. Has he, like Isi, moved significantly to the right? Did he support the Netanyahu government? Even Isi had called for Netanyahu to step down after he had failed again to form a government after the second Israeli general election in 2019. Mark responded:

> I do not live in Israel. Isi does and so he is free to say and write whatever he likes. I have always believed that Jewish leaders in the diaspora should not express support for any particular Israeli government—we don't vote. If we want to give the government advice on security issues, we have to either go live in Israel or give that advice privately. Israel has enough critics.

When I interviewed Isaac Herzog, former leader of the Israeli Labor Party, during his visit to Australia in 2018, he told me that he was pretty certain that Mark Leibler's views are centrist on Israel and the Palestinians. Unlike Isi, he said, who had moved far to the right. "Yes, Isi has written some very sharp things about me personally and about the Labor Party in general. We have no contact anymore. But it has not affected my relationship with Mark. I admire and respect him."

I asked Isi why he thought his brother had never made Aliyah. He said that Mark had a tremendous law practice that he could not have rebuilt, in middle-age, in Israel:

> To come to retire made no sense. He would become a vegetable. And, while Mark was a significant Jewish leader, if he had tried to get into politics in Israel, he would have been disappointed. It was impossible. All his involvement in Keren Hayesod and the Jewish Agency would have counted for nothing.

In his opinion, Mark was right not to make Aliyah, though he would have liked his brother to come and Mark would have been happy in

Israel. Asked whether he had ever talked to his brother about making Aliyah, he replied:

> Mark gets kind of locked up when you talk about Aliyah because you feel that he is thinking that as a Zionist, a Zionist leader, making Aliyah is the fulfilment of your Zionism. It was for me. We don't talk about it much. I understand his position and he understands mine. I did and he didn't.

Allan Leibler, the youngest Leibler brother, who had run the Leibler family diamond business before he made Aliyah, lives within walking distance of Isi in Jerusalem. Asked about his brothers, he said that he had never really had their leadership ambitions. He had always been a committed religious Zionist, however, and had often thought about making Aliyah, but that personal circumstances— a difficult divorce when he was young—had made it hard. He and his second wife had decided to move to Israel because, given the trends towards assimilation in America and increasingly in Australia, they believed it was the only way they could ensure that their children would be fully Jewish.

Mark and Rosanna's eldest son, Anthony, lives in the same Jerusalem area as his two uncles. He is a partner at Herzog, Fox and Neeman, one of Israel's largest law firms, and is a widely recognised tax and succession planning lawyer. He and his wife are Modern Orthodox and, with their four children, share a passionate commitment to Israel. In so many respects, Anthony has followed his father's path. They were both dux of Mount Scopus College, and Anthony was the head of Bnei Akiva in Melbourne, the religious Zionists youth movement. After a gap year in Israel, he went to Monash University rather than the University of Melbourne, but like his father, and his brother Jeremy after him, he won the Supreme Court Prize awarded to the university's top law student. He had done his articles at ABL, then a Masters in Law at Harvard University, rather than at Yale as his father had. While at Harvard, he met his wife, Elisheva, also a law student. For six years he worked in New York at Skadden Arps, a firm established by Catholics and Jews who had been excluded from the major establishment law firms, beginning his focus on tax law there. His eldest son, Yair, was born in the United States, not long before the family moved back to Australia so that Anthony could work at ABL in the tax area and spend time with his family.

The family spent only two years in Australia. After a second son, Yehuda, was born, Rosanna tried to convince him to stay in Melbourne and at ABL, where he would have a bright future, but he was determined to make Aliyah. His gap year in Israel before university had been vital to Anthony's decision. Even more important was a trip to Israel that his father had taken him on when he was 11. Together the two of them had toured the country for two weeks, from top to bottom. Anthony says that, from the age of 15, he had known that he would live in Israel.

Asked why had his parents not made the same decision, Anthony thought for a while before replying:

> My father had always been passionately Zionist. I think the only reason he's still in Australia is because my mother is less so, in the sense that she had never wanted to go live in Israel. I have always found it fascinating, her attachment to Melbourne. From a distance, from Israel, it doesn't make sense.

He remembers his parents' differing responses to his decision:

> My father was mindful of my mother's discomfort with us leaving Melbourne, so he did not verbalise it very much, but I knew my father well enough to see he was so excited and so proud. He

couldn't quite contain it, even when my mother was around. It was an absolute thrill for him.

So, did he still consider himself to be Australian? Anthony Leibler said he had roots in Australia, and yes, in some ways he still saw himself as Australian, but his life was in Israel and that meant he was an Israeli. In August 2018, Anthony came to Australia with three of his four children, for the bat mitzvah of Jeremy's daughter, Ella. His 19-year-old son, Yehuda would report for his compulsory three-year military service when he returned to Jerusalem. He is an intelligent and precocious young man, who set up a technology company in his teens, while writing regularly on Israeli politics and society for a number of Israeli newspapers, including the *Jerusalem Post*.

Yehuda Leibler has three nationalities—Australian, American and Israeli—but he sees himself unequivocally as Israeli. His connection to Australia was strong, but only in the sense that his family was there. When he thought about Australia, he thought about his family and the Jewish community. The fact that he was a citizen of Australia, or of America, did not mean much to him. On his 2018 visit to Melbourne, Yehuda was on the verge of commencing compulsory military service in an elite unit of the Israeli Defence Forces. His older brother, Yair, was already a commander in an army combat unit. During the riots and deaths along the Gaza border in May 2018, Mark Leibler said that he thanked God that his grandson had not been posted to the Gaza border, quickly adding that he was speaking as a grandfather and not being critical of the Israeli military.

The danger to which army service might expose her children and grandchildren has given rise to the fear that has stalked Rosanna Leibler from the time she married Mark more than 50 years ago.

CHAPTER 27

What she has never come to terms with is that one consequence of her husband being a Zionist leader was that one or more of her four children, having a father like Mark and going through a youth movement like Bnei Akiva, would fulfil the Zionist dream and make Aliyah and settle in Israel. She could not come to terms with the fact that, in time, her children's children would serve in the Israeli army, as two of them are now doing.

There were times, she said, when the worry about them was unbearable. And if any of her other children, Simone or Ilana or Jeremy, and their families made Aliyah, what would she do? Move to Israel, where she had never wanted to live and where she would feel alien, unable to speak the language, and with none of her friends or her sisters and their families who lived close by in that enclave of streets in North Caulfield? For 50 years she had supported her husband not only in his ambitions as a leader of the Jews, but in his instilling in their children a love both for Israel and for the gathering of the Jews there—the Zionist dream.

It was not, however, and had never been, her dream. She had never really contemplated making Aliyah, not even when Mark had raised the possibility of it when they were young. When Anthony had told her he was going to make Aliyah with his family, she had tried to talk him out of it, but she knew that her efforts would be in vain. She knew that her husband was proud of Anthony and supported him in his decision, even if, as she also knew, he would miss his son and his grandchildren terribly, and would worry about them when they were required to serve in the Israeli army.

One time, as she sat on a couch in her husband's study sipping instant coffee, she told me she had never considered going to live in Israel, never. She was a Zionist, she said, but not as engaged and passionate about it as Mark. She said that they had not actually discussed going to live in Israel since they were young. Was that, I asked, because Mark knew that she would never contemplate leaving Australia?

> I don't know. Maybe. But I don't think he seriously considered it either. You know it was a matter of controversy from time to time. He was once accused of being a hypocrite for advocating Aliyah but not making Aliyah himself. It was never an issue for me because of course I was not as involved in the Zionist movement as Mark. I wasn't a leader.

In October 2015, at the age of 103, Rachel Leibler died. Until the last few years of her life she had remained active in Emunah, the international women's organisation of religious Zionists. She was buried in Jerusalem. Her son, Mark, could not attend her funeral, as the Jewish custom is to bury the dead as soon as possible. In Israel, there are virtually no exceptions to this rule, so there can be no delay. A month after she died, Leibler flew from Australia to speak at her shloshim marking the end of the first stage of the mourning process. Rosanna stayed in Melbourne. Leibler expressed his regret at

> not being able to participate in your *levaya*. But at least I was able to watch on video the beautiful and meaningful eulogies by Isi, Allan, Tamara, and my son Anthony. Many visitors came during the *shiva* period. And nearly all of them only remembered you from the days prior to your Aliyah to Israel.

I asked Leibler whether his mother's making Aliyah had made him think about taking his family to live in Israel. "No, it didn't," he replied. "That decision was made a long time ago. The time to go had passed."

Why, then, had he not moved with his family to Israel when he was still young enough to do so? He had once said that Israel was the only place where you could live a really complete Jewish life. In the end, this was a question that Leibler could not answer. He had thought about it often. He had wondered, and still did, whether the decision to stay in Australia had been the right one. When pushed, he said that, in some ways, he felt that the fact he had not made Aliyah represented a personal failure, even though he had spent a lifetime dedicated to supporting Israel and doing whatever he could to ensure its survival. He had thought about making Aliyah, but never much more than that because his social roots, his family roots, his legal practice—what would he have done with himself in Israel?

I asked him whether that meant that, while Israel was central to Jewish life, the idea of all Jews going to live in Israel, in a Jewish state, which was once at the centre of Zionist ideology, no longer applied? Leibler replied that he had come to accept that not all Jews were going to pull up roots and go live in Israel, and that this was particularly true about the American Jewish community and the Australian community. Being a Zionist increasingly meant being connected in some way to Israel, visiting the country, sending children on birthright visits, donating to appeals like the United Israel Appeal. In a sense, this was really an expression of post-Zionism.

Israeli writer Amos Oz, who died in late 2018, once said that, for all the country's shortcomings, only in Israel could a Jew be fully Jewish without compromise and without worrying what gentiles thought of them. They were free to fully express their Jewishness. Oz was pointing to a fundamental tenet of Zionism; only in their own land could Jews be free to be fully Jewish. Leibler said that he agreed with Oz. How could he not, given his life-long love of Israel and of the Jewish people, and his concern about Jewish continuity at a time when European Jews face growing anti-Semitism and many American Jews, young American Jews, are less attached to Israel. Yes, he agreed with Amos Oz and his brother Allan; only in Israel could a Jew fully and unabashedly be a Jew.

Nevertheless, he did not feel that he had hidden his Jewishness, not ever. He had felt no restrictions, never needed to apologise or hide anything about who he was. The life that he and many Jews had managed to live in Australia was not possible everywhere. Indeed, it was becoming less and less available to the Jews of many countries, such as the Jews of Europe. And somehow, unlike America, the ravages of assimilation had not threatened Jewish continuity in Australia.

But what about the future? What about anti-Semitism? Does he agree with Isi that the Jews of Europe have no future because of anti-Semitism? Does he believe, given the violent anti-Semitic attacks on Jews in the United States, that America is no longer the golden land for Jews? Does he believe that British and French Jews have no future as Jews and that all diaspora Jewish communities face existential threats?

He does not believe this, though he says that Jews are now far less safe in some diaspora communities, including in the United States, than he thought would ever be possible a decade or two ago:

> Anti-Semitism has been on the increase for three decades and has accelerated in the past few years. Who could imagine even a few years ago that a major party in Britain would be led by an anti-Semite or, at least, by someone who has made numerous anti-Semitic remarks and has tolerated the growing number of anti-Semites in his party? I still can't believe it, that Jeremy Corbyn was the leader of the British Labor Party and could well have been the prime minister.

What about France? The United States? He continued:

> Well at least in France, none of the major parties that could form government are like the British Labor Party. But as far

as grassroots anti-Semitism is concerned, it's probably worse in
France than in England. In America, there has undoubtedly been
an alarming increase in violent extreme anti-Semitism from the
left and the right. What is happening there was unimaginable
a few years ago.

Is Donald Trump responsible? Has he made right-wing anti-Semitism
more acceptable? "Perhaps. But anti-Semitism on the left is also
growing, in the US, especially in the universities. It is expressed as
anti-Zionism but this so-called anti-Zionism invariably traffics in
anti-Semitic canards about the money power of the Jews for instance."

In Australia Leibler says, there is the threat of violent right-wing
anti-Semitism and Islamist anti-Semitism, encouraged and supported
by the far left, who pose the bigger threat in Australia to the safety
of Jews than the far right anti-Semites. It is true that virtually every
Jewish school in Australia, for instance, has an armed guard and there
are armed guards at most major Jewish institutions. The armed guards
are there at the recommendation of the government security services,
who have told community leaders that there have been credible threats
of violence.

Asked whether the increase in anti-Semitism around the world and
even in Australia scares him, Leibler replied:

> Of course it's a concern when there are Jewish communities
> under threat, but nowhere near the concern we would have had
> if not for Israel. The fact that Israel is there...I have said this
> many times to you, the fact that my efforts as a Jewish leader
> have been directed towards supporting Israel is because Israel
> is the best thing going for the Jewish people. Yes, we need to
> build our defences against anti-Semitism, but on the other hand,
> with Israel there, never again, never again will we be defenceless
> victims.

What about the future of the Australia's Jewish community. Will it, as his brother Isi argues, inevitably face the same sort of assimilation trends as the Jews of America. Will diaspora Jewish communities disappear?

> Look, nothing is inevitable. I believe the problems in the American Jewish community, the assimilation issue, the apparent weakening of ties to Israel, are all down to failures of leadership, their failures in education, Jewish education and Zionist education. Look at our Jewish schools and our Zionist youth groups. It is a different ball game here.
>
> As for the diaspora, over thousands of years, since the destruction of the Second Temple by the Romans and the dispersion of the Jews, there have been pogroms big and small, persecution and discrimination, the Holocaust, assimilation, but the Jewish people have survived. I think we should not be too hasty in predicting the end of the Jewish diaspora. It has been around for a long time. Jewish life in the diaspora will be around for a long time.

Like their father and mother, three of Mark and Rosanna Leibler's children have opted to stay in Australia rather than make Aliyah. They have managed to live the sort of Jewish lives that their parents have lived and, to a great extent, their grandparents. Simone Wenig and her husband Jonathan, a partner at ABL, live with their children in the street next to Simone's parents. A back fence separates their homes, and Mark Leibler often wanders over to see his grandchildren. Her parents come for the Friday night Sabbath meal and the Wenig family goes to the Leibler's home for Sabbath lunch the following day. Jeremy Leibler and his wife Andy and their four children live a short walk away.

What Simone remembers best about her father in her childhood were the Friday nights when, instead of going to synagogue for the start of the Sabbath services, Mark Leibler would call all the children into his study. Mark, Rosanna and the children would sit on couches and do the prayers for the beginning of the Sabbath and then they would sing the Sabbath songs. On Saturdays, after returning from Sabbath services at the Mizrachi synagogue, they would sit around the dining room table, often with Isi and Naomi and their children, for Sabbath lunch. "It was a real mix of, you know, real family time but also a lot of talk about Israel and Jewish issues. There was a lot of banter between dad and Isi," Simone said.

Asked what she had felt when her son, Ari, made Aliyah, Simone did not directly answer that question and instead said that she was sure that her father was very proud of him. She went on to say:

> I mean, the centrality of Israel to the Jewish people was really ingrained in us from a very early age. We have this joke with some friends and relatives whose children have made Aliyah. What did we expect? We sent them to Bnei Akiva, we sent them to Yavneh, we sent them on a year away to Israel and then when they come and say they want to move to Israel, we are like, "No! Don't leave." Really?

The Leiblers' third child, Ilana, also lives with her husband Gerard and three children within walking distance of their parents. Ilana said that her father was a regular visitor, mostly to see his grandchildren, one of whom was away on a gap year in Israel when we spoke in 2018. She said her father knew everything that was going on in all their lives. He was her "go-to person" when she had a problem; it had always been that way. Like her siblings, Ilana has grown up a religious Zionist and Israel is embedded deep in her heart and in her sense of herself as a Jew. Yes, she has sometimes thought about whether her children will make Aliyah, just as her nephew Ari had done and her brother Anthony and his family and her uncles Isi and Allan and their families. She did not know. Her children, she said, were still too young to make that decision.

Jeremy and his wife Andrea and their four children live within walking distance of Mark and Rosanna's home. Jeremy is not only a rising star in the law, but also increasingly recognised as a Zionist leader in Australia and internationally.

Each of Leibler's children, and his grandchildren too, spoke of him with affection, but also with something approaching awe. Somehow, they said, he had not been an absent father or grandfather, though he was often away and often working deep into the night, surrounded by billowing cigar smoke. All three children in Australia are members of the Mizrachi congregation, and their children are either at Leibler Yavneh College or are graduates of the school. All four children have followed in their parents' footsteps: each married a Jew; none has weakened in their commitment to Zionism and to the continuity of the Jewish people; none has ever doubted that they would.

I asked Mark Leibler on that February morning in 2019, almost two years after we, subject and author, had started on this book, what sort of father he had been to his children. His children had said that he had been an attentive and affectionate father, there for them when they needed him. Always there for them. How had he managed that?

> Two ways. Number one, I slept only four hours or so a night. So I left the office early and worked at home, late into the night. My door was always open to them. And then there was Shabbat. From sundown on Friday until sundown on Saturday, there were no meetings, no phone, no television, just the family together. I was completely there. Friday nights, we did the prayers together in my study and then we sat and talked and ate our meal together. Saturday mornings we walked to *shul* together. Ate our Sabbath

lunch together. Saturday afternoons, we played games like chess and read books together.

You know you have asked me several times to reflect on my achievements. I have always said, and I feel it more as time goes by, you have all these accomplishments and you have a successful career and you have done all this stuff for the community but at the end of the day, what do you really leave behind, you leave behind your kids and grandchildren.

Helene Teichmann, when asked what she had witnessed about Leibler and his family, said that Leibler, in her experience, was different from many of the public figures, including politicians that she had known over decades. He was, she said totally devoted to them. She said that she had travelled with Leibler often and worked closely with him:

> Rosanna used to refer to me as his second wife. But she did not have any concerns about us. How could she? Mark Leibler is the least sexist man, the least likely man to sexually harass any woman that I have ever met. I think he barely noticed that I was female. If I had walked into the room wearing black lingerie, he would have looked up and said "so where's that list for today?" With powerful men, in my experience, this is very unusual to say the least.

We were sitting in his office at ABL, Leibler and I on the eve of his next summer visit to Israel, with the sun high in the sky so that the suburbs stretching into the distance through the windows are heat-bathed and hazy. Leibler sat, as he did most weekdays, at his round table and ate lunch, a sandwich, a salad and some herbal tea, brought to him by a young man dressed in a black outfit.

He was 75 years old and the Jewish world into which he had been born and in which he had lived so much of his life had changed in so many ways. Israel, which he had always believed was central to Jewish life and continuity and self-respect—Israel too had changed and so too had attitudes to Israel, not just in the non-Jewish world, but amongst Jews as well, even though most Australian Jews overwhelmingly remain committed to Israel's future and refer to themselves as Zionists.

The post-Holocaust world, in which anti-Semitism, given the horrors of Nazism and the consequences of virulent Jew hatred, had been banished to the fringes of small and loony right-wing groups in the West, was no more. But Mark Leibler did not feel pessimistic about the future for the Jews of Europe and America and Australia. His brother may be convinced that assimilation is inevitable. Perhaps this is because Isi Leibler has made Aliyah and lives in Israel, the only place, according to Zionist ideology, where Jews can be fully Jewish and where the Jewish future is assured. The diaspora, on the other hand, has no long-term future.

His life and the way he has lived it suggest that Mark Leibler believes there is a future for the Jews, especially the Jews of Australia. Unlike Isi, he did not, as he said many times, really experience anti-Semitism. He has lived his life never needing to hide or apologise for his Jewishness or his Zionism. He has lived a full Jewish life, he often said, and his children too, those who stayed in Australia, are leading full Jewish lives. Australia, Leibler said, was truly a *goldene medine* for the Jewish people. This position marks a major difference between Isi and Mark Leibler; Isi Leibler never moved beyond being a leader of the Jews, both in Australia and internationally. He never felt the need to do so. He was always going to end up making Aliyah.

Mark Leibler too, until he was 50, was essentially a Jewish leader, a Zionist leader to be precise, who lived most of his life, outside of his professional life, among Jews. But when he was 50, after Ron Castan brought the Yorta Yorta case to ABL and after he developed such a close, even loving, relationship with Noel Pearson, Mark Leibler became an activist and an advocate for Indigenous justice, recognition and reconciliation between Indigenous and non-Indigenous Australians. It consumed a large part of his life. It changed him. It changed the way he saw Australia and its history. It changed the way he saw himself as a Jew and an Australian. "My involvement with Indigenous people, with Indigenous issues was very important to me," he revealed. "I got to understand things that the vast majority of Australians don't get to understand. I had found the right balance between my Jewishness and my being an Australian. The two were not separate."

One of the great moments of his life was when he was there, over four days in May 2017, at Uluru, where Indigenous leaders had gathered to debate, and eventually pass unanimously, their Uluru Statement from the Heart that called for a referendum on an amendment to the Constitution which would set up an Indigenous body that would advise the federal parliament on issues that affected Indigenous people. Leibler was one of only a handful of non-Indigenous people invited to the gathering. He had supported the proposed amendment from the time that Noel Pearson had raised it with him. He was immediately convinced that only a substantial constitutional amendment like this could address the injustices that Indigenous Australians had suffered for more than 200 years. He had not made Aliyah, and here he was at Uluru, an Australian Jew, witnessing what he believed was an historic day for all Australians, having done what he could—and what he would continue to do—to turn the Uluru Statement into political reality.

That summer's morning in 2019, he was not very forthcoming when asked to list his achievements as a Jewish leader. It was as if doing so would acknowledge the implicit assumption in the question—that his time of achievements was over. He was looking forward during this trip to the time he would spend with his brothers, with his son, Anthony, with Anthony's family and with Simone's son, Ari. His achievements in the law and his achievements as a leader of the Jews—well, in a way, he said, time would tell.

ABL was in good shape and yes, there was satisfaction in the fact that his son and his son-in-law were partners and that the children of the firm's other senior partners were also at ABL. Not that this meant the leadership of the firm when he and the other long-time partners were gone would be decided dynastically—not at all.

As for the Jewish community, it did face challenges, but he was more than a little proud that Jeremy Leibler had been elected president of the Zionist Federation of Australia in November 2018, becoming, at 39, the youngest president since he, Mark, had been elected as the youngest president in 1984. The ZFA, he said, was in good hands. He smiled broadly when he said that, as if "good hands" was an understatement. He said again what he always said: the quality and impact of any organisation almost always depended on the quality of its leader.

Asked whether he thought that there would ever be another three generations of Jewish leaders in Australia like the Leiblers, he said he didn't know: "Probably not. My father and my brother and I came out of a very special, even unique Jewish community that was formed by absolutely unique circumstances. Those circumstances won't be repeated."

It was 2pm. He had spent the time he had allocated for talking about these things and had to get back to the next set of tasks on his list of things to do that day. The next morning, he would be driven to Melbourne Airport to catch the flight to Israel. He would be travelling for close to 24 hours. When he arrived at Ben Gurion Airport in

CHAPTER 27

Tel Aviv, he would, even as he waited to get off the plane, check his phone. If there were messages from Rosanna or his children, he would call immediately. If there were messages from his secretary about calls from clients, he would answer those too, before he had travelled the hour and a half from Tel Aviv to Jerusalem. Only then would he, once again, take in the special light of this city, holy to Jews and Muslims and Christians, but, in all probability, he would not think about that for very long. Instead, he would once again be thinking of the work that lay ahead of him. Perhaps, for a moment, he would then think about the momentous journey from Australia to Israel that he had never made.

GLOSSARY

AIJAC: Australia/Israel & Jewish Affairs Council.

AIP: Australia/Israel Publications.

AIPAC: American Israel Public Affairs Committee.

Aliyah: Hebrew for "going up". Making Aliyah means moving to Israel, one of Zionism's most fundamental tenets.

ALP: Australian Labor Party.

ASIO: Australian Security Intelligence Organisation.

ATO: Australian Taxation Office.

bar mitzvah: ceremony at which Jewish boys, when they turn 13, become adults and are able to perform the rituals of Jewish religious observance.

bat mitzvah: ceremony at which Jewish girls, when they turn 12, become adults.

bechor: Hebrew for the first-born male child.

Bnei Akiva: international religious Zionist youth movement.

bris: circumcision ceremony at which boys, at eight days old, are circumcised and given their Hebrew name.

broyges: Yiddish word that roughly translates to a serious falling out.

Bund: international Jewish workers' party that was a mass movement in Eastern Europe before World War 2. It was anti-Zionist, anti-religious and socialist. It believed in Jewish peoplehood and was committed to fostering Yiddish culture and a sense of belonging to the Jewish people among its working-class supporters.

Chabad: one of the best-known Chasidic sects and the biggest in Australia, with thousands of followers. Sometimes referred to as Lubavitch, because of its origins in Lubavitch, a small town in Lithuania in 1775. The sect's leader, called the Lubavitcher Rebbe, has for hundreds of years chosen his successor. Chabad's headquarters is in Crown Heights in Brooklyn, New York.

Chasidism: a mystical strain of Judaism founded in the 1750s in Poland by rabbi and mystic Israel ben Eliezer, who was known as the Ba'al Shem Tov. Chasidism places emphasis on prayer, religious zeal and the expression of joy, in part through dancing and singing.

ECAJ: Executive Council of Australian Jewry, the peak body of the Australian Jewish community.

Emunah: Israel's largest religious welfare NGO. There are Emunah organisations throughout Jewish communities in the diaspora.

gevir: Yiddish for flamboyantly rich man.

gmar tov: Hebrew for a good ending. It is used to wish for a good conclusion to the high holidays.

goldene medine: Yiddish for golden land. The term was earlier used by Jews who migrated to America from Eastern Europe and Russia at the end of the 19th century.

goyim: Yiddish colloquial term for Gentiles.

Halacha: Judaism's religious laws.

Keren Hayesod: Israel-based international body that distributes the funds raised by the United Israel Appeals in diaspora Jewish communities.

Ketubah: marriage certificate signed by a bride and groom before a Jewish wedding ceremony.

kibbutzim: collective communities in Israel, largely based on agricultural production.

levaya: Hebrew for funeral.

Liberal Judaism: a major Jewish denomination that emphasises the evolving nature of the faith and the need for constant reinterpretation and updating of Judaism, its laws and rituals.

madrich: Hebrew for leader, especially in youth groups.

Mizrachi: international organisation of religious Zionists founded in 1902 in Lithuania. It went on to form the Religious Zionist party in Israel.

GLOSSARY

Modern Orthodox: in the main, it is the home of Jews who believe that strict adherence to Jewish law is entirely consistent with being a full member of modern society; it generally includes support for Israel and for the Zionist mission. There are various strains of Modern Orthodoxy in Judaism.

Mossad: Israel's national intelligence agency and security service.

PLO: Palestine Liberation Organisation.

RAP: Reconciliation Action Plan.

Shabbat: Hebrew for the Sabbath.

shabbes: Yiddish for the Sabbath.

shiva: Hebrew term for the week-long mourning period following the death of a close relative.

shlichim: Young Israelis trained and funded by the Jewish Agency to live in diaspora communities for several years where they work in schools, synagogues universities and Zionist youth movements. Their mission is to foster a love of Israel and to support and encourage Aliyah.

Shoah: Hebrew term for the Holocaust.

shtetl: Yiddish term for the small villages and towns of Eastern Europe where most of the inhabitants were often Jewish.

shtibl: Yiddish term for small house used for communal prayer.

shul: Yiddish for synagogue.

SKIF: Sotsyalistishe Kinder Farband (Socialist Children's Organisation), the youth movement of the Bund.

shloshim: ceremony marking the end of the month of mourning for someone who has died.

UIA: United Israel Appeal.

ultra-Orthodox: Orthodox Jews who are very strict in the observance of the minutiae of Jewish law. They prefer to be called Haredi because they consider the term ultra-Orthodox to be pejorative.

Yom Ha'atzmaut: Israel Independence Day celebration.

ZFA: Zionist Federation of Australia.